The Quest for the Historical Israel

The
Quest
for the
Historical
Israel

GEORGE W. RAMSEY

John Knox Press
ATLANTA

Unless otherwise noted, the Scripture quotations in this publication are from the Revised Standard Version Bible, copyright 1946, 1952 and © 1971 by the Division of Christian Education, National Council of the Churches of Christ in the U.S.A. and used by permission.

Library of Congress Cataloging in Publication Data

Ramsey, George W   1937–
   The quest for the historical Israel.

   Bibliography: p.
   Includes indexes.
      1. Jews—History—to 1200 B. C.—Historiography.
   2. Bible. O. T.—Criticism, interpretation, etc.—
   History—20th century.   I. Title.
   DS121.R33   933′.01   80-82188
   ISBN 0-8042-0187-0

ACKNOWLEDGMENTS

Acknowledgment is made for permission to quote from the following:

Abraham in History and Tradition by John Van Seters, copyright © 1975 Yale University Press.
Antiquity: "Invasion, Diffusion, Evolution" by William Y. Adams, Vol. 42 (1968).
Archaeology and Old Testament Study, ed. by D. Winton Thomas, copyright © 1967 Oxford University Press.
The Bible in Modern Scholarship, ed. by J. P. Hyatt, copyright © 1965 by Abingdon Press. Used by permission of the Society of Biblical Literature.
The Biblical Archaeologist: "Biblical Customs and the Nuzu Tablets" by Cyrus H. Gordon, in *The BA Reader No. 2*; "The Hebrew Conquest of Palestine" by George E. Mendenhall, in *The BA Reader No. 3*.
Biblical Archaeology by G. Ernest Wright. Copyright © 1962 by G. Ernest Wright. Used by permission of The Westminster Press.
The Biblical Period from Abraham to Ezra by W. F. Albright, copyright © 1963 by Harper & Row.
The Book of the Acts of God by G. E. Wright and R. H. Fuller. Copyright © 1957, 1960 by G. Ernest Wright. Used by permission of Doubleday & Co.
Catholic Biblical Quarterly: "Archaeology and Early Israel: The Scene Today" by John E. Huesman, January 1975.
Christian Apologetics by Alan Richardson, copyright © 1947 SCM Press Ltd.
Death in the City by Francis A. Schaeffer, copyright © 1969 InterVarsity Press.
The Early History of Israel by Roland de Vaux. English Translation: © Darton, Longman & Todd Ltd., 1978. Printed in the U.S.A. by The Westminster Press. Used by permission.
Early Israel in Recent History Writing by John Bright, copyright © 1956 by Alec R. Allenson, Inc.
Forschung am Alten Testament by C. Westermann, copyright © 1964 by Chr. Kaiser Verlag.
From Joseph to Joshua by H. H. Rowley, copyright © 1950 by Oxford University Press. Used by permission of Oxford University Press.
God Who Acts by G. Ernest Wright, copyright © 1952 by Alec R. Allenson, Inc.
The God Who Is There by Francis A. Schaeffer, copyright © 1968 InterVarsity Press.
He Is There and He Is Not Silent by Francis A. Schaeffer, copyright © 1972 by Tyndale House Publishers. Quoted by permission.
Hebrew Origins (Torchbook edition) by Theophile J. Meek, copyright © 1960 Harper & Row.
The Historian and the Believer by Van A. Harvey, copyright © 1966 by Van

THE QUEST FOR THE HISTORICAL ISRAEL

A. Harvey. Used by permission of Macmillan Publishing Co.
The Historian's Craft by Marc Bloch, translated by Peter Putnam, copyright ©
1953 by Alfred A. Knopf, Inc.
Historian's Handbook: A Key to the Study and Writing of History, Second Edi-
tion, by Wood Gray et al. Copyright © 1964 by Wood Gray. Reprinted by
permission of Houghton Mifflin Company.
The Historicity of the Patriarchal Narratives by Thomas L. Thompson, copy-
right © 1974 by Walter de Gruyter, Inc.
History and Christian Apologetic by T. A. Roberts, copyright © 1960 by
S.P.C.K., London.
History and the Gods, by B. Albrektson, copyright © 1967 by Bertil Albrekt-
son. Published by AB CWK Gleerup Bokförlag.
A History of Israel by John Bright. © MCMLIX, W. L. Jenkins. © MCMLX-
XII, The Westminster Press. Used by permission.
The History of Israel by Martin Noth, copyright © 1960 by Adam & Charles
Black, Ltd.
A History of Israel in Old Testament Times by Siegfried Hermann, copyright
© 1975 by SCM Press Ltd. Reprinted by permission of Fortress Press.
Interpretation: "Revelation Through History in the Old Testament and in Mod-
ern Theology" by James Barr, April 1963; and "Moses and the Foundations
of Israel" by E. F. Campbell, April 1975.
The Interpreter's Dictionary of the Bible, Vol. 1 (1962), Supplementary Vol-
ume (1976), published by Abingdon Press.
Josephus, Jewish Antiquities, Vol. 9, tr. by Louis H. Feldman (in The Loeb
Classical Library), copyright © 1965 by Harvard University.
Journal for the Study of the Old Testament, issues of April 1977, May 1978.
Journal of Egyptian Archaeology: "The Hyksos Rule in Egypt," by T. Säve-
Söderbergh, 1951. Used by permission of the Egypt Exploration Society.
The Making of Luke-Acts, by H. J. Cadbury, copyright © 1927 by the Macmil-
lan Co. Used by permission of the Estate of H. J. Cadbury.
Myth and Reality in the Old Testament by Brevard S. Childs, copyright ©
1960 SCM Press. Used by permission.
The Nature of Nomadism, by D. L. Johnson. Published 1969 by the University
of Chicago Department of Geography. Used by permission of D. L. Johnson.
The Old Testament Against Its Environment by G. Ernest Wright, copyright ©
1950 by SCM Press Ltd.
The Old Testament and the Historian by J. Maxwell Miller, copyright © 1976
by Fortress Press. Reprinted by permission of Fortress Press.
The Old Testament and Modern Study, edited by H. H. Rowley, copyright ©
1951 by Clarendon Press.
Origins and History of the Oldest Sinaitic Traditions by Walter Beyerlin, copy-
right © 1965 Basil Blackwell & Mott Ltd.
Redating the Exodus and Conquest, by J. J. Bimson, copyright © 1978 by
JSOT, Univeristy of Sheffield.
Set Forth Your Case by Clark H. Pinnock, copyright © 1968 The Craig Press.
The Settlement of the Israelite Tribes in Palestine by Manfred Weippert, copy-
right © 1971 SCM Press Ltd.
The Suicide of Christian Theology by John Warwick Montgomery, published

and copyright 1970, Bethany Fellowship, Inc., Minneapolis, Minnesota 55438. Reprinted by permission.

Supplement XXVIII to Vetus Testamentum, published in 1975 by E. J. Brill, Leiden.

The Tenth Generation by George E. Mendenhall, copyright © 1973 by Johns Hopkins University Press.

Treaty and Covenant by Dennis J. McCarthy, S. J., copyright © 1963 by Pontifical Biblical Institute; revised edition published 1978.

The Tribes of Israel by C.H.J. de Geus, copyright © 1976 K. Van Gorcum & Company, B.V., Assen, The Netherlands.

Understanding the Old Testament by B. W. Anderson, copyright © 1975 Prentice Hall, Inc.

The Westminster Historical Atlas to the Bible, edited by George Ernest Wright and Floyd Vivian Filson. Copyright © 1945 by The Westminster Press. Used by permission.

What Is History? by Edward H. Carr, copyright © 1962 Alfred A. Knopf, Inc.

To
R. B. Y. Scott
with affection and esteem

Foreword

The helpfulness of friends is one of the most gratifying aspects of the experience of writing a book. I have been especially fortunate in having a large number of friends who were willing to give their time and assistance to me during the preparation of this book, and I hereby extend my thanks to them.

Colleagues in the faculty and administration of Presbyterian College helped me in various ways—loaning me books, reading and discussing with me various parts of the manuscript, and taking part of my teaching load to make possible a sabbatical leave during which much of my work was done. These colleagues include: President Marc C. Weersing; Librarian Lennart Pearson; Pete Hay, Jack Presseau, Tom Stallworth, and David Moorefield of the Department of Religion and Philosophy; and Ron Burnside and David Needham of the Department of History.

I also owe a debt of gratitude to those from outside the college who advised me on various aspects of the work: John Rogers, Jr., minister of the First Presbyterian Church of Shreveport, La.; James L. Mays, of Union Theological Seminary in Richmond, Va.; and my father, Harmon B. Ramsey, of Richmond. Editor Dick Ray of John Knox Press has been most encouraging throughout the process of bringing my work to publication, and the work of copyeditor Joe Baggett has been most helpful and thorough. The library staffs at Presbyterian College and Union Theological Seminary in Virginia were of great assistance in providing me with necessary materials and with bibliographical expertise.

All of my work would have been impossible without the understanding and encouragement I received from my wife Ellen, who, in addition to typing much of the manuscript, endured months of seeing books and papers piled in untidy ways around our home.

It is with a great deal of pleasure that I dedicate the book to R. B. Y. Scott, who was the director of my doctoral studies in Old Testament at Princeton University. As the one who "oversaw" my graduate work, he embodied fully the traits of the ideal "overseer" (*episkopos*) detailed in 1 Timothy 3:2ff. He has been, for example, dignified, sensible, hospitable, above reproach, temperate, the husband of one (very gracious and lovely) wife, an apt teacher. I am deeply appreciative of everything he has given me as mentor, pastor, and friend.

Contents

Introduction   xiii

Part 1:   The Historical Method   1

  Chapter 1: The Historian's Craft   3

Part 2:   Recent Study of Israel's Early History   25

  Chapter 2: The "Patriarchal Period"   27

  Chapter 3: Exodus and Covenant   45

  Chapter 4: The Settlement in Canaan   65

  Chapter 5: Historical Research: Literary Study
             and "External Evidence"   99

Part 3:   Theological Dimensions of the Quest   105

  Chapter 6: If Jericho Was Not Razed,
             Is Our Faith in Vain?   107

Abbreviations   125

Notes   128

Selected Bibliography   176

Scripture Index   181

Name Index   185

Subject Index   190

Introduction

A major part of any course in Old Testament is the study of the history of Israel. Quite apart from whatever interest the history of the Israelite people might hold in itself, the fact that it constituted the context out of which the Scriptures of the Old Testament emerged gives it special significance. Much emphasis is placed, in modern study of the Old Testament, upon the importance of understanding the Old Testament writings in the light of the times which produced them. This is a major concern of what we call the *"historical*-critical study" of the Bible. How can we really appreciate the messages of the Old Testament authors unless we are familiar with the situations which produced them and to which they were addressed?

The task of setting forth the history of Israel in Old Testament times is not so simple as it might at first seem. The obvious question which a layman might ask is, "Why not simply follow the narrative presented in the Bible?" Why can't we just re-tell the story of Israel's past as it is recorded in the historical books of the Old Testament? Until the rise of historical science in the last couple of centuries, this was exactly what one would do if he wished to write a history of the Old Testament people.

As the methods of analyzing and evaluating historical sources have been refined in modern times, certain things were discovered about the Old Testament narratives which make it impossible simply to read Israel's history straight off the pages of the Bible. Literary analysis of the Old Testament has revealed that most of the narratives which we have there were put into their final form long after the time of the events they describe. Early in his study of the Old Testament, the student learns that the prevailing scholarly opinion concerning the origins of the Pentateuch is that this block of material is composed of at least four distinct strands or sources (J, E, D, and P), all of which were

written *at least* three centuries after the events which they narrate.
similar situation prevails with regard to the books of Joshua through
Kings, although the "time lag" is not quite so great between event an
writing in the later sections.

The period of time separating the events from the final writing wa:
probably spanned in many cases by oral transmission of the stories, anc
one has to reckon with the obvious likelihood that they were altered ir
various ways during the course of transmission. (Even when narratives
were written down, this did not stop the process of alteration, as an
examination of the differences introduced by the author of 1 and 2
Chronicles when he used material from the books of Samuel and Kings
will show. The same can be seen in a comparison of the first three
gospels of the New Testament, where it is commonly held that Matthew and Luke used—and revised—much material from Mark.)

A careful study of the Old Testament narratives sometimes reveals
conflicts or inconsistencies in the reports of certain events, suggesting
that several different versions of a given occurrence grew up. Such is
apparently the case, for example, with regard to the episode of the
plagues in Egypt (Exodus 7–12), the stories of how the Israelite tribes
acquired their territories in Canaan, and the battle of Deborah and Barak (Judges 4–5).

Any storyteller is guided by his own interests as he reports the past.
This is unavoidable. But it means that we cannot assume that a given
report is an unbiased account or that this is all that needs to be said
about a given event or era. The modern historian is always desirous of
locating reports by persons with different interests or data of a disinter-
ested sort to help in the reconstruction of the past. Since the biblical
storytellers were, more than anything else, providing a religious testimony, their religious interests influenced their choice of events to be
reported and the way in which they described these events.

These reasons make it impossible to move in a straight line from
the stories in the Bible to a description of Israel's history. In this present century especially, biblical scholars have held high hopes that
archaeological discoveries would shed light upon the biblical accounts
and clarify for us which portions of the Old Testament narrative give a
reasonably accurate account of what really happened in the Old Testament era. The inscriptions and artifacts recovered by archaeologists
provide independent testimony to the times of the Bible. If characters
or events mentioned in the Bible should be mentioned in datable documents discovered by the archaeologist, we are given a means of estab-

lishing a chronology and checking the historical reliability of Old Testament accounts. A study of the annals of Assyrian and Babylonian kings, for example, frequently supplements biblical data concerning the period of the Israelite monarchy and enables us to assign rather precise dates to Old Testament events, and information from these annals helps us to round out our reconstruction of the monarchical era.

For the earliest period of Israel's history, however, archaeologists have recovered very little material that can be correlated with certainty with the Old Testament narratives. There are no inscriptions mentioning the arrival of Abraham or Jacob in a certain place, or of the escape of Hebrew slaves from Egypt, or of Joshua's attack on any of the cities of Canaan. Such archaeological evidence as there is for this early period is frequently susceptible to several different interpretations, and it sometimes raises as many problems as it solves.

The chapters that follow are designed to give some insight into the way modern historians proceed in their efforts to reconstruct Israel's past. For no period of biblical history is the task of reconstruction so difficult as for the period from Abraham to the settlement of the tribes in Canaan. The recent history of research into this era illustrates well the ways historians tackle their task and the kinds of problems that confront them. The reader will see that the writing of ancient history is a continuing process of developing a thesis from the available pieces of evidence, testing it, and subjecting it to the analysis, criticism, and revision of others.

A question that is bound to arise in the study of this topic is the relation of one's religious faith to the enterprise of writing biblical history. Can one be a believer and a good historian at the same time? Does one's religious faith influence his historical conclusions? What are the implications for one's religious faith if he discovers inaccuracies in the biblical reports of events? What if a narrative turns out to be a historical fiction, with no basis in historical facts? Can a religious faith be based on such reports? These questions will be explored in chapter 6.

ONE
The Historical
Method

CHAPTER

1

The
Historian's Craft

The historian working on the earliest period of Israelite history proceeds in principle in the same way as an historian working on any other era of the past. The historian of Israel is obligated to carry out his research and his reconstruction according to the rules followed by any other historian. There are certain procedures he must follow and certain standards to which he must adhere if his work is to earn the respect and consent of other scholars.[1]

For example, he cannot simply accept, without question, the testimony of anyone and everyone who reports on the events in which he is interested. The historian must have good reasons for believing his witnesses to be credible. He is obliged to examine all evidence which has a bearing on the period or events in question, and not restrict himself only to that which might be consistent with his pet theory. He cannot be arbitrary in deciding which witnesses to heed; he needs to have sound reasons for preferring witness A's account over that of witness B, if they differ. He cannot draw conclusions from the evidence without good reasons, and he should lay his reasons out clearly for public examination and testing.

The historian has aptly been compared to a detective.[2] Like a detective, the historian attempts to reconstruct events which he was not present to observe. He may have the reports of witnesses. For the historian of early Israel, the principal witnesses are the narratives of the Old Testament. He has certain other evidence, or clues, available to him. His clues may include pottery remains and burned debris from Palestine, royal inscriptions from Egypt, legal and economic tablets from Mesopotamia. The evidence is present; the events themselves are not. The evidence represents the "tracks" left by past events.[3] The historian/detective has to assemble the testimony of witnesses and all other clues, sift them in a process of evaluation and analysis, and then apply his best common sense to piece together what happened to cause these tracks. It is this threefold process of gathering, sifting, and reconstruction which we will discuss in these next pages. In actual practice the process does not usually develop in three clearly separate stages. While the historian is gathering evidence, he may well have a tentative hypothesis in mind which will determine the kinds of evidence he seeks. But for the purposes of understanding the historian's work, it is helpful to consider these three operations individually.

Collecting the Evidence

What constitutes evidence for the historian? Quite simply, anything which he is able to use may serve in this capacity. Clues to what happened in the past and why it happened may be discovered in all sorts of places.[4] The ingenuity of the historian is often able to turn the unlikeliest material into a clue. Seemingly "unhistorical" artifacts like pottery have yielded significant information about historical changes to those who know the right questions to ask. Place names can reveal information about the date, circumstances, and identity of the settlers. Legal customs or burial praetices can attest to the presence of differing social groups in an area at a certain time.

Historians distinguish between "intentional" and "unintentional" evidence. The former category includes records deliberately prepared to inform readers about the past (battle reports, chronicles, etc.). With this kind of evidence one always has to consider the possibility that the account has been shaped by the author's special interests which might have introduced a distorting bias. (See further below.) Remains from the past which disclose historical information not directly intended by the persons who produced them constitute "unintentional" evidence. People who produced pottery or coins or economic documents unwittingly made available to later historians certain bits of information about the era in which they lived. Historians generally assume this type of evidence less likely to be contaminated by bias or deceit. Even written narratives which would properly be regarded as "intentional" evidence can be interrogated by the historian so as to reveal things other than what the author intended explicitly to say, sometimes things contrary to what the author explicitly says. For example, the book of Deuteronomy—which purports to be a series of speeches by Moses—has revealed to biblical critics information about the seventh century B.C., the time at which the book was actually drafted.

The historian highly values material from independent sources (frequently referred to as "external evidence") which can supplement, clarify, or correct what is learned from the primary witnesses. Such "external evidence" has been called on much in recent decades in biblical studies to enlarge and clarify the picture drawn from the biblical record. The discipline of archaeology has rendered major service to Old Testament scholarship in this regard. Finds from Palestine and the other Near Eastern countries—remains of both an artifactual and an epigraphic nature—have greatly enhanced our understanding of the Old Testament era. Comparative data from other cultures (both ancient and modern) about such things as economic structures, ecological factors, processes of social change, or legal customs may help the historian better understand how the people of the Old Testament times lived and how changes occurred in their lives. The discipline of comparative literature has given a broader perspective from which to examine the Hebrew literature: to compare the tales or laws or hymns in the Old Testament with similar material from neighboring cultures of similar antiquity frequently sheds new light on the origin and meaning of the Old Testament material. Such external evidence as these disciplines provide can supply an independent check on the primary sources, i.e., the biblical record.

In order to keep his research in perspective, the historian has to remember that the evidence available to him is but a very small fragment of the total remains of the past. This is more crucial with regard to ancient history than with the history of recent times, when more systematic preservation of significant data has been achieved. Consider, for example, what we do *not* know about ancient Israel. We are told virtually nothing about the process of education in early Israel. What kinds of artistic and architectural skills the early Hebrews possessed we are not told. About their organized worship we are told next to nothing. The manner of government under which the Hebrews lived in the centuries prior to the monarchy is by no means clear.[5] There is nothing like a systematic description of their religious beliefs. And what information we do have about early Israel in the records of the Old Testament is a selective fragment preserved by the literate elements in the society; what did the non-literate majority do and think?

Sifting the Evidence

After the various kinds of evidence have been gathered, then comes the process of "sifting" to determine the likely value of the respective pieces of evidence. The obvious place to start in the effort to reconstruct biblical history is with the witness which purports to tell of that history, namely, the Old Testament narrative.

Textual criticism

An important preliminary step in this process is the clarification of what the biblical text actually says. The science of textual criticism developed for the purpose of reconstructing the original wording of the text. This is not commonly a problem in the use of sources such as monumental inscriptions, legal or economic tablets (except where there is a defaced or broken monument or tablet). But, with the biblical text, we have no autographs (i.e., the copy produced by the original author); all we have are copies and translations, which frequently diverge from one another. The textual critic attempts to determine the most accurate reading of the source in question.[6]

Genre analysis and literary criticism

Another basic question that needs to be asked of written materials at this stage of "sifting" is the question of genre. What type of writing have we here? Is it a military report? a liturgical piece? a hero tale? Different genres are composed in different settings and with different intentions. The identification of genre, setting, and intention is the province of the method of literary analysis known as "form criticism."[7] By comparing the structure, content, and mood of a particular text with those of similar texts, the form critic can frequently infer much about what kind of social context produced this text (a worship setting? a judicial proceeding? a didactic situation?) and what the author was trying to accomplish (elevate the religious spirit of the community? evoke repentance from a sinner? entertain? instruct?). To treat a text that bears signs of legendary embellishment or liturgical hyperbole as if it were a straightforward historical report is an error which has sometimes led researchers into absurd reconstructions.

It is further helpful if the historian can at this stage draw on the results of a study of the literary qualities of his written sources. The *literary critic* studies narrative design, plot devices, the use of imagery, the development of character, and the like.[8] Attention to the literary features of a work can give insight into what the author was trying to do, and this may, for example, alert the historian to the fact that here is a composition in which certain characters or events were introduced simply to enhance the aesthetic appeal of the narrative or to move the plot along and do not correspond in any way to actual persons or events.

Evaluating the witness

Once the original text has been reconstructed with a reasonable degree of certainty and the historian is satisfied that his sources are historiographical in nature, he seeks to determine the value of these sources for reconstructing history. Just how reliable a witness do we have here? Written materials from the past can be at once the most helpful and the most misleading resources for the historian. Written records are less ambiguous in what they have to say than is a layer of ash or a fragment of pottery. Written materials refer to specific occurrences, peoples, places, transactions. But the competent historian knows that he cannot take all statements at face value. Witnesses frequently distort the past in their reporting of it.

In common with any scholar who aspires to be scientific in his method, the historian requires competent observation if his hypotheses are to be adequately drawn and tested. Unlike the laboratory scientist, the historian cannot make his own observations (of the past) nor control the data essential to his undertaking, since the object of historical research is past. So he must subject his observers (i.e., his witnesses) to careful examination. The first requirement of a good historian is a healthy streak of skepticism. Like a good detective, the able historian interrogates witnesses carefully before making use of their testimony to reconstruct the past. The historian does not want to be duped.

Among the questions which the historian needs to ask about each of his sources, including the biblical witness, are the following.

Provenance. One of the historian's first tasks with regard to the evidence accumulated is to determine the circumstances attending the production of his sources. Is the testimony what it appears or claims to be? Is it the work of the person whose name is associated with it as the reporter or author? A document which turns out to be in fact the work of the person whose name appears in it is labeled "authentic" or "genuine"; if the document is the work of someone other than the purported author, it is considered "inauthentic" or "spurious" (which is not necessarily a judgment on the value of its contents).

Students engaged in critical study of the Bible learn rather early that certain biblical books were not written by the persons who have traditionally been regarded as the authors. Sometimes no statement is made in a biblical book as to the identity of its author (e.g., Exodus, Joshua, Matthew, Luke), but synagogue or church tradition has theorized as to the author (viz., Moses wrote the Pentateuch, Joshua the book that bears his name, and Matthew and Luke the gospels carrying their respective names), and the tradition became accepted as fact through the centuries. In some cases an author is named in the biblical book, but critical study has uncovered evidence that at least part of the book was produced by someone other than that author (e.g., Isaiah, Amos). In still other cases, we have books which fall in their entirety into the category of pseudonymous writings, or writings purporting to be the work of someone entirely different from the actual author (e.g., Daniel).[9]

Obviously, views different from our own prevailed in ancient times regarding attribution of authorship. If a modern writer were to compose a narrative or a letter or a speech and attribute it to a notable person from the past, this would contravene our notions of literary propriety (and we might even consider it grounds for legal action). If an editor or translator revised or supplemented the manuscript of an earlier speaker or writer without clearly indicating the changes, we should regard this as wrong. But it is rather clear that such procedures as these were commonly undertaken in ancient times, without any sense of impropriety.[10] In light of the prevailing customs of those times, we might regard these practices as justified and honorable enough. In some cases the scholar might, on the other hand, conclude that false attribution of authorship was derived from dishonorable or deceitful motives. However we may judge the motives, the historian *as historian* recognizes that determination of the actual author could be an important factor in assessing the historical reliability of the account.[11]

When a work is recognized as partially or totally pseudonymous, it is useful to uncover, as far as possible, the motives for the false attribution of authorship. The account might include deliberate historical inaccuracies designed to subserve the real author's vested interests. Or, it might be that the report is reliable with regard to historical data, and the false attribution is employed simply to gain a wider audience by crediting the report to a famous and respected figure.

Especially useful in this effort to establish the provenance of the work are the techniques of "source criticism" and "tradition criticism." The *source critic* tries to determine whether a given piece of writing is the work of a single individual or whether there are signs of unevenness, changes in style, interruptions, or inconsistencies which indicate that originally separate materials (or "sources") have been joined together to form a composite work. He also looks for telltale clues which will reveal the dates of the respective contributors. The *tradition critic* concerns himself especially with the process by which certain materials (stories, laws, customs, etc.) are passed along from one person or people to another. He tries to reconstruct the original form of the material and the stages of revision and redaction through which it passed in the process of its development into the form which we now have.[12]

Once it has been determined *whose* account the historian has before him, the next questions relate to the *reliability* of the account. Can the historian expect the source to yield reliable information about the events on which it reports?

Proximity of witness to events. How close was the author of the account to the events described? Did he have the opportunity to observe what he reports? If not, by what process was the information transmitted to the author? Those familiar with the history of Pentateuchal studies will know that a number of different hypotheses have been produced about the dates and process of Pentateuchal composition, but most scholars have concluded that the stories in the "books of Moses" were written down at a time rather distant from the time of the events narrated, and that an extended process of oral transmission preceded the writing.

In biblical studies it is universally recognized that many stories, hymns, sayings, and such in the Bible were passed down orally from one person or generation to another before they were written. After they were put in writing, many of them were subjected to further stages of copying and transmission. In the following pages the term "tradition" is used as a quite neutral term to refer to any material (in our study, mostly stories) which is thus passed along. The term is not intended in itself to imply any judgment about the historical value of the material. It will often be used to refer to material relating to a particular theme or to a particular individual, such as "the exodus traditions" or "the Jacob traditions."

It is also commonly recognized that changes of various kinds could and often did occur as a tradition was transmitted—additions, deletions, "updating," combination with other traditions. Modifications could be made at either the oral or the written stage, or both. Each new audience which received a tradition might "hear" in it fresh insights or read into it new applications for its situation, and these insights or meanings were often incorporated into the tradition when it was passed on. Whenever in the following pages a reference is made to revisions that were made in a tradition at a "secondary" stage, this refers to the stages subsequent to that at which the tradition originated (which would be the "primary" stage).

Ability. How able is the witness as an observer and as a reporter? Is the report internally consistent? Are there apparent omissions? Does the report appear to have been embellished in the telling? In cases where material was transmitted orally over a period of time, the accuracy of the transmission might be specially questioned. A reporter might have distorted reality quite unintentionally by uncritical reporting[13] or by concentrating on certain aspects of the past to the neglect of other equally vital aspects. In the stories of Israel's settlement in Canaan, for example, non-militant means of settlement are generally ignored, since the stories concentrate on the more dramatic military episodes, which naturally would attract more attention from both storyteller and audience.

Bias. What biases might have colored the witness's perception[14] or reporting? The reporter might have had some special interest to advance which prompted him to distort the facts. It is generally believed by Old Testament scholars that the stories of the conflict between David and Saul were preserved in pro-Davidic circles; one wonders how the story would have been told differently in the circle of Saul's supporters. The nature of the audience for which he was writing might have led the reporter to slant his account in a particular way. It is the historian's task to expose the biased, skewed, or uncritical aspects of the stories.

Hypothesis and Critique

Once the historian has satisfied himself as to the value of his evidence and how much he can rely on the respective pieces of evidence, he constructs a theory from that evidence about what actually happened in the past and why. The evidence might include a fragment of pottery from a Middle Bronze Age stratum in Jericho, or differing types of tombs at several Middle Bronze Age sites, or the relative location of wells to a particular mound of ruins; there might be a vague reference to "Israel" or general references to "Asiatics" in texts from Egypt, or

conflicting biblical accounts of the Hebrew conquest of Canaan. From
these bits and pieces the scholar has to postulate things that the bits and
pieces do not tell him directly.

The Old Testament historian, exercising his reasoned judgment,
pieces together observations and inferences about the biblical account
and the extra-biblical evidence to produce an hypothesis about the
course of events. Was there a real Abraham? If so, when did he live,
how did he make a living, and why did he move to Canaan? Which
of the Israelites' ancestors were put to slave labor in Egypt? For how
long? Under which Egyptian ruler did the escape of the Hebrew
slaves occur? Was there in fact a Moses, and, if so, did he do all that
is reported of him in the Pentateuch? Did the Hebrews of the pre-
monarchical period conceive of their relationship with God as a
"covenant," or is the notion of the covenant a theologumenon which
developed only in the first millennium B.C.? What degree of historical truth is there in the picture of Joshua's army storming into Canaan
and conquering the land in several swift maneuvers? When did this
influx of Israelites into Canaan take place? What really bound the
Israelite tribes (which even according to the biblical record were rather independent of one another) together, and when did their sense of
unity emerge?

The historian sets forth his hypothesis, along with his supporting
arguments as to why he interprets a certain biblical text as he does,
why he reckons Moses to have been an actual person, why he relates
this archaeological data to the invasion of Joshua, why he prefers this
account of a battle to that account, and so on. One thing that is standard throughout the study of history is the obligation of the historian
to give the reasons for his inferences, the warrants for his conclusions. What is the evidence on which he bases his conclusions? How
did he get from the evidence to his conclusions? If not in his more
popular presentations, at least in his scholarly publications, he owes
it to his peers to explain how he has reached his conclusions.[15] Only
then can these peers judge the value of his evidence and the cogency
of his reasoning. (Footnote references in historical works are not inserted just "to give credit where credit is due," but also to enable
other scholars to know what evidence the author is drawing on and
where fuller expositions of the evidence for a given position may be
found.)

In popular treatments the evidence and the process of inference
are often not fully laid out before the reader. It could become rather

burdensome to have to wade through all the stages of hypothesis and argument that led a scholar to a relatively simple-sounding statement like the following about the story of Joshua's attack on the city of Ai (Joshua 7–8): "From excavations it is known that the city involved was not Ai, but rather the nearby Bethel."[16] Lying behind this statement are judgments about the genre of the story in Joshua, the meaning of archaeological remains at the sites of Ai and Bethel, the general timing of the arrival of Joshua's army in Canaan, and the reliability of scholars who have studied the evidence.[17] None of these judgments is beyond dispute, but the general reader could get lost in the often technical discussion supporting the writer's position. To take another example, a scholar writing about the people known to us as the "Amorites," who exerted pressure on Mesopotamia about the year 2000 B.C. (and are often associated with the ancestors of the Old Testament Hebrews), says, "That their presence was felt even earlier to the West is testified to in Egyptian literature in the Instructions of Merykare ca. 2100 B.C., when the sage issued his warning about the rampaging Asiatics."[18] This sounds like a statement about certain undeniable facts, but it is based on inferences about the meaning of certain terms in the Egyptian text, the dating of the text, and the correspondence of a people mentioned in the Egyptian text with a people mentioned in Mesopotamian texts—and all these inferences are arguable. The stages of argument have usually been developed in professional journals or technical monographs, and, even if the average reader took the time to consult these works, it would frequently be beyond his competence to evaluate the scholar's interpretations of epigraphic or artifactual data and the soundness of his inferences.

By means of his peers' analysis and criticism—and his own ongoing self-criticism—the historian's hypotheses are subjected to testing. Weak points in the construction are exposed—fallacies in reasoning, relevant evidence misconstrued or overlooked or unaccounted for by the hypothesis. Through a process of debate other historians propose and argue for different hypotheses. A different form-critical analysis of the patriarchal narratives might be offered, with attendant implications for the historical reliability of the stories; a more congenial context for the events of the conquest of Canaan might be suggested; a different model for the form of government in early Israel might be proposed. Unlikely reconstructions of the past are eliminated and more likely reconstructions are developed and improved. Through this process we progress toward a better understanding of the past.

The Historian's Reasoning

At every stage of his work and with all his pieces of evidence, the historian—like a detective trying to reconstruct a crime—has to supplement the evidence with reasoned inferences of his own. The evidence does not "speak for itself." (Some of the evidence is genuinely mute, such as archaeological remains or topographical data; but even with written records, the historian must go beyond what the record says.) The scholar has to make the evidence "talk," rather like Sherlock Holmes inferring a man's nationality, occupation, and recent travels from observing the man's hat.

This use of inference begins at the "sifting" stage. Certain inferences are necessary in the exercise of textual criticism; where manuscripts of the Old Testament have variant readings, the textual critic must judge which is most likely the original; where the reading, even if found in all extant manuscripts, does not make sense, the critic must reason his way to an appropriate correction of the text. In the form critical phase of his work, the researcher must infer the genre and intention of a text, much as we today might study a newspaper clipping and determine whether the writer intended the piece as a straightforward news report, a piece of satire, or a piece of fiction. In determining the date and manner of a text's composition, the use of inference is required. The Pentateuch does not declare itself to be a literary composite, but biblical critics have been able to deduce this, in Holmesian fashion, from observing details in the narrative (such as inconsistencies, stylistic differences, and doublets).

When he comes to the interpretation of his evidence, the historian likewise applies inferential reasoning. Sites dug by archaeologists frequently do not yield unambiguous evidence as to which biblical settlement stood on this site or that; the scholar must study evidence from the site (such things as location, topography, artifactual remains) and compare this with information in the Bible so that he can hypothesize an identification. Is biblical Pithom to be identified with this site or that? Which of these two places was the Debir of the Bible? From the jewelry or art objects or weapons found in tombs, the historian may infer the origin of the people buried therein or the identity of the trading partners of that people, partners from whom such objects could have been obtained.[19]

Even with written records, the historian must go beyond what the record says and make inferences. If he simply pieces together the testimony of various witnesses and accepts the result as "history," he deserves the epithet coined by the British philosopher of history R.G. Collingwood, "scissors and paste historian,"[20] which is to say that he is no historian at all, but simply a collector and transmitter of tradition.

Records from the past such as government archives, royal inscriptions, or biblical narratives seldom if ever give us all the facts we need for an accurate reconstruction. Every account of past events is selective and, therefore, necessarily incomplete. Moreover, many accounts are the work of someone with a vested interest to promote. As noted above, various conscious or unconscious motives might have led the writer to give an account which is at variance with the facts.

> No document can tell us more than what the author of the document thought—what he thought had happened, what he thought ought to happen or would happen, or perhaps only what he wanted others to think he thought, or even only what he himself thought he thought.[21]

Another historian writes:

> Students of military history are familiar with the remark that on the day of battle Truth stands naked, but that as quickly as possible thereafter she begins to wrap herself in the garments of self-justification and myth.[22]

One has only to compare the accounts of a battle prepared by the opposing sides (e.g., the reports of the battle of Kadesh, 1286 B.C., between Egypt and the Hittites)[23] to verify the truth of this!

There is further the possibility of a record's being ambiguous. What group exactly is it that is referred to as "Israel" in the Merneptah stele of ca. 1220 B.C. from Egypt?[24] Do the accounts of Abraham and Jacob and their children in the book of Genesis reflect the activities of actual individuals, or do they reflect—as is often the case with folk traditions—the activities of groups disguised in the form of individual exploits? Another form of ambiguity confronts the historian when he has conflicting testimony, as we have, for example, in the narratives of Joshua's conquest of Canaan; he has to weigh probabilities and conjecture the truth out of the disparate accounts.

There is much indirect or unintentional testimony that the astute historian can wring from the written record. He learns much of importance by "reading between the lines." By analyzing the structure and meaning of personal and place names in a document, the historian often can infer from the linguistic characteristics of these names the ethnic composition of the community to which the document relates. The reference in Genesis 46:34 to the settlement of Joseph's family in Egypt implies that the Hebrews were not settled near the court of the rulers of Egypt; although neither the date of the Hebrew settlement in Egypt nor the identity of the Pharaoh then in power is given in the Bible, many scholars have inferred from this passage that the settlement must have occurred at a time when the Egyptian capital was *not* located in the delta region, near the Hebrew settlement in Goshen. From Genesis 36:31 the historian is able to infer that that passage could have been written only by someone who knew that kingship had come to the Israelite nation; an inadvertent comment in the text assists the scholar in his efforts to date the material.

Like a detective, the historian, has to "go beyond the evidence" in order to reconstruct what happened. When direct observation is lacking, when evidence is incomplete, when the meaning of a document or artifact is ambiguous, or when witnesses' testimonies clash, the historian has to hypothesize, interpolate, weigh probabilities. A work of history is a series of reasoned arguments and can be considered "factual" only to the degree that the historian's reasoning is defensible.

Let us look a little more closely at some of the types of reasoning used by historians. Although our discussion will be developed with special reference to biblical materials, the historian uses these types of reasoning when interpreting non-biblical evidence as well.

Commonsense judgments

Many of the inferences made by the historian may best be labeled simply commonsense judgments, based on generalizations about the laws of nature or human nature. One process of reasoning judges the credibility of a report by its coherence with what we know of the "laws of nature."[25] We recognize that the story told by Jotham (Judg. 9:7–15) is a fable, since trees do not talk. A similar judgment is made about the story of Balaam's ass speaking (Num. 22:28–30).

When the author of Exodus 13:17 writes that God did not lead the Hebrews out of Egypt "by way of the land of the Philistines," common sense tells us the earliest possible date at which the writing could have been set down (what scholars like to call the *terminus a quo* for the writing): this phrase could not have originated before the arrival of the Philistines in that part of the world.

Human nature likewise is considered to be fairly constant, so that, in reconstructing the past, the historian often extrapolates from what he knows of human behavior. Of the biblical account of the Hebrew slavery in Egypt, an historian writes: "The Biblical tradition a priori demands belief: it is not the sort of tradition any people would invent!"[26] He is generalizing from his own experience of human behavior, namely, that people do not invent stories which reflect in an ignominious fashion upon themselves. Suppose, for another example, one discovers a passage such as Genesis 15:7, in which God is quoted as saying to Abram,

> I am Yahweh* who brought you from Ur of the Chaldeans, to give you this land to possess

and a passage such as Exodus 6:2–3, in which God is quoted as saying to Moses,

> I am Yahweh.* I appeared to Abraham, to Isaac, and to Jacob as El Shaddai,** *but by my name Yahweh* I did not make myself known to them.*

Common sense tells one that these passages likely came from separate authors; one has drawn a generalization to the effect that a single author is unlikely to write two passages which contradict each other so blatantly. Most biblical critics have drawn this commonsense inference.

In the work of the textual critic, when two manuscripts give differing readings of a passage, sometimes the principle of *lectio difficilior* is used to reach a decision as to the more original. According to this commonsense principle, the version that is most awkward or difficult is considered likely the original, since copyists have a tendency to "smooth out" awkward passages when they find them, and it is not natural for a copyist to introduce an awkward reading into a passage.[27]

Arguments from analogy

Arguments based on analogy are widely used in the study of history. What we have above called "commonsense" inferences are in fact forms of arguments from analogy. One assumes that something contrary to the laws of nature or of human behavior with which we are familiar is, by analogy, highly unlikely to have occurred in biblical times.[28] Other types of analogical argument include the following.

Form criticism. The practice of form criticism, whereby the scholar determines the genre, setting, and intention of a text, is based on the

---

*RSV: the LORD
**RSV: God Almighty

use of analogy. The form critic analyzes the structure of a passage and then, by noting similarities of that structure to recognized genres of speech or literature, identifies the genre of the passage under study and draws certain conclusions accordingly about the interpretation of the passage. For example, certain accusatory passages in prophetic literature exhibit similarities in form to speeches used in Hebrew law courts, and we infer that the prophet intended to create a "lawsuit" atmosphere by using this genre of speech.[29] A particular text is understood by comparing its form with that of other texts from the Bible and elsewhere. The genre and meaning of certain biblical psalms have been clarified by classifying them according to formal types and comparing them with hymnic compositions from other Near Eastern cultures.[30] Inferences about the age and meaning of covenant passages in the Old Testament have been drawn by comparing their structure with examples of the treaty genre attested in texts from the Hittite and other ancient empires.[31]

Cross-cultural studies. Since the people of the Old Testament period cannot be observed directly by modern scholars, it is not uncommon for scholars to fill in the gaps of information that can be drawn from the Old Testament by drawing analogies from what is known of cultures similar to that of the Hebrews. For example, by discovering how genealogies were constructed and used among other primitive peoples, certain inferences are made about the Hebrew genealogies and what sorts of information can legitimately be drawn from them.[32] From field studies of oral performance and transmission among modern primitives it is hoped to gain insight into these phenomena in ancient Israel.[33] Studies of tribal structures in the modern Middle East have been used to construct models by which the Hebrew society could be better comprehended.[34] How enlightening one finds such comparisons depends on how valid one feels the analogy to be between the Hebrews of the premonarchical period and peoples removed in time or geographical context. The general tendency among scholars has been to bestow respect upon such analogies in direct ratio to the geographical and chronological proximity of the other people to the biblical Hebrews.

"Congenial context." Yet another type of analogical argument has been utilized in the effort to fit the events of the early Old Testament into their proper chronological context. Much of the historical work relating to ancient Israel has centered around dating the events described in the early books of the Bible. Approximately when did the patriarchs live? (Late third millennium B.C.? Early second millennium?

Mid-second millennium?) When did the family of Jacob begin its sojourn in Egypt, which is reported in the last chapters of Genesis? (Hyksos period? Amarna age?)[35] At what date did the exodus occur?
(Fifteenth century? Thirteenth century?) What about the date of the
"conquest" of Canaan? (Fifteenth century? Early thirteenth century?
Late thirteenth?)[36] Since none of the characters or events in the early
Old Testament books are mentioned in extra-biblical sources which
have come to light, scholars have commonly chosen what we may term
"the congenial context argument" as the most promising way to establish a dating. By comparing what is told of Hebrew life and society and
history in the Bible with what is known of life and society and history
in the ancient Near East at various periods, researchers have tried to
find the historical setting into which the Old Testament stories best
"fit." The process has been described as follows:

> Historians, having deduced from the biblical narratives that a period of
> Israel's history with characteristics A, B, and C should be placed into
> period Y, have considered themselves methodologically obliged to verify
> or falsify their profile by testing it out against the relevant extra-biblical
> data. If the extra-biblical data for period Y indicate that conditions A, B,
> and C do in fact exist in period Y, they would accept that the proposed
> profile would thereby be verified to a greater or lesser extent. The degree
> of verification would depend upon such factors as the exactitude of the
> conditions involved, and whether or not conditions A, B, and C existed in
> other periods. But if, on the other hand, it is shown from the extra-biblical
> data that period Y does not contain conditions A, B, and C, but reveals
> conditions M, N, and O which are antithetical to A, B, and C, then the
> proposed reconstruction is obviously falsified and should be immediately
> abandoned.[37]

In the study of the patriarchal era, a number of customs exemplified
in the stories of the patriarchal families (who are supposed to have
come originally from Mesopotamia) have been compared to customs
attested in tablets from early and mid-second millennium Mesopotamia. Many scholars have concluded that the similarities confirmed that
the early or mid-second millennium was the most congenial context in
which the patriarchs with these customs could be located. It was argued
by some that this was the *only* context in which the patriarchal customs
"fit"—in short, that the era up to about 1500 B.C. provided an *exclusive* congenial context. A similar argument was made about the types
of personal names found among the patriarchal families and name-
types from second millennium Mesopotamia. On the other hand, some

scholars have utilized the same form of argument to claim that the only possible context out of which the patriarchal traditions can be explained was the mid-*first* millennium B.C.[38]

Considerable debate has taken place as to whether the notion of Israel's covenant with Yahweh really dated back to the time of Moses or whether it was introduced centuries later, in the first millennium B.C., from which time it was "read back" onto the Mosaic period. In the 1950s it was discovered that biblical passages describing Israel's covenant with Yahweh resembled in their structure treaties used by the Hittite empire in the second half of the second millennium B.C. The form of these treaties, it has been claimed, differs significantly from treaty forms commonly used in the Near East in the first millennium; consequently, it is argued, the Hebrew covenant passages must have been framed in the late second millennium, when the Hittite treaty type was in vogue.[39] Efforts to date the Hebrew conquest of Canaan under Joshua have commonly proceeded by trying to match up the course of attack described in the book of Joshua with an archaeological context in which destruction of the cities said to have been attacked by Joshua is attested.[40]

This type of argument can seldom *prove* the date of particular biblical events. All that can usually be concluded is that there is nothing to disprove a given dating.

Typological arguments

We are all familiar with the way fashions in clothing or automobile design change and evolve. If you were given photographs of six styles of women's dress or models of Chevrolet automobiles from six model years during the past half century, you could in all likelihood arrange them with little difficulty in the proper chronological sequence. What you would have done is to set up a "typology" of clothing styles or automobile designs.

Scholars who have studied ancient cultures have discovered that phenomena like pottery designs, styles of writing (i.e., scripts), and poetic forms change and evolve in similar ways. If a scholar has specimens of pottery or writing from enough known dates, he can arrange them in a sequence; and then, if a specimen of unknown date comes to him he can, by comparing it with those in his typological sequence, infer the probable location of the new specimen in the sequence. Through the use of typological analysis, therefore, one can infer the relative dating of artifacts or poetry or even theological ideas: this specimen appears to be later than that one, but earlier than that other one. If enough of the specimens can be assigned *absolute* dates,[41] the new specimen can then be assigned an approximate absolute date.

Argument from silence

When something is absent which one might naturally expect to be present, the scholar will frequently conclude that the absence is significant. The German scholar Gerhard von Rad discovered that numerous creed-like statements in the Old Testament, in reviewing the great events of Israel's past, move directly from the exodus to the conquest of Canaan, with no mention of the Sinai theophany and law-giving. Von Rad inferred from the silence of these passages regarding Sinai that the Sinai material had not originally been connected with the story of the exodus from Egypt, and that the two experiences belonged to originally separate groups of people.[42] The Old Testament is strikingly silent about any battle by Joshua's armies in the area of Shechem—the site where, according to Joshua 24, a nationwide convocation of the Israelites was held following the conquest. Many historians have inferred from this that the inhabitants of Shechem proved friendly toward the Hebrew invaders (possibly because of ethnic ties), so that coexistence was achieved peacefully.[43] Arguments from silence are notoriously slender reeds to lean upon unless they are corroborated by arguments of a more direct and positive nature.

Degrees of Certainty in Historical Study

The reader should not be misled by the inferential and hypothetical nature of historical study into thinking that the whole enterprise is nothing but untrustworthy guesswork. Because of the tentativeness of historical conclusions, some people have reasoned as follows:

> Those acquainted with the nature of historical inquiries, the uncertainty of testimony, the prejudice of witnesses, the doubtfulness of documents . . . may easily assure themselves, without entering far into the laborious inquiry, that its results are bound to be in the highest degree tentative and uncertain, that scholars to the end of the chapter will continue to disagree and dispute and that, in fact, there is not evidence sufficient in quality or quantity, to establish any unquestionable final truth.[44]

One should not assume that historical conclusions, because they are inferential and hypothetical, are for that reason subjective and arbitrary and unreliable. Historians, like experts in any field, advance their hypotheses on the basis of objective evidence and reasoning conducted according to accepted principles of logic.

Both scientific and historical constructions are meant to account for known data which exists independently of the investigator. In both cases, the constructions stand or fall by their adequacy in explaining the known evidence. No construction, on the other hand, is a final solution to a particular problem. History shares with science the characteristic that its new constructions are always open to revision, either because new data may come to light or because new interpretation or construction of the already established and known data may be possible.[45]

Experts in many fields of endeavor which affect our lives proceed by inference and hypothesis. For example, economists, meteorologists, judges, government officials, and medical doctors all draw inferences in their interpretation of relevant data and form hypotheses which most of us are neither in a position nor competent to check. But when we have satisfied ourselves as to the competency of these experts, we act on the basis of their judgments. We do not wait upon "unquestionable final truth."[46] It is unrealistic to measure knowledge in any field against the ideal of *perfect* knowledge,[47] which is humanly unattainable. We cannot know the historical past with absolute and total accuracy, but neither can we attain total and absolute accuracy in medical diagnosis or economic analysis or the system of criminal justice. The most we can usually hope for in such investigations is the establishment of an hypothesis or proposition "beyond a reasonable doubt."

No inferential argument can be posited with absolute and total certainty. The degree of confidence or assent that an argument or hypothesis can elicit will vary (and this holds true whether we are dealing with physicians or lawyers or historians). The conclusions in one instance may be more persuasive than in another, not because the reasoning is better in the former, but because of variables such as the nature of the evidence, the quantity of evidence, the ambiguity or absence thereof in the evidence, and the number of possible alternative inferences from the evidence. The person presenting the argument should consider how strong a case the evidence and reasoning make and qualify the argument (hypothesis) appropriately. In one case the evidence may be so overwhelming that he can declare, "Undoubtedly . . . ," but another conclusion may be only "probably" or "possibly" valid. Genuine disagreements break out in historical studies when an historian claims more certainty for an hypothesis than the evidence warrants.

Any responsible person will be prepared to submit his evidence and his reasoning for scrutiny if his conclusions should be challenged.

> All claims are implicit appeals to other persons. And our respect for persons is directly proportionate to the degree to which we make clear the worthiness of our claims.[48]

One cannot specify in advance exactly how a person should justify his conclusions. The type of evidence or the chain of reasoning which will lend credibility to an hypothesis will vary from case to case. A judgment about the proper translation of an ancient document will require one sort of justification, whereas a conclusion about the cause of an ancient city's destruction will require a different kind of justification. Van Harvey uses the illuminating analogy of a lawyer presenting his case in court.[49] The lawyer may employ arguments about handwriting analysis, medical arguments about the cause of death, psychological arguments about the defendant's state of mind, or legal arguments about the admissibility of certain evidence, to mention some of the possibilities. In each instance the lawyer is expected to adduce reasons, or justification, for his arguments. But the sorts of evidence in these different arguments, and the chain of reasoning, will be quite varied.[50] One cannot establish an exclusive category or type of "legal argument." There is not just a single type of statement or argument that the lawyer specializes in.

One cannot measure the validity of a medical argument by the same criteria used for measuring the certainty of an argument about the defendant's motives. Statements about motives are in a different "field" from statements about medical factors. Similarly, statements about physical possibility (e.g., can a person travel from city A to city B in a specified length of time?) are different from statements about the constitutional rights of a suspect.

The historian, like the lawyer in court, must employ arguments of the most diverse sorts. His studies encompass hypotheses (arguments) about such widely divergent matters as the dating of artifacts, the translation of documents, the verification of occurrences, the dating and sequence of events, the motives of historical figures, the motives of those who report on historical figures, natural laws, and laws of human behavior.

The element which is common to all the arguments of the lawyer or the historian (or anyone else) is the obligation to give reasons for his conclusions. The nature of the evidence and the line of reasoning, however, will differ from argument to argument—as will the degree of certainty.

The best way to gain an understanding of how historians work is to observe the process of historical study. The next three chapters present a discussion of recent historical work on the earliest history of the Israelite people. What kinds of decisions are required as the scholar reconstructs the past? What kinds of evidence does he draw on? How does the historian move from the evidence to a reconstruction of what actually happened? What are the alternative ways of interpreting the available evidence? Just how reliable is the Old Testament narrative as an historical source? What light can extra-biblical evidence, such as the findings of archaeology, shed on this early period?

TWO
Recent
Study
of Israel's
Early History

CHAPTER

2

The "Patriarchal Period"

Ever since the rise of source-critical study of the Pentateuch, with its dating of even the earliest written sources a number of centuries after the time when Abraham, Isaac, and Jacob were supposed to have lived, the reconstruction of the "patriarchal era" has been recognized as problematical. Julius Wellhausen provided the most convincing arguments that the Pentateuch was a composite of four sources—represented by the symbols J, E, D, and P—with the earliest of them, J, originating in the ninth century B.C. It was Wellhausen's well-known belief that the Pentateuchal sources bore witness only to the times in which they were written, and had no value with regard to informing us about the age they purport to describe.[1]

While generally accepting the findings of the source critics, many scholars in the twentieth century have attempted to penetrate behind the period at which the Pentateuchal material was reduced to writing. Practitioners of "form criticism" and "tradition criticism" have sought to determine what the material looked like and how it was used in the pre-literary stages.[2] But still historians were hesitant to ascribe much historical value to the traditions about the patriarchs, even if they could be traced to pre-literary stages which were chronologically closer to the times purportedly described.

In recent decades, with a constantly expanding store of material being uncovered by the archaeologist's spade, much hope has been aroused that "external evidence" from this quarter will make it easier to decide about the historical value of the patriarchal narratives. Two

decades ago the American Old Testament scholar John Bright com-
plained that among those who wrote on the early history of Israel there
was "a surprising reluctance to call upon the results of archaeology" to
illuminate and evaluate the traditions of the patriarchal period.[3] Bright
belongs to a school which believes that the historical value of the patriarchal traditions must, in the face of evidence from archaeology, be
considered rather high.

Outright verification of the patriarchal stories is hardly to be expected. The happenings narrated in these stories are simply not the kind
which would likely find mention in any public record. The patriarchal
stories are family stories, with almost no mention of people or events
which would find their way into the sort of written records which have
survived from the ancient Middle East. Occasionally a scholar has
claimed that reference to some character from the book of Genesis can
be found in extra-biblical records, but responsible historians seldom
have claimed support of this order from the archaeologists' findings.
What is claimed is that information gleaned from archaeology about the
cultures and population movements of the Middle East in the second
millennium B.C. shows that the way of life and the movements of the
characters in Genesis 12–50 are "authentic," and not a fabrication of
later ages. This prompts claims that the "substantial historicity" of the
patriarchs has been established.

By the decade of the 1960s many scholars in the English-speaking
world became persuaded by finds unearthed at Middle Eastern sites
such as Mari, Nuzi, and Ras Shamra, as well as locations in Palestine,
to concede that the narratives of the patriarchs had indeed an air of
verisimilitude about them.[4] Much recent writing about the patriarchal
period has assumed that the evidence from archaeology, if it has not
verified the historicity of the patriarchs, at least has confirmed that the
narratives originated in a second millennium context. These stories (so
it is argued) bear the marks of a second millennium origin, not of some
later age.[5]

It should be noted that it is the *age* of the stories which is inferred
from this archaeological evidence. It is another inferential jump to conclude that the stories are non-fiction and that the described events actually happened. Sometimes it appears that scholars, having
demonstrated to their satisfaction that the stories reflected a second millennium milieu, automatically assumed that the stories were therefore
historically reliable.

Now there has arisen a volley of criticism, however, against the way in which archaeological findings have been called on to substantiate the antiquity of the patriarchal stories. Recent critics have argued that the evidence used to buttress the "authenticity" of the Genesis stories is either non-existent or has been distorted, and that, consequently, it has *not* been demonstrated that the patriarchal tales reflect a second millennium milieu.[6]

Patriarchal Customs

The most influential argument used to substantiate the patriarchal narratives has been the similarities detected between certain behavior recounted in the patriarchal stories, on the one hand, and social customs and legal procedures attested in documents from second millennium Mesopotamian cultures, on the other.[7] Very simply, the argument was that some of the customs reflected in the patriarchal narratives are paralleled by customs which prevailed in certain Mesopotamian cultures of the second millennium—and that comparable parallels are not to be found anywhere else! This line of argument seemed to establish (1) that the tradition about Abraham's family having originated in Mesopotamia was indeed reliable, and (2) that the patriarchal stories must have originated in a second millennium context in which these customs were current.

Customs attested in tablets excavated from Hurrian and Hittite sites were thought to parallel incidents in the Genesis accounts such as a childless wife beseeching her husband to have children by a maid,[8] the pretense by a patriarch that his wife is his "sister,"[9] the relationship of Jacob to Laban (believed to involve the adoption of Jacob by his uncle),[10] and Abraham's purchase of a grave site.[11]

Critics have charged that those who argued in this fashion have (1) seen parallels where none exist, (2) reconstructed either the biblical story or the extra-Israelite material or both in order to insert details necessary to create a parallel,[12] or (3) neglected to consider documents from later periods which provide equally good, if not better, parallels to the practices in the patriarchal stories.[13]

The childless wife. The theme of the childless wife offering her maid to the husband in order to get children is well known in Genesis. Among the tablets from Nuzi there are marriage contracts specifying that if a woman bears children to her husband, he shall not take another wife; but if she fails to bear children, she shall procure a slave woman as concubine.[14] In distinction from the Genesis stories, however, the Nuzi procedures are designed for the benefit of the husband instead of the wife (note Gen. 16:2).[15]

According to the Nuzi contracts which are supposed to parallel the Genesis practice, if the wife herself bears children after the concubine has borne children, all of the inherited property goes to the biological children of the wife; but in Genesis 29–30 the children of the hand-maids are reckoned among the heirs. If a Nuzi-like contract were in effect in the case of Abraham and Sarah, Sarah would have no cause to fear that "the son of the slave woman shall . . . be heir with my son Isaac" (Gen. 21:10).

The Nuzi tablets are specific marriage contracts, rather than examples of standard legal measures. Marriage arrangements—including such items as limitations on the husband's freedom to take additional wives, concessions by the wife if she bears no children (the husband may take a concubine), and stipulations concerning respective inheritance rights of children born to the wife and the concubine—vary from marriage to marriage. The variety of practices at Nuzi helps us understand the general background of the Genesis stories, but none of the Nuzi texts offers an exact parallel to either the Abraham or the Jacob stories; and the types of marriage contracts are not limited to the Nuzi culture.[16] Alleged similarities between the patriarchal stories and the Nuzi texts do nothing to demonstrate that the former depict practices that can be explained only by a second millennium origin of the stories.

The patriarch's wife passed off as his "sister." On three occasions in Genesis one or another of the patriarchs is portrayed as telling a foreign king that the woman who is actually the patriarch's wife is his sister.[17] E. A. Speiser initiated the interpretation[18] that this motif derives from a Hurrian custom which had become unfamiliar by the time the patriarchal stories were put into their written form. The custom is supposed to have been one whereby a man could adopt his wife as his sister, which heightened her status and security.[19] Speiser observes that the teller of the present form of the stories in Genesis obviously knew nothing of the "wife-sister" custom and instead presents the patriarchs' ploy as simple deception. What seems in the biblical story to be deception (viz., that Sarah/Rebekah is the sister of Abraham/Isaac) was, according to Speiser, originally the truth—but knowledge of the "wife-sister" custom had disappeared by the time the stories reached the literary stage.

Close scrutiny of the cited Nuzi texts shows, however, that a man who adopted a woman as his sister undertook therewith the obligation to arrange her marriage to *another* man. There is no clear case in which a man, upon taking a woman as his wife, simultaneously adopts her as his sister.[20] Therefore, it is an exceedingly fragile hypothesis to connect the "wife-sister" stories in Genesis with a supposed custom in Nuzi which is reckoned as unique to that culture. There are other possible sources for the motif in Genesis: for example, the numerous legends in the Near East which depict gods and heroes married to their sisters, or the use of the term "sister" as a term of endearment (cf. Song of Songs 5:1–2; Tobit 8:4).[21]

The "adoption" of Jacob by Laban. Regarding the interpretation of the Jacob-Laban story, one scholar wrote: "This story has been difficult to understand heretofore, but it is now easily explained by means of Nuzian customary law."[22] The Nuzi text which some interpreters have taken as a close parallel to the arrangement between Jacob and Laban is here quoted in full:

> The adoption tablet of Nashwi son of Arshenni. He adopted Wullu son of Puhishenni. As long as Nashwi lives, Wullu shall give [him] food and clothing. When Nashwi dies, Wullu shall be the heir. Should Nashwi beget a son, [the latter] shall divide equally with Wullu but [only] Nashwi's son shall take Nashwi's gods. But if there be no son of Nashwi's then Wullu shall take Nashwi's gods. And [Nashwi] has given his daughter Nuhuya as wife to Wullu. And if Wullu takes another wife, he forfeits Nashwi's land and buildings. Whoever breaks the contract shall pay one mina of silver and one mina of gold.[23]

The suggested correlations between the tablet quoted above and the Jacob-Laban story include the following: (1) Since no sons of Laban are mentioned when Jacob arrives in Haran, it has been inferred that Laban desired to adopt Jacob as his own, after the fashion of Nashwi's adoption of Wullu. (2) Laban's words of anger in Genesis 31:43 make sense if Jacob was a son (adopted) of his, which meant that Rachel and Leah still belonged to Laban also. (3) The insistence by Laban (Gen. 31:50) that Jacob take no wife in addition to his daughters has a counterpart in the contract quoted above. (4) The incident of Rachel's theft of the "household gods" (Gen. 31:19, 30–35) is illumined by the reference in this contract to the right to possess the gods.

The only one of these alleged similarities that has stood up under critical scrutiny is number 3; but this feature is common to Near Eastern marriage contracts of so broad a chronological period as to render the similarity useless insofar as verifying a second millennium dating for the traditions behind the Genesis accounts.

There is nothing of a direct nature to suggest that Jacob was adopted by Laban.[24] There are no adoption formulas in the story. To infer from the lack of any mention of sons of Laban in the early part of the story that he had no sons is but an argument from silence with little value in itself. The fact that Jacob is required to pay a bride price for Leah and Rachel (by the widespread practice of working off the bride price—in this case, seven years of service for each) shows that he is *not* the adopted son of Laban—in which case no bride price would have been required. Jacob is never shown as considering Laban as anything other than his father-in-law (cf. Gen. 31:4–13) and employer; throughout, Jacob regards Isaac as his father (Gen. 30:25; 31:18) and Canaan as his home (Gen. 30:25). When Jacob expressed a desire to return to Canaan, Laban raised no objection on the grounds of Jacob's obligation to his adoptive father (see Gen. 30:25–28). In the absence of any clear evidence to the contrary, the angry words of Laban in Genesis 31:43 can only be taken as the outburst of a frustrated man.

We have no proof whether Laban adopted Jacob or not, but the hypothesis that he did does not seem to "stand up"; the evidence against the hypothesis seems stronger than the evidence for it.

The argument has been made that Rachel's theft of the household gods is explained by the Nuzi text, from which it is inferred that, if property is to pass to someone other than a man's natural sons, possession of the household gods by that someone was essential.[25] This interpretation assumes that Jacob, having been adopted by Laban at a time when the latter had no natural sons, lost his status as chief heir when such sons were born. Rachel's theft is therefore designed (so the argument goes) to defeat the provisions of the contract by which Jacob was adopted and to gain for Jacob the chief inheritance portion and status as paterfamilias after Laban's death.

But mere possession of symbolic objects, such as the household gods, is not likely to have guaranteed the chief inheritance portion.[26] It is unreasonable to think that a potential heir can thwart the will of the still-living father by a theft of such objects.[27] Furthermore, nothing in the Jacob cycle suggests that Jacob, Rachel, or any others of the family had any design on Laban's estate. A much simpler explanation of Rachel's theft is suggested by a comment of Josephus, in connection with a similar incident (to be sure, from a time nearly 1,500 years later), "it is the custom among all the people in that country to have objects of worship in their house and to take them along when going abroad."[28]

Abraham's purchase of a grave site. In Ephron's offer (Gen. 23:11) to sell Abraham the whole piece of property instead of just the cave, some scholars saw a reflection of the Hittite law which provided that the feudal service attaching to a piece of property is transferred to the new owner only if the entire holdings of the original owner are sold. This is why Ephron wanted to dispose of the whole property and why Abraham did not want to purchase the whole.[29]

But there is nothing in Genesis 23 that mentions feudal service. Even if the Hittite parallel were legitimate, the parallel would not prove that this story had to arise out of the second millennium, since laws relating to feudal obligations cannot be considered as limited to one people or one period.[30] The account in fact bears greater resemblance to contracts from the neo-Babylonian and Achaemenid periods (sixth through fourth centuries B.C.), known as "dialogue documents," in which proposals and counter-proposals are recorded.[31]

Other parallels alleged to exist between customs in second millennium Mesopotamia and patriarchal practices have been similarly refuted.[32] In sum, none of the customs portrayed in Genesis which were formerly thought to be explainable only against a background of the second millennium have turned out that way after all. The customs— where they are illumined by material from Mesopotamia—are just as understandable if the stories originated at a later time.[33]

Patriarchal Names

A second example of the use of the "exclusive congenial context" principle may be seen in the comparisons drawn between personal names in Genesis 12–50 and name-types from second millennium Mesopotamia. The personal names found in the patriarchal stories (e.g., Abram/Abraham, Jacob, Nahor, Terah) were said to fit more readily into the nomenclature of the population of northwest Mesopotamia of the early second millennium B.C. than into that of any later period.[34] Since that is the region to which the traditions trace the patriarchal origins and the period of ancient history in which the traditions seem to date them, this seemed to be a significant confirmation of the biblical accounts.

In criticism of this line of argument it has, however, been observed that these types of names are found in the late second millennium and in the first millennium as well! The name Abram, far from fitting "best" into the early second millennium B.C. context, is of a quite common sort which "can be expected to appear wherever we find names from West Semitic peoples.''[35] The name Jacob is ''one of the most common West Semitic names of the ancient Near East,'' found from the early second millennium down through post-Christian times.[36] Evidence regarding Isaac and Israel, though less extensive, does not indicate a different situation.

Certain names which appear in the genealogy of Abram (Gen. 11:10–26), such as Serug, Nahor, Terah, and Haran, have been associated with place names which are clustered in northwest Mesopotamia, and this was taken as evidence that the traditions locating the patriarchal origins in that region were authentic. But some of these names are known from first millennium sources as well as second, and some others of them are known *only* from first millennium sources![37]

So it turns out that, although the second millennium context is one into which the names in Genesis might ''fit,'' it is not the only such context. The context is congenial, but it is not uniquely so. The historian is justified in arguing that the evidence *permits* location of the patriarchs in the second millennium. To claim more for this particular evidence is inappropriate.

The Patriarchal Mode of Life

The following words of John Bright are representative of a view which became widespread by the 1960s:

> The patriarchs are portrayed as semi-nomads living in tents, wandering up and down Palestine and its borderlands in search of seasonal pasture for their flocks and, on occasion, making longer journeys to Mesopotamia and Egypt. They were not true bedouin. . . . On the other hand, they did not (except for Lot) settle in towns, nor did they farm save, perhaps, in a limited way. . . . In other words, the patriarchs are depicted not as camel nomads, but as ass nomads, who confined their wanderings to the settled land and its fringes.[38]

This description would make the patriarchs a perfect fit in the cultural and political milieu of the early second millennium, says Bright.[39] We know of similar seminomadic stockbreeders from the Egyptian Tale of Sinuhe, the Mari texts, and the wall painting of the Beni-Hasan tomb.[40] In this instance the historian's argument is not that he has located an *exclusive* congenial context for the portrait of the patriarchs, but that the mode of life attributed to the patriarchs is not alien to the second millennium setting. The argument from analogy is used here to *"non-falsify"* the picture of the patriarchs in Genesis.

The common assumption has been that this seminomadic way of existence was the normal and natural antecedent to the development of a settled, agrarian manner of life. In portraying the Hebrew ancestors as pastoral nomads, the Genesis story provides precisely what we would expect of this people recently arrived as migrants from Mesopotamia and not yet settled in Canaan (so the argument goes).

However, a closer examination of the socioeconomic features of the patriarchal stories and a more thorough knowledge of nomadism derived from anthropological studies have led some scholars recently to argue that we must now abandon the understanding of the Hebrew patriarchs as wandering seminomads in the process of making a transition from a desert economy to an agricultural mode of life.[41]

Pastoral nomadism has long been thought of as a stage in the evolution of peoples preliminary to their settling down to an agricultural economy. Studies in the anthropological disciplines have shown, however, that pastoralism is an *offshoot* of an agricultural economy, not a stage prior to it.[42] Pastoralism is a diversification essential to the livelihood of those engaged in the tilling of the soil, which could be a precarious enterprise.[43] The pastoral nomad does not, therefore, represent a mode of life which should be contrasted with the agricultural, as in the familiar contrast between "the desert and the sown."[44] Sometimes farmers developed nomadic herds secondarily; sometimes one part of a community would farm and the other herd; sometimes the whole community would alternate in semiannual cycles between the agricultural and the pastoral.[45]

Certain features which are often regarded as exclusively nomadic—such as tents,[46] tribal structures,[47] asses, flocks and herds—are now known to have been characteristic of other modes of life in the ancient Near East as well.[48]

Moreover, a careful inspection of the patriarchal stories in Genesis reveals features which point away from a nomadic conception of the early Hebrews. Their way of living is compared with that of settled groups and contrasted with the manner of life of the nomadic Ishmaelites.[49] The Genesis stories contain signs of a more sedentary lifestyle than has commonly been assumed.[50] The social grouping around Abraham seems less built on kinship relationships than was common in nomadic groups.

> The patriarchs represent single households augmented by various levels of subordinates, including bought and house-born slaves. . . . There is nothing in the second millennium sources to suggest that nomads retained slaves as part of their social way of life.[51]

There is very little evidence of the nomadic practice of transhumance (seasonal movement from winter to summer pasture).[52] Most of the migrations in the patriarchal narratives are motivated by causes other than seasonal search for pasture.

Several scholars have proposed that the mode of life depicted in the patriarchal stories be classified as a "dimorphic society" in which herdsmen and farmers achieve a symbiosis. This sort of society is represented in the seminomadic population reflected in the Mari texts of the eighteenth century B.C.[53]

The arguments summarized here do more to disprove the old model of the patriarchal communities as a people in the process of evolving from (semi)nomadic origins to a settled agricultural existence on their way to becoming a state, than they do to disprove a second millennium origin for the patriarchal narratives. The mode of life of the patriarchs—even if it has been mistakenly characterized as "seminomadism"—nevertheless exhibits no essential features which demand an origin for the traditions in the first millennium. If the patriarchal families are better interpreted as examples of a sedentary (or "dimorphic") than a nomadic people,[54] one would have to show that it is a type of settled life unknown to the second millennium in order to disprove the second millennium origin of the traditions.[55]

The understanding of the patriarchs as nomadic which has long prevailed in Old Testament studies needs revision, but the patriarchs' mode of life has not been shown to be a decisive factor in regard to the dating of their traditions or their historical value.

The Amorite Migration Theory

The movement of the Hebrew patriarchs from Mesopotamia and Syria to Canaan, reported in Genesis 12 (cf. also Genesis 24; 28–33) has been reckoned by many Old Testament scholars to be plausible and historically likely when placed in the context of the movements of the "Amorites," who are believed to have been active throughout the Near East at the end of the third millennium B.C. and the beginning of the second millennium.[56]

From Mesopotamian sources[57] it is known that, during the latter part of the third millennium, Semites infiltrated Mesopotamia from the northwest; their original home seems to have been the Syrian-Arabian desert.[58] A number of individual kingdoms ruled by these West Semites were established after the turn of the millennium, and for several more centuries the Amorites continued to play an important role in Mesopotamia.[59]

The story of Abram's migration from Ur to Haran (Gen. 11:31) has been located by some historians[60] in the context of this Amorite infiltration which contributed to the downfall of the Ur III kingdom (dated ca. 2060–1950 B.C.) in Mesopotamia. However, records of this infiltration point to movement from peripheral regions into settled areas, rather than from one urban center (such as Ur) to another (Haran); and there is no trace of a movement of these peoples in the direction of Ur-to-Haran. "Ur, rather than being the source of these migrations, is among the prizes sought."[61]

Many scholars who doubt the historicity of the migration from Ur to Haran nevertheless are prepared to argue that the story of the migration from Haran to Canaan (Gen. 12:1–9) is historically grounded in one or another movement of Amorites into Palestine (and Egypt) just before or just after 2000 B.C.[62] Although there is no documentary evidence of such an Amorite movement, such a movement has been hypothesized by numerous scholars, some of them seemingly motivated by a desire to find an extra-biblical parallel to the story of Abraham's migration to Canaan.[63] The influx of Amorites into Palestine is hypothesized on the basis of (1) archaeological remains from late third and early second millennium Palestine which attest cultural changes in that region, including some cultural features derived from Syria, and (2) texts from Egypt which contain references to nomadic Asiatics who might be identified with the Amorites.

Various inscriptional and artifactual data from the Early and Middle Bronze Age have therefore been used to reconstruct what is believed to have been a migration of Amorites from Mesopotamia to Palestine and Egypt, and this hypothetical migration is depicted with features which seem to correlate with the movement(s) of Abraham and his family from Mesopotamia.

From archaeological findings, there are several junctures in the period from ca. 2300 to 1800 B.C. at which scholars have inferred that there was an infusion of new cultural elements into Palestine. It is primarily changes in the pottery repertoire and metal implements, new burial procedures and new weapons which are adduced as evidence;

cultural similarities with remains from Syria have been detected.[64] One period of "new arrivals" is the so-called "Middle Bronze I" period (ca. 2200–1950 B.C.),[65] which followed a general interruption of culture at the end of the Early Bronze Age.[66] Middle Bronze I is characterized as a time of widespread nomadic occupation, tribal distinctions, and unfortified villages, and primitive as regards material culture and the standard of living.[67] Another period in which some archaeologists have postulated a new cultural influx is the time of the reviving urban culture (Middle Bronze IIA) following 1950 B.C.[68] For each of these two periods there have been scholars who proposed that the bearers of the new cultural elements were Amorites who had migrated from Mesopotamia or Syria.[69]

In whichever of the two above-mentioned archaeological periods one sought to locate the arrival of the Amorites, there are Egyptian texts which offered hope of providing some corroborating evidence. If one could correlate archaeological evidence for an infusion of new population elements from the direction of Syria at a time when written texts testified to the presence of Asian nomads newly arrived in Palestine with Amorite names, the theory of Amorite migration(s) would have impressive circumstantial support.

Egyptian texts ranging in date from close to 2200 down to the 1800s B.C.[70] contain references to people called "Amu," who appear to be Asiatics who made incursions into Egypt and the surrounding area. The tomb painting of Beni-Hasan (from ca. 1890 B.C.)[71] is believed to depict Asiatics coming to Egypt from "the land of Shutu," taken to be the southern Transjordan;[72] the nomads here represented are called "Amu."

Another group of documents from Egypt, known as the "Execration Texts,"[73] contain lists of what appeared to scholars to be newly arrived nomads bearing Amorite names in Palestine. Many of the personal and place names mentioned in connection with the Palestinian area are West Semitic, and it has been argued that these names are identical in type with those of the Amorites. It is further argued that the West Semitic peoples named in these texts were newcomers in a process of transition from a nomadic way of life to a sedentary urban existence.[74] In the earlier stages of study of the Execration Texts, the texts were dated to a time that coincided with the MB I period, and they were used to support a theory of Amorite arrivals during that time of nomadic occupation and unfortified villages. Subsequent study has resulted in a re-dating of the texts to the 1800s, and now they are called on to support the theory of Amorite migration in MB IIA.[75]

The above-mentioned inferences from both the archaeological data and the Egyptian texts have been seriously challenged. Whether the archaeological evidence from the MB I period reflects the arrival of new population elements or not is debated. Some critics believe that there are sufficient indications of *continuity* between MB I and the culture preceding it, as regards pottery styles and burial customs, to inhibit the historian from speaking too quickly of new peoples arriving with a new culture.[76] These critics argue that cultural changes attested by archaeological discoveries have in the past been taken more often than is justified as evidence for changes in population. Natural causes can be just as much responsible for the disruption of a culture. Climatic or economic conditions have been suggested as likely reasons for the urban crisis which appears throughout the Mediterranean region toward the end of the Early Bronze Age.[77] It may be that the Early Bronze population simply maintained itself on a more primitive level in the wake of this crisis.[78] Similarly, it has been averred that there are signs of continuity between MB I and MB IIA;[79] and it has also been suggested that changes in the pottery repertoire could be attributed to new techniques and heightened trade, neither of which would necessitate an infusion of new population elements.[80]

The evidence of the Egyptian references to the "Amu" are not very conclusive. The ethnic affiliation of these "Asiatics" is not indicated. It is possible that the term "Amu" referred to peoples found for many centuries in the desert east of Egypt, with whom the Egyptians had sometimes friendly, and sometimes hostile, relations, and whose presence became more threatening in periods of Egyptian weakness.[81]

Similarly, the value of the Execration Texts for the "Amorite migration" theory is questionable. It cannot be shown conclusively that the West Semitic names in these texts belong to the same linguistic branch as the Amorite names known to us from Mesopotamian texts. Since the orthography of the texts is Egyptian (which does not distinguish certain dialectical differences among the West Semitic languages) it is difficult to identify, in these particular texts, the precise branch of the Semitic languages to which these names belong.[82]

The argument that the bearers of the Semitic names were *newly arrived* in Palestine is weak. These texts are the earliest historical sources relating to Palestine, so there are no previous texts with which a comparison can be made. Here in these earliest texts the Semites are already present in Palestine; one scholar observes there is some evidence which suggests that they might have been present there from as early as 3000 B.C.![83]

Even if it turns out that an Amorite migration into Palestine near the beginning of the second millennium can be demonstrated,[84] the value of this for clarifying the historicity of the patriarchal narratives is most uncertain. The fact remains that the movement of Abraham to Canaan (and the same goes for the movement of Jacob after his sojourn with Laban) is *not* depicted as part of a larger movement. Much of the pathos of Abraham's trek derives from the fact that it involved *separation* from his people. To argue that there was an Amorite movement from Syria or Mesopotamia to Canaan, and that Abraham belonged to that movement despite the biblical testimony that his migration occurred under quite different circumstances seems a curious way to secure an "historical foundation" for the biblical material.

Arguments for Lateness of Traditions

The criticisms summarized in the preceding sections do not *disprove* a second millennium provenance for the traditions about Abraham, Isaac, and Jacob, but they have seriously damaged the case which had been built up to verify such a date by the utilization of "external evidence." The assorted criticisms have shown that a congenial context for the patriarchal traditions cannot be located exclusively in early second millennium Mesopotamia. Much of the "external evidence" is *consistent* with such a dating, but none of it *demands* such a dating. The external evidence does not offer as much support for the theory of the traditions' antiquity as some scholars had claimed, but on the other hand, the criticisms do not in themselves falsify the Genesis accounts. However, there are further considerations which do indicate that a *later* origin for the traditions must be considered, which would render suspect the historicity of the traditions.

(1) It has long been recognized that the Genesis stories contain some late elements. Some of the individual stories are best understood as traditions which grew out of historical circumstances in the period after the settlement (or "conquest"). For example, those parts of the Jacob cycle which have as their theme the subjection of Edom (Esau) to Israel (Jacob)[85] likely reflect a period subsequent to David's subjecting Edom.[86] Elements in the "promise" to the fathers which relate to the growth of Abraham's family into a "great nation"[87] apparently presuppose the development of Israel into a world power.[88] These passages are believed by many scholars to fall into the cate-

gory of *vaticinium ex eventu* (prophecy after the fact).

(2) Although the point is not stressed in many of the widely used Old Testament handbooks in the English speaking world,[89] it is widely held among Old Testament scholars that the arrangement of Abraham, Isaac, Jacob, and the twelve sons of Jacob in a genealogical chain is an artificial connection made at a relatively late stage in the growth of the Genesis traditions. Originally separate traditions about these patriarchs have, in the opinion of many critical scholars, been joined together by redactors at a secondary stage of transmission. The stories of Abraham and Jacob, in particular, are concerned with different themes, and the narratives of the two men are centered around separate geographical areas where they likely circulated at one time independent of each other.[90]

(3) The linking of the twelve eponymous ancestors of the Israelite tribes to each other and to Jacob is artificial and late. The various tribes acquired their respective homelands in Palestine at different periods of time, in various ways, and from diverse backgrounds.[91] The sense of unity among these tribal groups evolved on Palestinian soil in the period of the judges.[92] Obviously the notion of the twelve tribal fathers being sons of a single man named "Israel" (Jacob) must be a fiction which grew up in the period of the judges or later.[93]

(4) The Philistines, who are referred to several times in the patriarchal narratives,[94] did not arrive in Canaan until shortly after 1200 B.C.[95] The references to them in Genesis are usually dismissed as anachronisms which were inserted into the narratives at a late stage in their transmission. Such an explanation would not be necessary if the traditions originated in the late second or in the first millennium.[96]

(5) John Van Seters has argued that the various terms used to designate the pre-patriarchal inhabitants of Palestine—"Amorites," "Hittites," "Horites," and "Canaanites"—are best explained if the patriarchal stories originated in the first millennium B.C.[97] Van Seters' argument is that by the first millennium these terms had lost their specific ethnic or political connotations and were used in Assyrian and Egyptian sources as general archaic designations for the peoples of Syria, Phoenicia, Palestine, and Transjordan—which is how the terms are used in Genesis.[98]

(6) A number of ethnic relationships of the patriarchs reported in Genesis could not have been conceived before the late second or first millennium.[99] A close relationship is perceived with the *Arameans,* among whom a wife for Isaac is sought,[100] a place of asylum for Jacob

is found,[101] and the mothers of the sons of Jacob/Israel are found.[102] The Arameans did not appear with certainty in Mesopotamian texts until almost 1100 B.C.[103] In genealogies[104] and in the story of Hagar and Ishmael,[105] Abraham is depicted as the father of the *Arabs,* who arrived on the scene only in the 800s B.C.[106] The association of Abraham's origins with the *Chaldeans*[107] can only have originated after the appearance of this people in the early first millennium.

(7) It is difficult to find a time in the early or mid-second millennium at which all the places said to have been frequented by the patriarchs were in fact settled. At least one of the sites where, according to Genesis, the patriarchs sojourned, namely Beersheba, was uninhabited before the thirteenth century B.C. Many of the other places mentioned in the patriarchal stories (e.g., Shechem, Bethel, Hebron) have left no archaeological traces of any MB I existence,[108] so that a provenance in that period would seem to be excluded for the patriarchal stories. On the other hand, archaeological findings in the Negeb (where patriarchal wanderings are also reported) indicate that this region, though settled in MB I, was devoid of occupation *after* MB I until the late second millennium.[109] These archaeological data prompt the historian to look for a later time period when the places were settled and when, therefore, it would have been natural for storytellers to utilize them as locales for the patriarchal tales.

(8) Finally, Van Seters, in the second part of his recent study on the Abraham stories,[110] has developed an extensive literary analysis of the stories which leads him to conclude that the Abraham traditions must be dated—on the basis of internal, literary criteria—to the first millennium. For example, he believes that many of the genres, or forms, used in the Abraham stories presuppose royal or prophetic models which did not exist until the first millennium.[111] Moreover, he finds at the core of some of the Abraham traditions certain concerns (or what some writers would call "kerygmatic intentions") that reflect the circumstances of the Israelite people in the exilic period and later.[112]

Indications of Antiquity

On the other hand, however, there are certain features in the Genesis stories which point in the direction of an *early* dating for the patriarchal traditions. Therefore the Old Testament historian should not immediately conclude from the aforementioned arguments that the patriarchal traditions must be dated in toto from the period after the settlement.

(1) A matter that will require further examination has to do with the

portrayal of the religion of the patriarchs.[113] The Pentateuchal traditions exhibit a consciousness of a distinction between the religion of the patriarchs and the religion of Israel in later times. The two versions of Moses' call imply that the religion of the pre-Mosaic era was different from that of the religion of Moses.[114] There are other indications that the worship of the patriarchs was directed to deities other than Yahweh. There are frequent references in Genesis to "the god of my/your/his father," or to "the god of Abraham/Isaac/Jacob," and these have long been taken to reflect the worship of clan deities who were believed to have revealed themselves first to the eponymous ancestors of the respective clans.[115] The god traveled with the clan and was considered related to the clan.[116]

In addition, the Genesis traditions indicate that the individuals depicted there worshipped various manifestations of the Canaanite high god El after their migration into the land of Canaan.[117] Several scholars believe that the form of the El religion which influenced the patriarchal traditions was an earlier form of that religion than is depicted in the fourteenth century Canaanite texts from the site of ancient Ugarit.[118]

How can these vestiges of earlier and distinctive types of religion be explained except as recollections of practices actually followed by the forefathers of Israel? If the content of the patriarchal stories was purely a product of later centuries, why did the Hebrews of those later centuries ascribe to their pre-history types of religion which were inconsistent with the Yahwism to which they were pledged? Common sense suggests that it would have been more natural to ascribe to that earlier era the form of religion which they themselves practiced. If they "read back" into the patriarchal period their own relations with Arameans and Chaldeans, and if they "read back" customs they themselves followed, why should they not also have imposed on the picture of the forefathers the religion which they themselves practiced?

(2) If the traditions are of a late origin, with no historical basis in fact, one wonders why the immediate father of the Israelite nation, Jacob, is portrayed in such an unflattering way. Jacob's character is at best questionable, and at several points he engages in activity which is in direct contravention to later laws and customs.[119] If such a portrayal of Jacob had some basis in fact and was handed down from antiquity, it is easier to account for the presence of these traits. But if we are asked to think of the tradition as a late fabrication, it is more difficult to conceive of a people deliberately constructing an eponymous ancestor along these lines.

(3) The kinship association of the Israelites with the Arameans

which is reflected in the patriarchal narratives is held by both Van
Seters and Thompson to be artificial and of late origin. [120] It is, however, somewhat hard to understand how this notion would have arisen
and been given credence at a time when Israel was so often engaged in
hostilities with the Arameans.[121] The Arameans are not portrayed simply as peripheral relatives; the very mothers of the Israelite tribes are
said to have been Arameans! If there was in fact nothing in the background of the people of Israel to link them ethnically and geographical-
ly to northwest Mesopotamia, why would they trace their origins to
that region?

(4) As Thompson himself notes, the names Abraham, Isaac, Jacob,
Israel, and Ishmael belong typologically to a class of West Semitic
names which is earlier than the class of names to which the majority of
biblical names belong.[122] Since these types of patriarchal names were
not limited to the earliest period in which they occurred, they cannot be
taken as proof of the antiquity of the traditions of the patriarchs. But it
is worth noting that names of the type more common in the later periods of history were not used of the patriarchs.

Students of the patriarchal period will now, in the light of recent
criticisms, review and refine previous delineations of probably late and
probably early elements in this material. Once analysis has identified
the material which is clearly late, the scholar must seek to determine if
the remaining material is (1) substantial enough to represent an earlier
stage of tradition, and (2) sufficiently early and reliable enough to be of
historical value. Are the late features numerous enough and of a sub-
stantive enough nature to compel us to conclude that nothing of any
consequence in the patriarchal stories derives from the era purportedly
described by these stories? Or is there embedded in these stories reliable information which, although refracted through generations of re-
telling and re-interpretation, can be used to reconstruct the course of
events and the manner of life from the pre-exodus period? Even if we
succeed in establishing an early dating for some of the material, should
we expect family stories of this type to yield historical information?
The patriarchal stories are mostly family stories,[123] and episodes of
family life have a certain timeless quality about them (cf. the stories of
Ruth and Tobit); are they in fact stories which were composed to report
about particular people living in particular times? Figures like Abraham
and Jacob became in time paradigmatic figures rather like the figures of
the "prodigal son" or the "good Samaritan" of Jesus' parables; were
they such from the beginning?[124] These are some of the questions now
before the scholars laboring on this earliest period of Israel's history.

CHAPTER

3

Exodus
and Covenant

At the end of the Genesis narrative we read that the Hebrew people have migrated to Egypt, approximately seventy in number (Gen. 46:26–27), to settle under a friendly ruler. At this point the narrative in the book of Exodus picks up (Exod. 1:1–5). The story goes on to tell of a change in attitude on the part of the Egyptian government toward the family of Jacob, which led to enslavement for the Hebrews. Under Moses' leadership and the providence of Yahweh, we are told, the Hebrews escaped from this predicament. They made their way to Mount Sinai, where they entered into a "covenant" (Exod. 19:5; 24:7; 34:10, 27) with Yahweh. Then followed a wandering through the wilderness, extended to a period of forty years as punishment for the people's lack of faith in their god. Much of this forty-year period was apparently spent in the vicinity of Kadesh-barnea (cf. Num. 13–14; 20; also Deut. 1:46; Judg. 11:16). Finally, following a march into southern Transjordan, the invasion of Canaan was launched.

The energies of many historians have been devoted to the analysis of these biblical narratives to determine how much they accord with actual events, when these events took place, and what portion of Israel's ancestors experienced these things.

This section of the biblical narrative has given rise to numerous historical problems, and it is beyond the scope of this book to deal with all of them: whether Moses was in fact an historical figure, the circumstances of his birth and upbringing, the date and nature of the Hebrews' sojourn in Egypt, the relationship of the Moses group to the Midianites, the content of the revelation granted to Moses in his call experience, the historicity of the plagues which were visited upon Egypt, the circumstances of the exodus from Egypt, the route of the Hebrews through the wilderness, the facts lying behind the Sinai accounts, the location of Sinai, etc. For a thorough discussion of these problems, the reader is referred to the recent magnum opus of Roland de Vaux, *The Early History of Israel*. In what follows I shall attempt to delineate some of the problems which have occasioned the most interest and discussion in recent years.

Into and Out of Egypt

It is obvious that only a fraction of the people who became the nation Israel could have had its actual forebears involved in the episodes of slavery in Egypt[1] and exodus and wilderness wandering under Moses. The biblical traditions themselves imply this. We are told that seventy persons immigrated to Egypt in the time of Joseph (Gen. 46:27; Deut. 10:22). According to the genealogy given in Exodus 6:16–20, Moses belonged to the third generation following the descent into Egypt; clearly seventy persons could not in three generations have multiplied into anything like the number of two million or more implied by the statement in Exodus 12:37.[2] The experiences of a rather small group were in the course of time adopted by a much larger group as a part of their folk heritage.

Date of entry

The date at which the ancestors of Israel entered Egypt remains very uncertain, for there are no clear external reference points by which the entry can be dated. A popular theory has been that the entry of Israel's ancestors into the land of the Nile (as recounted in the Joseph narrative) took place in the period of the Hyksos regime in Egypt (ca. 1720–1570 B.C.).[3] One strand in the biblical traditions states that the Israelites remained in Egypt for about four hundred years (Gen. 15:13; Exod. 12:40–41).[4] If the exodus is dated in the 1200s, as is most common now (see below), a four-hundred-year sojourn would have had its beginnings during the reign of the Hyksos. Other data taken as evidence for this dating of the entry include the appearance of the names Jacob and Hur among the Hyksos,[5] and the fact that there were Semitic elements present among the Hyksos population, which (it is inferred) would have disposed the Hyksos to receive fellow Semites such as the Israelites kindly[6] (and, it is sometimes added, would have provided a context in which a Semite like Joseph could rise quickly to power). Further, it is argued that the proximity of the Hebrew settlement in Goshen to the pharaoh's court (cf. Gen. 45:10; 46:28–29) accords best with conditions in the Hyksos period, at which time the capital was located in the delta region rather than up the Nile at Thebes, its former location.[7]

A number of criticisms, however, have been raised against this theory of the Hebrews' descent into Egypt during the Hyksos period, and it does not now appear the most likely possibility. There is the separate biblical tradition referred to above that the sojourn in Egypt lasted only four generations (Gen. 15:16; note the sequence of generations in Exod. 6:16–20: Levi-Kohath-Amram-Moses).[8] A considerable chronological gap is created between Exod. 1:8 and 9 if verse 8 is taken to refer to the re-establishment of native Egyptian rule following expulsion of the Hyksos (ca. 1570 B.C.) and verse 9 to refer to the institution of slave labor shortly before the exodus of the Hebrews in the early 1200s.[9] In the period of the Hyksos, it has been further argued, it would have been no honor to bestow upon Joseph the daughter of a priest of On (Gen. 41:45), the temple where the sun god Ra, despised by the Hyksos, was worshipped.[10] Some have also argued that Gen. 46:34 implies that the residence assigned to the Hebrews upon their entry was *far from* the court of the pharaoh.[11]

Several arguments both for and against a date in the Hyksos age are premised on the assumption that the Joseph story contains historical reminiscences. It needs to be recognized that this assumption is itself a hypothesis. If, as some recent students of the Joseph story hold, that story is a fiction—especially if it is a late fictional novella—[12] items such as the distance of the Hebrew settlement from the Egyptian court, or the marriage of Joseph, are of dubious value for historical judgments about the era of Hebrew settlement in Egypt.

Several recent important histories of Israel assert that we should not think of a once-for-all entry of the Israelite ancestors into Egypt, but of a *series* of entries during the several centuries preceding the exodus.[13]

Date of the exodus

The consensus opinion now for the date of the exodus from Egypt is that this event occurred in the thirteenth century B.C. It was not long ago, however, that a fifteenth century date was frequently assigned to the exodus.[14] A principal piece of evidence used was the dating of Jericho's fall to about 1400 B.C. by the archaeologist John Garstang.[15]

Other evidence which seemed to support a fifteenth century date were certain extra-biblical texts and chronological notations in the Old Testament. Some Egyptian vassal kings of the fourteenth century, living in Canaan, wrote to the Egyptian court of "Hapiru" groups who were attacking Canaanite cities.[16] A number of scholars associated these references with the attacks of the invading Hebrews, moving into Canaan under Joshua's leadership. Other Egyptian texts from the 1300s mention "'Asaru" who were then present in Canaan, and these references were thought to be connected with the tribe of Asher.[17] The statement in 1 Kings 6:1 that Solomon began to build his temple (dated to about 957 B.C.) "in the four hundred and eightieth year after the people of Israel came out of the land of Egypt" would indicate a date in the 1400s for the exodus. In Judges 11:26 the "judge" Jephthah, commonly dated about 1100 B.C., refers to three hundred years that the Israelites had already dwelt in Canaan.[18] Scholars are much more cautious now about easily identifying the Israelites with groups mentioned in extra-biblical texts from the 1300s,[19] and the notorious difficulties with chronological notations in the Old Testament[20] make it extremely hazardous to put much weight on them in reconstructing the history of ancient Israel.

A date in the 1200s is now claimed for the exodus by most scholars, although there is disagreement as to when in that century it should be located.[21] An important factor in this thirteenth century dating has been the mention, in Exodus 1:11, that the Egyptians "set taskmasters over them to afflict them with heavy burdens; and they built for Pharaoh store-cities, Pithom and Ra-amses." Even the German scholar Martin Noth, who was generally very skeptical about the historical reliability of the traditions in the Pentateuch, acknowledged this to be "a reliable tradition" giving "strikingly concrete information"[22] which enables us to relate the slave labor of the Hebrews to the building projects known to have been undertaken by Sethos I (ca. 1305–1290 B.C.) and Rameses II (ca. 1290–1224 B.C.).[23]

Other evidence frequently cited to support a thirteenth century date for the exodus include: (1) the archaeological indications that the kingdoms of Edom and Moab, with whose inhabitants the Israelites migrating toward Palestine had to deal, according to Numbers 20:14–21 and Numbers 22–24, were uninhabited between the nineteenth and the thirteenth century B.C.;[24] (2) the archaeological evidence that numerous towns in Palestine reported in Joshua and Judges to have been targets of Israelite attacks were in fact destroyed in the thirteenth century, with resettlement by people with a poorer material culture;[25] (3) the stele of the fifth year of Pharaoh Merneptah (ca. 1224–1211 B.C.), containing a reference to what seems to be a military engagement in Canaan with a freshly settled people named "Israel";[26] (4) Egypt's defeat by the Hittites at Kadesh in the fifth year of Rameses II, which set off a series of revolts that would have created a favorable situation for the Hebrew slaves' escape.[27] We shall look further at this chronological question in chapter 4 when we discuss the matter of dating the conquest, which is intimately related to the dating of the exodus.

Which tribes were in Egypt?

With regard to the question of which of the Israelite tribes were represented in Egypt, the biblical traditions suggest principally the *Joseph* tribes (Ephraim and Manasseh), and most scholars assume this to have been the case.[28] Since Moses is claimed for the tribe of *Levi* and since numerous Egyptian names (e.g., Moses, Hophni, Phinehas) are found in the tribe of Levi,[29] many have concluded that Levites were also present.[30] Some have suggested that Genesis 42:24, which speaks of *Simeon* being held hostage in Egypt, grew out of a recollection that Simeonite elements were also in Egypt.[31] Bright and Noth both suggest that it may be that the persons who sojourned in Egypt represented elements that were eventually absorbed into *all* the tribes.[32] A writer's opinion on this question is always related to his theory about the dates and circumstances of the various tribes' entry into Canaan, which will be discussed in chapter 4.

What Happened Between Egypt and Canaan?[33]

Following the escape from Egypt, the biblical narrative reports a march to Mount Sinai, where the law was given to the Hebrews through Moses, and then a wandering through the wilderness for forty years, with a great deal of time spent in the vicinity of Kadesh-barnea, and finally, a march into Transjordan, whence the invasion of Canaan was launched.

For several decades it has been debated whether or not the traditions relating to the Sinai experience were originally connected to the traditions of the exodus. Scholars engaged in literary analysis detected features in the traditions which led them to suspect that the Sinai material might have had a separate provenance from the story of the exodus and that the two traditions had been joined together at some later time in the course of their transmission. This raised the historical question, did the same group which escaped from Egypt in fact proceed to Mount Sinai and receive the law, or *were these the experiences of two separate groups?*

It was observed by source critics that the narrative and legal passages relating to Sinai are integrated somewhat awkwardly into the present context of the Pentateuch, and that the narrative reads smoothly if one excises these passages and presumes a march directly from Egypt to the oasis of Kadesh.[34] Gerhard von Rad, in an influential article in 1938,[35] called attention, further, to the fact that mention of the Sinai events is strikingly absent from certain creed-like summaries of Israel's early history (Deut.26:5–9; 6:21–23; Josh. 24:2–13) as well as some hymnic accounts of the same (1 Sam. 12:8; Pss. 78, 105, 135, 136). It is only in late compositions (such as Ps. 106 and Nehemiah 9) that Sinai is incorporated into the recital of God's redemptive works with and for Israel.[36] Von Rad used techniques of form criticism and tradition criticism in the effort to identify the earlier stages of the traditions which lay behind their being taken up into the completed narrative as we have it. He advanced the thesis that the events summarized in the credal passages (principally exodus and conquest) constituted a sort of "canonical history" which was fixed at an early date and celebrated in the Israelites' annual Feast of Weeks (which von Rad believed was centered at the shrine of Gilgal), whereas the Sinai material constituted a completely separate tradition and was originally celebrated, perhaps every seven years, in a covenant ceremony at Shechem.[37] He believed that the "canonical history" originated during the period of the judges (roughly 1200–1000 B.C.) and that this "credo" served as the "skeleton" for the first fully developed history of early Israel, namely the work of the "Yahwist," who composed his account in the tenth century B.C. and who was responsible for inserting the Sinai material into the story of the exodus and the conquest.[38] The "credo," then, was the nuclear statement of faith which was eventually elaborated, in the time of the monarchy, into the history now preserved in the books of Genesis through Joshua.[39] The absence of any reference to Sinai in such an early summary of Israel's history under Yahweh seemed strong evidence that those who first lived through and recited the events of the "credo" knew nothing of any revelation of the law at Sinai.

If the nation Israel developed from diverse elements which acquired their land in quite separate periods (see chapter 4) and pursued separate histories for a considerable period of time, it is at least a logical possibility that the present form of the biblical tradition, which links exodus,

Sinai, wandering, and conquest together, is the result of a secondary fusion of traditions which had quite separate historical foundations and histories of transmission.

Since, however, the present form of the tradition tells of a single group which experienced the escape from Egypt and the revelation at Sinai, and since the figure of Moses is intimately associated with both traditions, the burden of proof rests on those who would maintain that the exodus and Sinai traditions originated with separate groups. Von Rad's thesis, which relies heavily on the assumption that the creed-like texts which fail to mention Sinai are summaries of the Israelite tradition at an early stage, has been heavily criticized in recent years.[40]

Critics have pointed out that the credal passages exhibit linguistic and stylistic features common to the book of Deuteronomy and related writings which are usually dated to the seventh century B.C. The extensive deuteronomic features in these passages are too pervasive to permit the theory that an ancient tradition has simply been touched up or revised by Deuteronomists.[41] Rather than being an ancient summary of faith which formed the basis for the narrative in Genesis through Joshua, the tradition represented in the credal passages is more likely a late summary, composed by Deuteronomists, of that narrative in the Hexateuch. The absence of Sinai from the "credo" passages must be explained on other grounds than a separateness of the traditions, since by the Deuteronomic era exodus and Sinai were certainly linked together.

It has also been argued by critics that the credal passages recite *Yahweh's mighty acts on Israel's behalf,* and that the Sinai events, which have to do with the *revelation of Yahweh's law and Israel's response to Yahweh's deeds,* would not logically belong in such a recital.[42]

Another argument has been that the credo passages do not actually attest a separation of the Sinai theme from the exodus theme, since each passage in which the "credo" is found recalls in some fashion the covenant law.[43] This can be seen clearly in Deuteronomy 6:20–25: following a discourse summoning Israel to obey the laws of the Lord (cf. Deut. 6:1), the text (which is supposed to be a speech of Moses) says, "When your son asks you in time to come, 'What is the meaning of the testimonies and the statutes and the ordinances which Yahweh our God has commanded you?' " and there follows as the appropriate response the "credo" reciting Yahweh's mighty deeds. Deuteronomy 26:5–9 and Joshua 24:2–13 also appear in contexts dealing with acts of obedience deriving from the Sinai law. The credal summary of God's mighty acts is in each case used to motivate an act of obedience to his law. The intention of the passage in Nehemiah 9 is different. Ezra is reciting, in a prayer of confession, the long history of Israel's repeated disobedience despite the Lord's repeated acts of benevolence. Ezra's summary by its nature must include explicit reference to both the mighty acts of God and the covenant laws which Israel disobeyed.

Some have claimed, in arguing against the separation of the exodus and Sinai events, that the exodus has no purpose or "natural outcome" apart from Sinai, and that the Sinai events have no motivation if separated from the exodus.[44] This argument, however, is rather weak. The theophany of a god, such as the one reported in the Sinai narrative, does not have to have an antecedent history of the god's benevolent deeds to ground it (compare the theophanies granted to the patriarchs). Nor does divine lawgiving have to presuppose a history of benevolent deeds.[45] Similarly, it is difficult to see how one can say that apart from the Sinai events the exodus from Egypt would have no goal or "natural outcome." The "goal" which Yahweh mentions to Moses at his call (Exod. 3:8; 6:6–8) is possession of the land of Canaan.

Finally, in support of the thesis that the exodus and Sinai originally belonged together as the experiences of a single group is the argument that several passages commonly judged to be old link together the events of exodus and Sinai (Exod. 15:13, 17; 19:4–6)[46] and that Sinai and the march of conquest are linked in others (Deut. 33:2; Judg. 5:4–5).[47] And there remains the fact that the figure of Moses is deeply woven into the whole sequence of exodus, Sinai, and march to the promised land.

On balance, the case for the unity of exodus-Sinai-conquest is stronger than the case for separating the experiences among separate groups, and the majority of scholars now seems to favor the "unity" thesis.

Was a Covenant Established at Sinai?

In the influential nineteenth century school of biblical criticism associated with the name of Julius Wellhausen, it was believed that the notion of a "covenant" between Yahweh and the Hebrew people developed late in Israel's history (in approximately the time of the great prophets) and was read back into the early history of Israel.[48] The more conservative view, that the Sinai narrative was historically reliable and that the covenant was established in the time of Moses, providing the basic structure of Israel's social and religious life from that time on, received a substantial boost in the 1950s and 1960s with the development of the thesis that Near Eastern suzerainty treaties (especially Hittite) of the second millennium B.C. provided the formal prototype for the Hebrew covenant with Yahweh.

Analogy of Hittite treaty-form

It was argued by George E. Mendenhall, who pioneered this thesis among English-speaking scholars, that the resemblance of the Sinai covenant, as described in the book of Exodus, to the structure of the Hittite treaties confirmed an early date for the adoption of the treaty form by Israel.[49] Mendenhall argued that the treaty pattern used by the Hittites disappeared from use after about 1200 B.C. and, consequently, could not have been available as a model to the Israelites at a later date. His arguments, which will be recognized as belonging to the "exclusive congenial context" type, were widely subscribed, especially among English-speaking scholars.[50]

There is almost unanimous agreement among Old Testament scholars that the Near Eastern treaty genre exercised an influence on the Old Testament traditions. But many scholars recognize this influence only on the later traditions, principally those emanating from the Deuteronomic school.[51] If the treaty influence cannot be clearly demonstrated prior to the time of Deuteronomy (seventh century B.C.), obviously this cannot be used to provide support for a Mosaic date of the treaty pattern in Israel.

The following discussion will attempt to show approximately how the debate has developed about the existence of the treaty form in Israel at the time of Moses.

Mendenhall's study identified nine elements in the structure of the treaty, as follows:

1. *Preamble,* or *titulature,* which identifies the author of the covenant, i.e., the suzerain, along with his titles and laudatory epithets.

2. The *historical prologue,* describing prior relations between the parties to the treaty, with emphasis on benevolent deeds performed by the overlord for the vassal. A primary purpose for this section seems to have been to instill a sense of gratitude in the vassal and, consequently, a readiness to adhere to the stipulations laid down by the overlord. Mendenhall pointed out the frequent use in this section of the "I-Thou" style, in which the suzerain addresses the vassal in personal terms of direct address.

3. The *stipulations* laid upon the vassal, typically such things as

prohibition of treaty arrangements with any other overlord, prohibition of hostile action against any fellow vassals, obligation to answer the suzerain's call to arms, extradition of any refugees fleeing from the suzerain, and regular appearance in the court of the overlord, with payment of tribute.

4. Provision for the *deposit* of a copy of the treaty in a temple and for *regular public re-reading* of the text.

5. A list of gods as *witnesses,* usually including gods of the vassal state as well as those of the suzerain kingdom's pantheon.

6. A formula of *curses and blessings*, which constituted the sanctions of the treaty.

These six items, according to Mendenhall, were regular components of the written text of the treaty. In addition to these, he observed three further factors common to the treaty proceedings:

7. The formal *oath* of obedience on the part of the vassal.

8. A *ceremony* accompanying the oath.

9. Some sort of *procedure for initiating punitive measures* against a disobedient vassal.

Studies by Klaus Baltzer and D. J. McCarthy followed somewhat later,[52] with essentially the same findings regarding the Hittite treaties. The scope of McCarthy's study was broader, encompassing treaty documents from a broader geographical area and a longer historical span. McCarthy emphasizes that the absolutely indispensable elements are the stipulations, the god lists (which imply that the obligations have been formally assumed), and the curse formulas. Baltzer and McCarthy both emphasize that it is essential to the treaty procedure for the party on whom the obligations are laid to assume them *under oath.*[53]

Can it be demonstrated that this treaty genre was in fact adopted in the Mosaic period as the structure of the Sinai covenant? Did the Israelites of Moses' time comprehend their relationship to Yahweh after the fashion of an oriental suzerain-vassal relationship, formulated in a manner akin to the treaty arrangements of the second millennium?

Alleged biblical parallels

Exodus 20:2–17. The Decalogue was one of the first Old Testament texts to be compared with the treaty pattern. The analysis was made as follows. Verse 2a, "I am YHWH your God," was identified as the *preamble.* Verse 2b, "who brought you out of the land of Egypt, out of the house of bondage," was considered the counterpart to the *historical prologue*, and it was noted that, just as in the Hittite treaties, the

"I-Thou" style was employed. The commandments (vss. 3–17) constitute the *stipulations*, and the apodictic style of the commandments was
thought by some to derive from the treaty genre, where this style was
sometimes used. Just as the stipulations of a Hittite treaty are called the
"words" of the Great King, so the Decalogue is introduced by the
statement, "And God spoke all these words" (vs. 1).

Obviously missing from this Decalogue text are three elements
cited in the treaty genre by Mendenhall: the deposit clause, the list of
witnesses, and the blessings and curses. The absence of the *witness-list*
is commonly explained by the exclusive worship of Yahweh, which
forbade the recognition of other deities. References elsewhere in the
Sinai traditions to the tablets of the covenant (see Exod. 32, 34) indicate the importance of writing the covenant text, and the well-known
preservation of the tablets of the covenant in the ark is supposed to
correspond to the *deposit* in a holy place (cf. Deut. 10:1–5). Deuteronomy 31:9–13 shows something of the procedures for the *rereading* of
the covenant that took place in Israel. The *sanctions* (blessings and
curses) are found by some in the references to a jealous God (Exod.
20:5–6; cf. also vs. 7b) or the promise attached to the commandments
about honoring parents (vs. 12),[54] and by others in the categorical, apodictic nature of the commandments, which imply (so it is argued) a
curse upon disobedience.[55]

Parallels have been seen between the first commandment and the
common stipulation in Hittite treaties that the vassal enter into no treaty
relationship with any other suzerain.[56] Also, it has been observed that
there is an analogy between the stipulation in the treaties that the vassal
shall engage in no hostile activity against a fellow vassal and the prohibition in the Decalogue of injurious action against any fellow member
of the covenant community (vss. 13–17).[57]

Beyerlin finds the parallels between the Decalogue and the Hittite
treaties "so numerous and so striking that one can hardly avoid the
view that the Ten Commandments are—formally—modelled on the
covenant-form that is revealed in the vassal-treaties of the Hittites and
was probably in general use in the Near East of the second millennium
B.C."[58]

However, the subjection of this hypothesis to scrutiny and critique
has resulted in its rejection by numerous scholars. As seen above, those
who claim an analogy between the Decalogue and the treaty pattern
have to draw on other texts to supplement Exodus 20:2–17 in order to
find all the elements of the treaty genre. It is questionable method to

presume that, if we can gather from the various "covenant" passages in the Hexateuch some form of each item in the treaty pattern, this would confirm the existence in early Israel of the whole pattern. In order for the proposed analogy to carry conviction, the various elements need to be demonstrated in a single text.

Several writers have challenged the comparison of Exodus 20:2a to the titulature on purely formal grounds: in the Hittite treaties the preamble, or titulature, was stated in the third person,[59] whereas in the biblical text Yahweh speaks in the first person.[60] Similarly, the identification of 20:2b as an "historical prologue" is questioned. To some critics it seems that this is simply the predicate portion of the theophanic self-revelation of God, characterizing and defining the deity. The history section in the Hittite treaties functioned differently; it served rather to persuade the vassal and provide grounds for his obedience. "The purpose in [Exod.] 20:2," McCarthy writes, "is not so much motivation as identification."[61] Moreover, many scholars have concluded that verse 2b is a late (Deuteronomic) insertion into the text and did not even appear in the original version of the Decalogue.[62]

The nature of the stipulations in the Decalogue do not closely resemble the sorts of stipulations set forth in the suzerainty treaties. In the Hittite treaties the number of apodictic "thou shalt not" stipulations in a series seldom exceeds five or six, and these commands usually appear alone. When they do appear in a series, they all deal with the same political matter (e.g., seizure and return of fugitives), in contrast to the Decalogue, where the commands form the whole moral law.[63] Although the apodictic style of the Ten Commandments has been thought by some to be derived from the treaty genre, this does not seem likely. Other likely sources outside Israel for the apodictic style have been found.[64]

The blessing/curse formulas, indispensable in the treaty genre, are missing from Exodus 20. The expansions to the second, third, and fifth commandments are, in the opinion of most commentators, secondary additions to the original Decalogue,[65] and therefore of no use in helping us to identify the genre of the original unit. Beyerlin's suggestion that the apodictic form of the commandments makes up for the absence of the sanctions is not convincing. Regarding this suggestion, McCarthy's remark is well taken: "Any law, apodictic or conditional, implies (or states) a sanction. The point is that the curse-blessing seems to have been felt as an essential separate member of the treaty form."[66]

Other Sinai texts. Several writers have seen in *Exodus 19:3-8* at least a partial outline of the treaty form, with vs. 3 representing the titulature, vs. 4 the antecedent history of benevolent deeds by the suzerain, and vs. 5a as the stipulations, with vs. 5b a statement of blessings.[67]

Exodus 24:3–8, likewise, has been reckoned by some to contain several components of the treaty pattern. Vs. 3 refers to the stipulations; vss. 4 and 7 allude to the covenant document; the oath of the people is seen in vs. 7; vss. 4–6 and 8 describe the ceremony of ratification, and the pillars established according to the note in vs. 4b would represent the witnesses (cf. Josh. 24:27).[68]

Another Sinai text that has been related to the treaty pattern is *Exodus 34:10–28*. Here several scholars have found a "historical prologue" (vss. 10–11), a basic stipulation (vss. 11a, 14) and more specific stipulations (vss. 17–26), as well as reference to the writing down of the covenant agreement (vs. 27).[69]

These alleged parallels have not proved convincing to many scholars. Aside from the fact that Exodus 19:3–8 is considered a late composition by many[70] (and therefore would not offer any evidence for religious or social conditions in the time of Moses), the statement in vs. 5a does not appear in the same form as the treaty stipulations, nor does it set forth detailed norms of conduct, as the treaty stipulations do.[71] The ratification of the covenant by *rite*, such as we find in the passage from Exodus 24, would, according to McCarthy, belong more to the treaty types of the first millennium B.C. than to the second millennium type, in which the emphasis was on the sworn *oath* (which is lacking in Exodus 24).[72] Finally, Exodus 34 lacks any reference to sanctions, there is no mention of an oath, and since vs. 10 deals with the *future*, it hardly fits the classification of historical prologue.[73]

Some of the criticisms of the analogy between the Sinai covenant passages and the treaty pattern may be blunted if we consider that (1) certain modifications would inevitably be made in adapting a political instrument (treaty) to express the relationship between a people and its god; and (2) the material in Exodus 19–24 and 34 constitutes a *narrative about* the enactment of the covenant instead of the covenant document itself. Nevertheless, the attempt to show, by means of this analogy, that the Hebrews *in the time of Moses* borrowed the Near Eastern treaty pattern to express their relationship to Yahweh has to be judged unconvincing.

Mendenhall's argument has the same fragile character as any "exclusive congenial context" argument which seeks to show that parallels

to a biblical event or concept are known from only one chronological
setting: if parallels subsequently turn up from other time periods, the
argument breaks down. It now appears mistaken to claim, as Mendenhall did,[74] that this treaty form passed out of use after the thirteenth
century B.C. and therefore must have been adopted by Israel in the time
of Moses. Further study has shown a basic continuity in the use of the
suzerainty treaty form in the Near East extending from the third millennium into the mid-first millennium B.C.,[75] so that, even if a connection
were granted between the structure of the Sinai covenant and the form
exemplified in the Hittite treaties, the Israelite people could have
adopted the form at almost any time in their history. It is *a priori* more
reasonable, as several writers have pointed out, that Israel would have
borrowed the treaty form in the era of her monarchy when she would
have used such legal instruments in her own international dealings,
than that the Israelites in the Sinai period of their history would have
been familiar with political treaties used by settled peoples.[76]

The book of Deuteronomy, it is generally agreed, reflects the treaty
pattern much more closely than anything in the book of Exodus.[77] The
common critical opinion is that Deuteronomy was written in the seventh century B.C. This gives rise to the supposition that the influence of
the treaty genre in Israel occurred principally in the first millennium
B.C. It is reasonable to surmise that, when this genre was adopted for a
religious use by the Hebrews (generally speaking, in the monarchical
period), materials such as the Sinai traditions, which originally were
not derived from or modelled on the treaty pattern, were re-shaped
under the influence of that pattern. This would explain why the Sinai
traditions exhibit a partial resemblance to the treaty form.

A different form of covenant?

Even if we cannot interpret the early Sinai traditions by the analogy
of the oriental suzerainty treaties, can we nonetheless still speak of the
events which transpired at Sinai as a "covenant"? Not all covenants in
ancient times had to be of the same type as the Hittite suzerainty treaties. Was a pact established at Sinai between Yahweh and Israel, with a
proclamation of the divine will laying obligations upon the Israelite
people? To what degree can we regard the narrative in Exodus as a
reliable account of what originally happened at the mountain?

Considerable portions of the Sinai narrative are, in the consensus of
critical opinion, secondary accretions to the story and, therefore, not
usable in the attempt to reconstruct the original Sinai events. *Exodus*

19:3–8 is adjudged a Deuteronomic composition by many.[78] The "Book of the Covenant" (*Exod. 20:22–23:19*) and the Priestly material in *Exodus 24:15b–31:18* and *35–40* and *Numbers 1–10* are almost universally recognized as later additions to the Sinai pericope.[79] The episode of the golden calf (*Exod. 32*) is thought by most scholars to presuppose the setting up of the golden calves by Jeroboam I at Dan and Bethel.[80] *Exodus 24:12–15a* prepares for the episode of chapter 32 by telling of Moses' call to come up on the mountain for a time. *Exodus 34* presents a very complex problem. In its present form, this chapter looks back to the episode of the tablet-shattering in chapter 32. Some of the commandments (vss. 18–26) parallel the closing verses of the "Book of the Covenant" (23:12–19) and presuppose the settlement of the Israelites in Canaan, observing the agricultural festivals borrowed from the Canaanites.[81] God is spoken of in the third person in some places, while other sections are formulated as divine speech. To all appearances, therefore, the chapter is a redaction of varied materials, some clearly later than the Mosaic period, so that it is difficult to use the chapter with confidence to reconstruct the original Sinai events. *Exodus 33* also contains materials of differing ages and concerns, and it would be hazardous to base any reconstruction on it; in any case, there is little here having to do with a covenant.

The Decalogue (*Exod. 20:2–17*) has always been thought of as the centerpiece of the covenant established at Sinai. But there has long been substantial scholarly opinion which holds that this passage also is a secondary insertion into the Sinai narrative. It seems to interrupt the narrative context; 20:21 follows more smoothly directly after 19:19 and very awkwardly after God's having already spoken in 20:2–17.[82]

Moreover, the Decalogue in its present form is the product of several stages of development. Up through 20:6 Yahweh is speaking; after that point he is referred to in the third person. In the opinion of some form critics, the "rules for daily life" which constitute the second part of the Decalogue originated in a different setting than did the opening commandments, which reflect a cultic setting.[83] Several of the commandments have been expanded from their original form; perhaps several have been abbreviated.[84] Some of the language in the present form of the passage is found elsewhere mainly in Deuteronomic writings, indicating a revision of the material in the seventh or sixth century.[85]

The Mosaic dating of the Decalogue is not lacking for defenders,[86] but more and more recent writers seem to be accepting a later date. Some of the content of the Decalogue may be of great antiquity,[87] but the shaping of the commandments into a *Decalogue* under the *rubric of divine speech* and the *insertion of the whole into the Sinai narrative* are now frequently dated to a time after the settlement of the Hebrews in Canaan or even in the monarchical period.[88]

What are we left with, then, as likely testimony from the Mosaic period to the original Sinai events? After the above-mentioned passages have been subtracted from the Sinai narrative, there remain three texts: *Exodus 19:9–19*[89] + *20:18–21; 24:1a*[90] + *9–11;* and *24:3–8.* Depending on their analysis and interpretation of these three passages (all of which are generally accepted as embodying early traditions about Yahweh and Sinai), some scholars conclude that the Sinai tradition originally had to do only with a theophany,[91] while others conclude that there was some sort of a covenant established, however different this covenant might have been from the kind of legislative enactment represented in the final form of the Sinai narrative.[92]

The dominating theme in these three texts is the theophany of Yahweh. This is especially clear in Exodus 19:9–19 + 20:18–21 and in 24:9–11. In neither of these passages is there any reference to a covenant, nor is there any mention of requirements laid upon the Israelites. The meal in 24:11 is often interpreted as an action to ratify the covenant between Yahweh and his people,[93] but if it is considered apart from the "covenant" context in which it is now fitted it does not give the appearance of being a covenant-ratifying ceremony. Meals did sometimes signify the ratification of a covenant (cf. Gen. 31:43–54), but a meal, even if eaten in the presence of God, did not *ipso facto* have this significance (cf. Exod. 18:12; 1 Chron. 29:22).

The third of our passages, Exodus 24:3–8, seems to make very explicit the celebration of a covenant ceremony. This passage refers to the people's (twofold) pledge of obedience to the "words of Yahweh" which are written in "the book of the covenant" (vss. 3, 7). This passage in its present form includes some features judged to be early[94] as well as some obviously late features.[95] *If* the references to the words and the book of the covenant belong to the earlier stages of this tradition,[96] we have a witness to an early association of covenant-making with Sinai.[97]

Several further lines of argument, however, converge to recommend the thesis that the notion of a covenant, built around the Decalogue, was not associated with Sinai in the earliest centuries of Israel's existence, but was a theological development of the monarchical period.

(1) As has been noted above, all of the law codes which now appear in the Sinai narrative show signs of having been inserted there at a secondary stage of the tradition's development. If there was a code of law associated with the original Sinai tradition, it has been displaced by the Decalogue and other codes which now appear there.

(2) None of the early references to Sinai outside the main Pentateuchal sources makes any mention of its being a place of law-giving or covenant-making. Deuteronomy 33:2, Judges 5:5, and Psalm 68:9 all associate Yahweh with Sinai, but the imagery is purely theophanic and has nothing to do with laws or covenant.

(3) It has always been recognized as curious that there is virtual silence about the Sinai covenant among the Hebrew prophets prior to Jeremiah (who was active at about the time the Deuteronomic theology was a growing influence). The Hebrew term $b^e r\hat{\imath}t$, which is commonly translated "covenant," occurs in the mouth of pre-Deuteronomic prophets only in 1 Kings 19:10 and 14[98] and in Hosea 6:7 and 8:1.[99] Some scholars have argued that the prophets used the idea of the covenant even though avoiding the term $b^e r\hat{\imath}t$. These scholars argue that the prophets' calling the people to account for disobedience is to be interpreted with reference to a "covenant theology"; the sins of the nation were violations of the Sinai covenant.[100] Their avoidance of the term $b^e r\hat{\imath}t$ might be explained by their fear that this usage would be misconstrued: in their time $b^e r\hat{\imath}t$ was applied especially to the unconditional promises of Yahweh to the house of David and was therefore associated with a sense of blasé self-assurance on the part of Israel which the prophets wanted to puncture.[101] It still seems exceedingly strange that, if the concept of a covenant established between Yahweh and Israel at the very fountainhead of the nation's life had existed in Israel, the great prophets of Israel should have made no clear reference to it. The ethical norms of the prophetic message could have been derived from other sources, such as ordinary legal procedures or wisdom traditions, besides the presumed covenant theology.[102]

(4) The use of the term $b^e r\hat{\imath}t$ becomes common in the literature of the Deuteronomic era and later, and it is in the writings of the Deuteronomic school[103] that we encounter the fully developed covenantal theology, according to which Yahweh's goodness to Israel was conditioned upon her obedience to the stipulations of the Horeb covenant.[104] Whether the $b^e r\hat{\imath}t$ concept originated with the Deuteronomic school, as Perlitt maintains,[105] is debatable,[106] but it did receive its greatest development at their hands.[107] Since the Decalogue and certain

other key passages in the Sinai narrative bear the marks of Deutero-
nomic handling,[108] it does seem quite likely that the re-shaping of the
Sinai narrative into a story about the origination of a covenant between
Yahweh and Israel was the work of the Deuteronomic school.

Three principal arguments have been used in recent years to support
the contrary thesis that the Sinai covenant is a concept that goes back to
the time of Moses. One is the "exclusive congenial context" argument
discussed above,[109] which held that the model for the Sinai covenant
was an international vassal treaty pattern unique to the second millennium B.C. Weaknesses in this argument include the following: (1) the
pattern was not in fact limited to the second millennium, (2) the resemblance between the Sinai narrative and the vassal treaty form is rather
weak, and (3) the best biblical imitation of the treaty pattern is found in
the book of Deuteronomy, a composition from the seventh-sixth
centuries.

A second argument is that the legal and prophetic literature of pre-
Deuteronomic Israel exhibits influences, in form and content, of the
vassal treaties.[110] This, it is argued, attests to the Hebrews' familiarity
with the treaty pattern and supports the theory that that pattern had been
adopted by pre-Deuteronomic Israel to give expression to its relationship to Yahweh. Some of the alleged influences are debatable;[111] some
of them can be explained as rhetorical devices which would confirm
only that the authors or prophets were familiar with the vassal treaty
form, and not that Israel had formally adopted this form as an institu-
tional expression of her relationship with Yahweh. It is quite conceivable that, just as the prophets used imagery from family relationships
(e.g., Hos. 1–3; 11:1–9; Amos 3:1–2; Isa. 1:2–3) to portray God's
dealings with Israel, so they also used imagery from the world of suzerain-vassal relationships, without being guided by a formal covenant
institution in Israel. Furthermore, almost all of the literature in which
these influences are suspected stems from the period of the monarchy,
so this would be relatively weak support for a Mosaic date for the adoption of the vassal covenant concept unless that hypothesis were demonstrable on other grounds.

A third argument is that the bond of a religious covenant is necessary to explain the existence of the Israelite nation in the period immediately following the time of Moses. G. E. Mendenhall's theory
about the origins of Israel posits the Sinai covenant in the time of
Moses as the indispensable element in explaining the origin of
"Israel."[112] He believes that the nation was forged, not out of wan-

dering nomads entering a new land (as most Old Testament scholars have conventionally believed), but mainly out of discontented citizens of Canaanite city-states who challenged the power ethic of their rulers with the higher ethic of the Sinai covenant. The kingship of Yahweh, manifested in the vassal covenant with Israel, provided a perspective for the structure of personal and societal relationships which transcended class interests. Mendenhall's theory is discussed further in our next chapter. Some bond of unity was surely necessary to give the infant Israelite nation coherence whenever and however it emerged. But a religious bond is not the only conceivable source of unity, and if the nation originated according to a different scenario from that projected by Mendenhall, the bond need not have been a vassal covenant whereby the overlordship of King Yahweh was institutionalized. We shall return to this point in chapter 4.

CHAPTER

4

The Settlement in Canaan

Most students of Israel's early history acknowledge that the arrival in Canaan of the people who were to comprise the Israelite tribes did not occur in the simplified and unified way suggested by the accounts in the biblical books of Genesis through Joshua. Rather, the settlement of the people occurred in several stages and the pre-settlement history of these people was diverse. Often the pre-settlement histories of the various groups can be reconstructed in only a tentative fashion from clues found within the biblical traditions and clues provided by corollary disciplines.

In recent years there have been numerous efforts, utilizing biblical data,[1] documents from the ancient Near East (especially Egyptian archival materials),[2] and archaeological findings relating to Late Bronze Age Canaan,[3] to piece together a coherent reconstruction of how the respective Israelite tribes arrived in the land of Canaan. In what follows it will be seen that much uncertainty still prevails about this topic which R. de Vaux called "the most difficult problem in the whole history of Israel."[4]

Complex Settlement History

It is commonly recognized that the settlement did not occur in the simplified and unified way suggested by the "conquest narrative" in Joshua 1–12. Within the Bible itself, first of all, the following indications of a more complicated process of settlement can be cited.

1. There are inconsistencies between the version of the conquest in

Joshua 1–12, where it is said that the taking of the land of Canaan was a thoroughly successful uniform national action by the army which invaded Canaan from east of the Jordan River under Joshua's command (Josh. 11:16–23; 12:7–24; cf. 21:43–45), and the picture which one derives from a critical reading of the whole narrative in Numbers, Joshua, and Judges.[5]

For example, Judah and associated clan groups are credited with taking areas (Judg. 1:11–20) which are said in Joshua 10:28–39 to have fallen to the march of Joshua's army. The taking of Hebron, which is credited to Joshua's armies in Joshua 10:36, was the work of Caleb, according to Joshua 14:6–15 and 15:13–14. Here and elsewhere it seems that accounts of land acquisition by individual tribes or clans have been superseded in the national tradition by accounts of acquisition by "all Israel."

Further, there are notations scattered through Joshua and Judges which candidly acknowledge the inability of the Hebrews to displace the Canaanites in places such as Jerusalem (Josh. 15:63), Gezer (Josh. 16:10; Judg. 1:29), and the Galilean region (Josh. 17:11–13; Judg. 1:27–28, 30–33).

In still other passages tradition critics believe that earlier forms of the tradition, telling of actions by individual tribes, have been subjected to later redactions with an "all-Israel" orientation. The spy story in Numbers 13–14 probably had to do, in its original form, only with a reconnoitering and taking of the Hebron area (cf. Num. 13:22–24; 14:24) by the Calebites,[6] but the later redaction of the passage has enlarged the scope of the spies' mission to include the entire land of Canaan; as noted above, the taking of the area of Hebron is attributed to Caleb in Joshua 14:6–15 and 15:13–14. The oldest parts of Numbers 32 appear to report individual tribal or clan actions to gain territory in the Transjordan, quite distinct from any campaign by the national Israelite army.[7] And many commentators believe that the stories in Joshua 2–10 derive from a nucleus of tradition which dealt only with the tribe of Benjamin (in whose territory all the stories are located), rather than with Israel as a whole.[8]

2. The present form of the Old Testament narrative, although it purports to tell us of the entire Israelite nation gaining its territory in military operations led by Joshua (Josh. 11:16–23), says nothing at all about the territorial acquisitions of some of the tribes. Settlement traditions are recorded for only the following tribal areas: Reuben and Gad (Num. 21; 32:2–5), Benjamin (Josh. 2–10), Judah (Josh. 10:28–39;

Judg. 1:1–20), Naphtali (Josh. 11:1–15), Dan (Josh. 19:47–48; Judg. 17–18), and the house of Joseph (Judg. 1:22–26). For some of these tribal areas we have stories relating the capture of only a single site. There is obviously much land acquisition not reported.

3. Although it is customary to follow the lead of the account in Joshua 1–12 and think of the conquest of the promised land as originating east of the Jordan, there are several traditions about an invasion of Canaan from the *south*. The capture of the Hebron area by the Calebites, referred to above, perhaps was the result of an attack from the south which is reflected in the traditions found in Numbers 13–14. Numbers 21:1–3[9] relates a successful attack (by "Israel") on Hormah. Judges 1:11–20, in the opinion of some commentators,[10] describes an invasion by Judah and her associates from the south.

4. Joshua 24 reflects the memory that many who belonged to the Israelite nation had not shared in the exodus and were integrated into the community after the various tribes had settled in their respective territories.[11] The story exhibits an awareness that many members of "Israel" had not been represented in the wilderness experiences with Moses and had settled their territory quite independently of the tribes involved in the exodus and wilderness wanderings.

5. The recurring friction between the tribes of the north and those of the south—evident, for example, in the divided monarchy which occurred at the death of Saul, the permanent division of the nation after the death of Solomon, and the repeated wars between the states of Israel and Judah—is easily understandable if their origins were diverse.[12]

6. There are several clues which point to settlement by some of the tribes in Canaan in the pre-Mosaic period.

(a) The figures of the patriarchs in Genesis sometimes clearly serve as personifications of the tribes of which they are the eponyms.[13] For example, a number of scholars think that the narrative in Genesis 34 derives from activities of the *tribes* of Simeon and Levi in that earlier period when these tribes were prominent.[14] Similarly, Genesis 38 has been interpreted by some as a tradition representing the residence and expansion of the tribe of Judah in Canaan in the period before the exodus.[15]

(b) Lists of the twelve tribes always record Reuben, Simeon, and Levi as the eldest sons of Jacob/Israel, implying that the tribes bearing these names held positions of prominence.[16] In the stories of the post-conquest period, these tribes play an insignificant role; by that period, these tribes appear to have diminished greatly in importance—or vanished. Their seniority is best explained, therefore, if their entry and residence and pre-eminence in Canaan occurred in the period *before* the exodus.[17] That period of their greatness remains obscure.

Archaeological Evidence

Archaeological research in the Middle East during the past century has raised the hopes of biblical scholars that finds uncovered by the digger's spade would facilitate an evaluation of the stories of the Bible. Some of the finds excited hopes of confirmation for the biblical record of conquest, but their value in this regard diminished or evaporated under more extended scrutiny. Excavator John Garstang announced that his digging at the site of Jericho (in 1930–36) had revealed the collapse of the city wall and the burning of the city, to be dated by his reckoning ca. 1400 B.C.[18] Letters from military outposts in Canaan to the Egyptian court telling of attacks by groups of "Habiru" (or, more correctly, "Hapiru") in the early 1300s[19] seemed to dovetail rather nicely with Garstang's findings to provide testimony to a conquest by Joshua's army shortly after 1400. Several texts from Egypt and Ras Shamra, from the 1300s, mentioned the presence of a people called "Asaru" in Canaan (= tribe of Asher?).[20]

Although these finds and others did not finally provide the hoped-for support, Old Testament scholars have nevertheless widely anticipated that archaeology would supply data useful for testing the reliability of the biblical story.

The Albright school

The school of Old Testament interpretation which took its inspiration from W. F. Albright[21] has steadfastly maintained that the question of a narrative's "historicity" can be properly settled only after the testimony of the "external evidence" of the archaeologist.[22] The material remains of ancient civilizations and written sources discovered among these remains provide an external check on the accounts of the Bible.

Members of the Albright school are convinced that the evidence turned up by archaeologists laboring in Palestine and elsewhere in the Middle East generally confirms the biblical stories of a substantial attack on Canaan by the Hebrew army under Joshua's command, and that this invasion is to be dated sometime in the 1200s B.C.

Surface explorations in the Transjordan led Nelson Glueck to conclude that the Transjordanian area south of the River Jabbok was "largely empty of civilized settlement for more than half a millennium" before the thirteenth century.[23] Before this time the kingdoms of Edom and Moab could not, therefore, have been present to grant or deny the Hebrews' request for passage through their territory (cf. Num. 20:14–21; 22–24; Judg. 11:17). These conclusions of Glueck's, along with the knowledge from Egyptian sources that building projects of the kind the Hebrew slaves labored on, according to Exodus 1:11, were undertaken by the pharaohs ca. 1300 B.C.,[24] were responsible in great measure for turning the attention of Old Testament scholars to the thirteenth century rather than earlier times to find a date for the exodus and conquest.

The stele of the fourth year of Pharaoh Merneptah (ca. 1224–1211 B.C.), which reports a campaign against the area of Canaan, includes a reference to "Israel" which implies that this is a people just settling down.[25] This information seemed to fit in with the above-mentioned evidence and strengthen the case for a thirteenth century dating.

With attention directed to the thirteenth century, verification of an invasion by the Hebrews seemed to many to be supplied by the archaeological findings that the Palestinian towns of Lachish, Bethel, Hazor, Debir, and Eglon—all reported in the Old Testament to have been attacked by the Israelites—were in fact destroyed in the late thirteenth century, often with resettlement by dwellers representing a poorer culture (as one would expect in the case of Hebrews coming in from the desert!). A number of villages also sprang up at the beginning of the Iron Age (ca. 1200 B.C.) on sites which had been either previously unoccupied or long uninhabited (e.g., Mizpah, Shiloh, Geba, Ai), and these have been identified as Israelite settlements.[26]

Dissent

In spite of the widespread acceptance of these arguments, there has been a growing chorus of dissent in recent years. It is now argued in rebuttal by a number of scholars, including archaeologists, that the findings of archaeology do not provide clear and compelling support for the biblical stories, after all. In fact, the evidence is exceedingly ambiguous in several ways.

For a couple of decades it has been known that Garstang's conclusions about the fall of Jericho's walls needed serious revision. The walls which he attributed to a fourteenth century destruction turn out to be structures which fell before the end of the third millennium.[27] Excavations at Jericho in the 1950s revealed nothing to indicate a habitation of any significance in the thirteenth century.[28]

Similarly, it has been known since excavations on the site of Ai in the 1930s (and confirmed by more recent expeditions)[29] that the city was uninhabited between the late third millennium and about 1200 B.C., so it could not have been the target of an attack like that described in Joshua 8 in the thirteenth century.[30]

Excavations at the sites of other cities mentioned in the biblical narrative of the Hebrews' march to and into Canaan have added the following to the list of places which archaeologists now believe to have been uninhabited in the Late Bronze Age (usually dated ca. 1550–1200 B.C.): Gibeon,[31] Heshbon,[32] Hebron,[33] Hormah,[34] and Arad.[35] There are only four cities which the Bible specifically identifies as having been destroyed by the Israelites: Hormah (Num. 21:3; Judg. 1:17), Jericho (Josh. 6:20–26), Ai (Josh. 8:18–28), and Hazor (Josh. 11:1–15); now it appears that none of the first three of these constituted anything like a fortified city in the 1200s![36]

Some of Glueck's methods and conclusions have lately been challenged,[37] and it now seems questionable as to how much weight can be put on his findings regarding the occupational gap in Transjordan. In any case, several scholars have queried the relevance of this evidence, observing that the narratives in the book of Numbers do not necessarily presuppose fortified cities and a settled population in Edom and Moab (as distinct from nomadic or seminomadic groups).[38]

Even in instances where there is evidence of thirteenth century destruction of Palestinian cities it is frequently doubtful that this constitutes significant support for the biblical stories of Joshua's conquest. The number of plausible alternative explanations for the destruction levels at a given site is usually larger than many historians, especially those concerned to secure an "historical substratum" for the biblical record, acknowledge.[39] In the Late Bronze Age widespread unsettled conditions prevailed in Palestine, with several possible candidates for the role of destroyer at a number of sites.[40] The destroyer need not in every case have been an invader from without, for the collapse of Egyptian control over Palestine and Syria in the thirteenth and twelfth centuries B.C. created a situation of inter-city conflict in the region.[41] Many Palestinian cities experienced multiple destructions in the Late Bronze Age.[42]

The destruction of *Lachish* could plausibly be attributed to the Philistines attacking an Egyptian garrison or to Egyptians conducting a punitive raid or executing a scorched earth policy in the face of invaders.[43] The identification of Tell beit Mirsim as biblical *Debir* now appears erroneous, and a better candidate for Debir seems to be Khirbet Rabud, where explorations indicate that the transition from the thirteenth to the twelfth century was peaceful![44] Tell beit Mirsim might have been the site of biblical *Eglon* (cf. Josh. 10:34–35), but even so, the destruction attested at this site from the thirteenth century could have been caused by the Philistines as well as by the Israelites.[45]

Hazor suffered destruction in the Late Bronze Age, but again there are problems with attributing this to the Israelite army of Joshua. The agent of Hazor's destruction is not specifically identified by the remains, and there is a possibility that the destruction was the work of the Sea Peoples who invaded Syria-Palestine in the Late Bronze Age.[46] Even if Hazor was destroyed by Israelites, it is doubtful that we can think of this being the same group which invaded central Palestine. A belt of Canaanite cities which stretched from the coast (Dor) to the Jordan River (Beth-shan)—a string of cities which the Old Testament itself acknowledges as unconquerable by the Hebrews (Judg. 1:27; Josh. 17:11–12)[47]—would have presented a considerable barrier limiting the northward march of the Israelite armies after they had established themselves in central Palestine. It seems more reasonable to suppose that if there was Israelite involvement in the burning of Hazor it was a tribal group (Naphtali?) whose exploits have been subsequently "nationalized" and attached to the Joshua tradition.[48]

Bethel suffered in the thirteenth century what one archaeologist has called "the most terrific burning yet seen in Palestine,"[49] but the Old Testament does not clearly say that Bethel was destroyed by the Israelites[50] (cf. Judg. 1:22–26; notice that the capture of the city is credited to an action by the "tribe of Joseph," and not by Joshua's army!), so caution is advisable in claiming archaeological support for the biblical record in this instance.[51]

Without written evidence archaeology cannot prove that the devastation evident in a particular stratum of a site was wrought by a particular invading force.[52] There are problems, first of all, with dating the stratum, and then the agent of the destruction must be identified, and finally the intention of the agent.[53] Renovation and the ridding of vermin are examples of non-malicious motives which might account for some destruction in primitive communities.

We have said nothing yet of natural catastrophes which might have been responsible for some of the destruction. Fire and earthquake merit consideration as possible causes.

Destructive fires can have many causes, and anyone who knows the closely-packed houses of Late Bronze Age cities in Palestine will not be surprised that . . . what started as a relatively small fire could reduce larger sections of a city and even whole cities to ashes.[54]

When all of this is taken into account, one's hesitation about correlating *this particular biblical report* with *that particular destruction level* has to be considerable.[55]

Many believed that additional archaeological support for the biblical conquest narrative existed in the indications that the Early Iron Age settlements which sprang up in Palestine, sometimes on top of Late Bronze ruins and sometimes on virgin soil, were culturally poorer than the Late Bronze Age settlements.[56] Some recent writers have suggested, however, that the cultural decline at the end of the Late Bronze Age—which was not limited to Palestine—might have had causes of a more widely ranging nature, such as deterioration of the climate or a general economic crisis.[57] No distinctively "Israelite" artifacts have been identified, by which the arrival of the Israelites can be determined archaeologically.[58]

Two other items of evidence used to date the conquest in the 1200s are not unexceptionable. (1) The reference in Exodus 1:11 to the Hebrews serving as slaves on the pharaoh's building projects at Pithom and Raamses has been thought to place the Hebrews there in the reigns of Seti I and Rameses II, who carried out construction projects at these sites.[59] The names Pithom and Raamses apparently originated in the Ramesside period, but they are also found in late texts, so the tradition could be a late one.[60] Or, on the other hand, the tradition could pre-date the Ramesside period, with the names Pithom and Raamses being substituted at a secondary stage in the history of the tradition.[61] In any case, given the diverse origins of the peoples who eventually constituted Israel,[62] we cannot assume that the tradition in Exodus 1 (even if based on actual datable events) originated among the same people who produced the traditions in the book of Joshua. If the traditions of slavery in Egypt arose from a different people than the traditions of the conquest did, affixing a date for the slavery would not establish a date for the events of the conquest.

(2) The reference in the stele of Pharaoh Merneptah[63] to the presence of "Israel" in Palestine by about 1220 B.C. has also been used to argue for a thirteenth century exodus and conquest. However, some scholars maintain that the Egyptian stele does not have reference to an

actual campaign by the pharaoh into Canaan.[64] The stele does, none-theless, attest to an "Israel" in the land in the late 1200s;[65] but once again, in light of the numerous groups which eventually comprised the nation Israel, it is impossible to know which of these is being here referred to.[66]

Re-dating the Conquest

With the increasing awareness in recent years that archaeological findings, far from supporting the thesis of an Israelite conquest of Canaan in the 1200s, tend strongly to falsify that thesis, it is not sur-prising that efforts have been undertaken to find another archaeological period which would provide a more congenial context for the biblical narratives.

J. A. Callaway has suggested lowering the date for the conquest into the twelfth century, primarily because this would make possible some degree of correlation between the archaeological findings at the problematical site of Ai and the biblical record of that city's destruc-tion.[67] Ai was rebuilt, after a thousand-year occupational gap, in the Early Iron Age, and the first phase of this rebuilt city suffered some destruction sometime in the twelfth century.[68] Callaway identifies this destruction with the story in Joshua 8. Callaway's theory has not gener-ally been found persuasive. For one thing, the extent of burning evi-denced in the Iron Age remains is rather limited, in contrast to the total destruction reported in Joshua 8:28.[69]

Various attempts have been made to establish an *earlier* dating for the exodus and conquest.[70] Of these the most extensive and impressive is that of J. J. Bimson.[71] Bimson begins by discussing (1) the discorre-lation between the biblical narratives of the conquest and the archaeo-logical evidence from the thirteenth century pertaining to the cities supposedly conquered by Joshua's armies; (2) the ambiguity of the evi-dence from sites which were destroyed in the thirteenth century; (3) the absence of criteria by which a distinctive "Israelite" culture can be identified archaeologically; and (4) the weakness of the argument based on Exodus 1:11.[72]

The most important part of Bimson's study argues that the archaeo-logical evidence from Palestine reveals the close of the Middle Bronze Age to be a more congenial context, archaeologically speaking, in which to fit the events of the conquest stories than is the Late Bronze Age. Many of the Canaanite cities which have left few, if any, traces of occupation in the 1200s (e.g., Jericho, Hebron, Hormah, Gibeon,

Arad) were occupied in the latter part of the Middle Bronze Age (commonly dated ca. 1750–1550 B.C.), and many of them suffered at the
end of that period destruction of a sort commensurate with that suggested in the Old Testament stories of the conquest. Since these places
apparently had no significant settlement in the Late Bronze Age (commonly dated ca. 1550–1200 B.C.), it is difficult to imagine opposition
arising from them for Joshua's army if it invaded the land in the 1200s.
But all of these sites exhibit signs of occupation from the latter part of
Middle Bronze, and several of them attest destruction at the end of that
period. Moreover, the few "conquest cities" which do evidence destruction at the end of the Late Bronze (and therefore seem to offer
some support for a thirteenth century dating of the conquest)—Hazor,
Lachish, Bethel,[73] Eglon, and Debir[74]—also experienced destruction at
the end of Middle Bronze, so the findings from these sites can support
a Middle Bronze as well as a Late Bronze dating for the conquest.

Bimson proceeds to argue that the date for the end of the Middle
Bronze Age should be lowered from the sixteenth century (where it is
commonly dated) to the fifteenth century, so that it can be correlated
with certain chronological information about the date of the exodus
given in the Old Testament, especially 1 Kings 6:1.[75] Heretofore, he
observes, the basic criterion for the sixteenth century dating has been
the assumption that the numerous destructions of Middle Bronze sites
in Palestine occurred as the Egyptian army campaigned into Canaan in
retaliation against the Hyksos, who were expelled from Egypt ca. 1570
B.C. after ruling there for about a century and a half. This would have
been a likely occasion for the destruction of cities like Jericho, Hazor,
and others which had been fortified by the Hyksos. As convenient as
this political explanation for the devastation may be, Bimson points out
that the evidence for such a campaign into Canaan is virtually non-
existent,[76] as is the evidence that cities such as Jericho and Hazor were
ever Hyksos fortifications in the first place.[77] If there never was a campaign of anti-Hyksos retaliation by the Egyptian army into Canaan in
the 1500s, the standard explanation for the destruction of so many Middle Bronze towns is eliminated (and a crucial reference point for dating
the end of the Middle Bronze period is also eliminated), and other al-
ternatives must be explored.

While Bimson's points about the weakness of present criteria for a
sixteenth century date may be well taken, his arguments for a fifteenth
century dating of the end of Middle Bronze will almost certainly be
greeted with less enthusiasm by Old Testament scholars and archaeolo-

gists alike. He cites no archaeological reasons for lowering the date. There is no archaeological evidence which is better accounted for by dating the end of Middle Bronze about 1450 instead of a century earlier. Bimson's criteria for the lower date are selected chronological notations in the Old Testament. If the date for the beginning of Solomon's temple is taken to be ca. 966 B.C., the note in 1 Kings 6:1 would result in a date of ca. 1446 for the exodus. Bimson also cites Judges 11:26, which says that by the time of the "judge" Jephthah (whom he dates to ca. 1130), the Israelites had held Heshbon, which they conquered from Sihon (Num. 21:21–31), for three hundred years. Bimson argues that besides being a problem for those scholars who would date the conquest in the late 1200s and therefore compress the total period of the judges into less than two centuries (between ca. 1200 and 1030), Judges 11:26 offers positive support to a fifteenth century date for the conquest.

Bimson adduces the overall chronology of the book of Judges to support his case. As is well known, the chronological notations in that book add up to a total of 410 years from the first "judge" (Judg. 3:7–11) through the last one (Judg. 15:20; 16:31).[78] When the years of wilderness wandering and the conquest are added to this figure, plus the years of office ascribed to Eli and Samuel, plus the years of reign of Saul and David[79] and four years of Solomon's reign, the total is obviously closer to the span of years in Bimson's thesis than to the span of time between a thirteenth century exodus and Solomon's temple.

Actually, a chronological span based on the notations in the book of Judges would total between 550 and 600 years for the period between the exodus and Solomon's temple.[80] (A span of this length would take us back to approximately the time of the expulsion of the Hyksos from Egypt and the currently accepted date for the end of the Middle Bronze Age. It will not be surprising if someone soon ventures a fresh hypothesis tying the exodus in with the departure of the Hyksos from Egypt, which hypothesis would surely bring forward as one supporting argument the report of the ancient historian Josephus, who identified the biblical exodus with the expulsion of the Hyksos.)[81] However, as many studies of the book of Judges note, the exploits of the major "judges" are local in scope, involving in each case only a few tribes, and none of them is a truly national leader.[82] It is not therefore unreasonable to suspect that some of the judges were contemporaries of each other, in which case the scheme representing them as comprising a chain of successive national leaders is artificial and therefore useless for the calculation of dates.[83]

Bimson makes much of the fact that serious encounters between Israel and the Philistines are not reported until the later sections of the book of Judges, and he says that if the Israelites moved into Canaan about 1200 B.C., we should expect continual clashes with the Philistines (who arrived ca. 1200) to be reported from the beginning of the book.[84]

To argue from the location of the Philistine episodes late in the book of Judges that the Israelites did not encounter Philistines early in the period of the judges (and, therefore, that the early part of the period of the judges must have fallen prior to 1200, when the Philistines arrived) rests too heavily on the assumption that the book of Judges is arranged in correct chronological order. Each of the major judges combats in turn separate enemy peoples: Mesopotamia (fought by Othniel), Moab (Ehud),[85] Canaan (Deborah and Barak), Midian (Gideon), Ammon (Jephthah), and the Philistines (Samson). This suggests a certain artificiality about the arrangement of the book, which renders it unwise to assume that the relative position of the Philistine stories in the book accurately reflects the relative date at which Israel began to experience difficulties with the Philistines. Furthermore, Bimson himself observes that "the book of Judges is not intended as a full history of the period,"[86] and so events which did not contribute to the author's theme of apostasy and punishment need not be expected to appear. Following this line of thought, we observe that the absence of references to the Philistines in the early part of the book need not mean that the Philistines were not in the land and disturbing the Israelites in the early part of the post-conquest period.

Bimson also cites the genealogical data in 1 Chronicles 6:33–37 which indicates that Heman (who served in the sanctuary of David's time) belonged to the eighteenth generation after Korah (who was a contemporary of Moses [Exod. 6:21–24]). Figuring twenty-five years for each generation, this would give a span of time between Moses and Solomon approximately equal to the figure in 1 Kings 6:1 and far too great to be squeezed into the period from 1200 to 1030.[87]

The fragility of Old Testament chronological data can be illustrated by citing, in rebuttal to the argument about Heman's genealogy, the genealogical information in Ruth 4:20–22 (which is intended to be complete at least from Boaz to David and Solomon),[88] from which we learn that Nahshon, who belonged to the generation of the exodus (cf. Num. 1:7), preceded Solomon by only six generations!

Although Bimson's method of establishing a biblical chronology as the norm for adjusting the dates of archaeological periods is highly questionable and the particular arguments from the Bible which he employs to re-date the end of the Middle Bronze Age are very weak,[89] his work merits attention. He has summarized well the problem which others have recognized, namely, that the Palestinian cities whose remains from the Late Bronze Age create problems for the theory of a thirteenth century conquest outnumber the cities which do not, and he has given a reasonable alternative archaeological context for consideration.

The Peaceful Entry Alternative

An alternative thesis of the *nature* of the Israelites' entry into Palestine was developed in the 1920s by the German scholar Albrecht Alt[90] and adopted by Martin Noth in his influential *History of Israel*. The thesis has recently been summarized and supported by M. Weippert.[91]

Alt examined references to Canaanite sites in Egyptian records of the fifteenth through the twelfth centuries B.C. and concluded that, despite changes in the overall political control of Palestine, certain territorial divisions remained constant. Two belts of city-states—one in the northern region stretching from Dor on the coast to Beth-shan by the Jordan River, and a second in southern Palestine extending from Jerusalem to the coastal plain—cut across the land, which was otherwise made up of large territorial units which were rather sparsely populated. By comparing this data with information preserved in the biblical books of Joshua and Judges, Alt deduced that the Israelites, upon entering Palestine, settled for the most part in the thinly populated areas between the belts of Canaanite city-states.

Military activity, according to these German scholars, did not play a significant role in this process of land acquisition. The process, as Weippert sums up the hypothesis, was essentially "a settlement growing out of the regular change of pasture on the part of nomads with small cattle."[92] They were not able to capture the cities,[93] so they claimed the territory where resistance to their coming would have been minimal. As time went by and the various Israelite tribes sought to extend their territorial holdings into areas of greater Canaanite presence, some local military engagements by individual tribes took place, and it is this activity which stood out more forcefully in the popular memory than the earlier peaceful infiltration.[94] Further, the holders of this theory suggest that the stage of territorial expansion, involving as it did some military activity, gave rise to conquest tales of a fictional nature to "explain" such striking phenomena as the ruins of Ai (Josh. 7–8),[95] the heap of stones in the valley of Achor (Josh. 7:26),[96] and the five trees before a cave near the town of Makkedah (Josh. 10:16–27).[97] The etiological [98] nature of these accounts was deduced especially from the frequently occurring phrase "to this day" (cf. Josh. 4:9; 5:9; 7:26 [twice]; 8:28, 29; 10:27) found near the end of a tale, suggesting to these scholars that the tale had been fabricated to explain the existence of some phenomenon known to Israelites of a later time.[99] The reference to the children's questioning as to "What does this mean?" (Josh. 4:6, 21) likewise seemed to point in this direction. No historical value is to be attached to these etiologies, it was argued.

Moreover, the leading role played by Joshua in the narratives of Joshua 1–12 was considered a fiction. In the course of Israel's development as an association of twelve tribes,[100] the etiological tales which had originated primarily among the Benjaminites (in whose territory are located the various phenomena "explained" by the etiologies) and the war tales of Joshua 10:1–15 and 11:1–15, which were originally traditions of the Benjaminites[101] and Naphtalites respectively, became the property of the whole tribal league and were given an "all-Israel" orientation which made it appear that the entire nation had been involved in the events described. In this process, Joshua, whose historical role was probably limited to the events described in Joshua 17:14–18 and 24:1–28,[102] was elevated to the leadership of the unified Israel in the tradition.

With regard to the reconstruction of the history of the Israelite settlement in Palestine, we are clearly quite a distance from the picture produced by the Albright school, which is based on the premise that the archaeological evidence establishes the credibility of the Old Testament narratives in essentially the form we now have them.

The two most extensive criticisms which have been directed against the views of Alt and Noth are (1) that they did not allow the witness of archaeological findings to influence their conclusions sufficiently, and (2) that they too quickly categorized the stories of conquest as etiologies, allowing this categorization to relegate the tales forthwith to the realm of fiction.[103]

The Germans, contrary to some of the more extreme assertions of their critics,[104] did not ignore the findings of archaeology;[105] but they did consider the findings too ambiguous to provide support for the stories in Joshua 2–11.[106] M. Weippert has picked up the line of argument of the Alt-Noth school and elaborated reasons why the value of archaeological evidence is rather limited.[107] He urges the sort of considerations mentioned on pages 69–72. The limitations to what archaeological finds can demonstrate are more and more stressed by a number of archaeologists themselves, such as Franken and de Vaux,[108] the latter a scholar whose views in many respects are closer to the views of the Albright school than to those of Alt and Noth.

The Alt-Noth school has also been criticized for drawing unwarranted conclusions about the fictitious character of the biblical conquest narratives from their literary analysis.[109] Once a narrative has been judged to be an etiology, their approach regards the events described in that narrative to be void of historicity. The rebuttal made by Bright has been subscribed by numerous other scholars, to wit: "Literary form does not . . . furnish a final test of historicity. . . . Historical value can be shown in certain known cases to vary within a given form."[110]

Dissenters from the Alt-Noth thesis raised the question as to whether the etiological factor (i.e., the intent to provide an explanation, by means of a past occurrence, for how some existing phenomenon, custom, or institution came to be) can ever be shown to have been the *primary* or *original* stimulus in the formation of a narrative.[111] The presence of etiological motifs in numerous narratives is readily acknowledged. But there is no *a priori* reason to assume that a given story which explains phenomenon X was non-existent until someone inquired "Where did X come from?" An already existent tradition may be employed for the purposes of etiology, without being dependent upon the etiological motive for its origination.[112]

B. S. Childs has shown that the presence of the phrase "(such-and-such is so) to this day," which frequently seems to have been for Alt and Noth the decisive clue that a tradition is etiological in origin, has in many instances been added to the tradition at a secondary stage simply to inform the reader that the phenomenon mentioned in the narrative of years past is still visible in the reader's day.[113]

Childs also argued that the concept of etiology has been used too loosely.[114] It has been applied to Old Testament stories in which the reported cause for an existing phenomenon is natural and historical as well as to stories in which the causative factor is mythical[115] (e.g., the sign of Cain, the diversity of human languages, Lot's wife turning into a pillar of salt). Childs questions whether the concept can appropriately be extended from the latter type of narrative (to which it was originally applied by Hermann Gunkel) to stories in which the causality principle is not mythical. There was a tendency in Israel to weaken the mythical elements in its inherited tradition; therefore, a resort to mythical causality (i.e., genuine etiology) would have been inconsistent. Although the stories in the book of Joshua provide explanations for certain existing phenomena, as do the myths in Genesis 1–11, there is a vast difference between the nature of the explanation in the myths (mythical causation) and the nature of the explanation in the conquest stories (historical causation). In the case of the etiologies in Genesis, recognition of the mythical causality principle rules out the possibility of the story's historicity. But it is unjustified simply to extend the genre of etiology from these Genesis tales to the stories in Joshua and assume that consideration of the historicity of the Joshua stories is irrelevant.

Claus Westermann approached the question of etiology in a somewhat different way. In his discussion of the types of stories in Genesis,[116] he defines a narrative (*Erzählung*) as a story which reports an event from its moment of tension to the resolution of the tension; the story line begins with the raising of a question or a problem and proceeds toward a conclusion which answers the question or deals with the problem. With reference to the question of etiologies, Westermann makes the point that if—and only if—the "eternal child's question 'Why?' " evokes the tension in a narrative and the story line is designed to provide an answer to this question, then the narrative is properly classified as an etiological narrative. An etiological narrative can only be one "in which the way from the question, which the etiology poses, to the answer, which the etiological conclusion gives, coincides with the arc (within the narrative) which leads from tension to resolution."[117] Is the arc of tension in the narrative produced by the concern to explain some existing phenomenon, or is this explanatory feature incidental to another, more basic, structure in the narrative? Westermann believes there are virtually no pure etiological narratives in the Old Testament. Etiological elements are usually secondary motifs attached to narratives arising from other concerns. Therefore Westermann's study also would support the criticism raised by Albright and Bright.

It has been healthy to have some scholars (viz., the Albright school) working with the presumption of maximum reliability of the traditions of early Israel until the reliability is disproved, while other scholars (viz., the Alt school) have been working with the opposite presumption that the reliability of these traditions is suspect until critical study and external evidence indicates otherwise.[118]

Each school has scored points vis-à-vis the other, and most recent writing on the settlement period has eschewed the more extreme tendencies of each school. The stories in the book of Joshua are not adjudged anymore to be lacking in historical value simply because etiological elements appear in them; it is recognized that the question of historicity is not decided simply by determining the genre of the narrative. (Score a point for the Albright school.) On the other hand, it is now recognized that archaeological evidence is subject to more alternative interpretations than the Albright school has commonly acknowledged. (Score a point for Alt-Noth.)

Although these two schools operate with different presumptions and with differing priorities regarding the types of relevant evidence, in the final analysis their conclusions about the conquest traditions turn out to be closer than appears at first.

1. Neither believes that the stories in Joshua are, in their present form, fully accurate. The tradition in its received form needs to be critically reconstructed in order to establish the original course of events.

2. Neither school believes that there ever was an invasion by "all Israel," i.e., by an army composed of the twelve tribes.

3. Each believes that the conquest tales in Joshua were inspired by the fact that some actual battles were fought. The German school reckons the military efforts to a secondary stage of occupation (i.e., the stage of "territorial expansion"), whereas the Albrightians believe the *initial* entry of some tribal groups to have been achieved by military force.

4. Each believes that a considerable segment of the Israelite people settled under different circumstances than those described in the book of Joshua.

Separate Tribal Settlements

Because of factors such as those mentioned in the opening pages of this chapter, most historians—including those who ascribe a high historical value to the narratives in Joshua 1–12—postulate a process of tribal settlement considerably more complicated than that implied in the book of Joshua. Reconstruction of this process is very hypothetical, and there are almost never two historians whose reconstructions coincide completely.

The Old Testament is our starting point in efforts to reconstruct the details of Israel's settlement in Canaan. Extra-biblical epigraphic materials and evidence of an archaeological, geographical, or anthropological nature may help us evaluate the usefulness of the Old Testament sources. The extra-biblical evidence can help us decide if a particular hypothesis is credible or not. If one should conclude that the Old Testament's testimony concerning this historical period is totally unreliable, he must learn to live with the fact that we simply cannot know, given presently available knowledge, what the historical facts were.

In addition to the tales of conquest and settlement in Joshua and Judges, scholars have used other biblical materials. Several stories in the book of Numbers, when later revisions are peeled away, seem to refer to events by which individual Israelite clans gained land in Canaan. Certain of the narratives and poems in Genesis, which ostensibly refer to individuals such as Jacob/Israel and his sons, likely originated as encapsulations of *tribal* experiences—tribal movements, occupations, changes in status. Some of the genealogical narratives and lists[119] found in various Old Testament books apparently contain, under the guise of individual kinship relationships, fragments of information about changing relationships between tribal and clan groups—for example, "marriages" indicating amalgamations of previously unrelated groups (e.g., Genesis 38;[120] cf. Num. 26:19–22), the description of one person as "father" of another indicating achievement of superiority by one clan over another (e.g., Josh. 17:1; Num. 26:29),[121] or the assigning of an "individual" to two different tribes indicating wanderings or migration from one territory to another (e.g., Carmi appears as belonging to Judah in Joshua 7:18, but to Reuben, according to Genesis 46:9 and Numbers 26:5–6).[122]

The following paragraphs attempt to show, by some typical reconstructions, the kinds of inferences which have been drawn from various biblical materials and the sorts of settlement patterns that have been hypothesized. Here we have some prime examples of how scholars attempt to elicit from the sources information which is not explicitly revealed.

Galilean tribes

Of the various groups of Israelite tribes, it is the Galilean tribes whose settlement is the most difficult to speculate about. Scholars concede that reconstruction of their settlement history is virtually impossible. The prevailing tendency is to assign the settlement of these northern tribes to a relatively early date, frequently in the Amarna age (early fourteenth century B.C.).

Some believe that Issachar (and perhaps Zebulun and Dan?) might have gained the right to settle the land by enrolling in the service of Canaanite cities in the region.[123] Genesis 49:15 speaks of Issachar engaging in "forced labor" to gain a pleasant land; the name Issachar has been explained by some as deriving from the Hebrew phrase *ish sakar* meaning "hired laborer."[124] Certain fourteenth century Egyptian texts speak of the use of corvée workers to till the land in the region which the Old Testament assigns to Issachar.[125]

There is also mention in Egyptian texts of the late fourteenth and early thirteenth century of an "Asharu" in the area where the Israelite tribe of Asher was later settled, and this prompts some to think that that tribe was settled in the region from an undetermined time.[126]

Concerning more precise circumstances of the settlement of the northern tribes, scholars admit "we are quite in the dark."[127] Several speculate that the concubine tribes were indigenous Canaanite peoples.[128]

Transjordanian tribes

The settlement of the area east of the Jordan River also has to be reconstructed from bits and pieces of data. Reuben's residence there might have been preceded by a period of occupation on the western side of the Jordan, which would account for a stone on the boundary between the territories of Judah and Benjamin named for "Bohan the son of Reuben" (Josh. 15:6; 18:17). Some interpreters also believe that the Song of Deborah connects Reuben with the tribes living west of the Jordan (Judg. 5:14–16).[129] The tribe's migration to the east, then, would have resulted from some catastrophe in the tribe's early history, alluded to in Genesis 35:22 and 49:4.[130] However, these arguments can be turned around the other way: perhaps Reuben originally settled east of the Jordan (as the narrative in Numbers 32 suggests) and only when the tribe was decimated did some families migrate west of the river.[131]

Some scholars hypothesize that the story in Genesis 31:43–54 concerning a treaty between Jacob and Laban reflects a settlement of Gad east of the Jordan from an early period.[132] Some believe that the "three hundred years" of Israelite settlement prior to the time of Jephthah mentioned in Judges 11:26 goes back to the settlement of Gad.[133]

It may be that the region north of Gadite territory served to accommodate the "overflow" of population from west of the Jordan during the period of the judges. Judges 12:1–6 mentions "fugitives of Ephraim," which may refer to Ephraimites settled in Gilead.[134] The Transjordanian "forest of Ephraim," in which the battle between the troops of David and Absalom was fought (2 Sam. 18:6), might have taken its name from this settlement.[135] The close relationship that existed between the tribe of Benjamin and the Transjordanian town of Jabesh (Judg. 21:1–14; 1 Sam. 11; 31:11–13; 2 Sam. 21:12) might also derive from some migration from the west side to the east.[136]

At some time in the later part of the period of the judges, the clan of Machir (which at the time of Deborah's battle with the Canaanites[137] was in the hill country of Ephraim [cf. Judg. 5:14]) had to migrate east of the Jordan, into the region of Gilead (cf. Num. 32:39–40). Following the migration of Machir, Manasseh became the chief clan among those who remained west of the Jordan and gave its name to the whole tribe. Machir was regarded as the "father" of Gilead (Josh. 17:3; 1 Chron. 2:21, 23) since he was the strongest of the clans in the northern part of the Transjordan, and Manasseh was considered the father of Machir (Num. 26:29; Josh. 17:1).[138]

The "Leah" and "Rachel" tribes

The two most influential groups of Israelite tribes are those whose eponymous ancestors were said to have been born of Jacob/Israel (Gen. 29:31–30:24; 35:16–18; 35:23–26) by Leah (Reuben, Simeon, Levi, Judah, Issachar, and Zebulum) and by Rachel (Joseph [represented in the tribes of Ephraim and Manasseh] and Benjamin). Most scholars believe that the grouping of these tribes in this way arose because the tribes in each group shared some common history which was distinct from the experiences of the tribes in the other group. Each group is thought to have entered Palestine under different circumstances. But scholars are not in agreement about either the relative or the absolute dating of these groups' entry into Canaan.

The "Leah first" theory. Most believe that the "Leah tribes" (principally Reuben, Simeon, Levi and Judah)[139] made the earlier entry, and this is usually thought to have taken place in the 1300s. The individuals bearing these names are said to have been the eldest sons of Jacob/Israel (Gen. 29:31–35), which suggests greater antiquity for these tribes. Moreover, by the time of the judges, the tribes of Reuben, Simeon, and Levi had diminished in significance to the point that they played no important role in the traditions of that period. Their preeminence among Jacob's sons (assuming that their listing as the eldest sons carried that connotation) can only be explained if their entry and residence in Canaan antedated the exodus-conquest period,[140] with this pre-eminence having been lost by the time of Joshua.

There are still other clues which have suggested an earlier entry of the Leah tribes. The location of the story of the attack on Shechem by Simeon and Levi (Gen. 34)—frequently interpreted as a reminiscence of tribal activities disguised as the exploits of their eponyms—in the period before the exodus would point in this direction.[141] There are several indicators in the Old Testament which suggest a residence of Reuben west of the Jordan at a time before the tribe settled in the Transjordan area, where its territory is allotted in the post-conquest period.[142] The story of Judah and Tamar (Gen. 38), if taken as a representation of the assimilation of Canaanite elements by the tribe of Judah, would indicate the presence of the tribe of Judah in the land prior to the time of the exodus.[143] Finally, there has been an effort to correlate the presence of the Leah tribes with references in the Amarna texts (dating from the early fourteenth century B.C.) to "Hapiru" activity in the area inhabited by the tribe of Judah and at Shechem, where Simeon and Levi, according to Genesis 34, were present.[144]

The direction from which the Leah tribes entered Palestine is a matter of dispute. Numerous writers believe that at least some of them entered the land from the south.[145] An entry northward from Kadesh might be reflected in the pericope of Numbers 21:1–3[146] and the accounts in Judges 1:1–20.[147] The Calebites, whose entry is associated in Judges 1 with Judah and Simeon, almost certainly gained their land by means of an invasion from the south which is reflected in the narratives of Numbers 13–14. Others posit an entry from the east, across the Jordan River, basing this on a different interpretation of Judges 1:1–20, and on the inference from Genesis 34 that this group of tribes attempted to settle in the central part of Cisjordan.[148]

The histories of these tribes subsequent to their entry are inferred principally from texts in the book of Genesis. Activities in the area of Shechem which lie behind the narrative in Genesis 34 might have led to the scattering of Simeon and Levi (cf. Gen. 49:5–7).[149] The Simeonites in time deteriorated so that, by the time of the judges, they were simply a part of the tribe of Judah (cf. Josh. 19:1–9). The Levites never gained a territory of their own and simply vanished, unless they are to be connected with the priestly Levites.[150] Reuben apparently suffered some misfortune about the same time (cf. Gen. 49:3–4)[151] and had to retire east of the Jordan River, leaving behind only scattered reminiscences of the tribe's one-time residence west of the Jordan.[152] Judah alone was able to maintain her territory[153] and she succeeded in expanding peacefully during the following period, absorbing elements such as the

Calebites and Simeonites, as well as Canaanites, whose assimilation is perhaps reflected in Genesis 38.[154]

The "Rachel first" theory. There are some scholars, however, who argue that the Rachel tribes entered prior to the Leah tribes.[155] A principal reason for a while was the dating of Jericho's fall around 1400 B.C.; that dating prompted the belief that, since Joshua's name is so inextricably associated with the capture of Jericho in the biblical tradition, the entry of the Rachel tribes[156] under his leadership had to be dated then.[157] There seemed to be too much evidence for an invasion in the late thirteenth century[158] to date the entire Hebrew invasion at the time Jericho was supposed to have fallen, so a later entry by the Leah group was held to have occurred ca. 1200, following the exodus from Egypt under Moses' leadership.

Even after more recent discoveries at the site of Jericho disproved a fourteenth century dating for that city's fall, it has been argued by some that the activity of Joshua and his armies had a "vital connection" with the activity of the Habiru in Palestine in the early fourteenth century.[159] T. J. Meek further takes the cultural superiority of the North Israelites, evidenced in various ways, as owing to the two hundred years of additional settlement.[160]

Some scholars who accept Joshua 10:28–39 as a reliable historical record reckon this as evidence that Joshua's (Rachelite) armies entered the land in advance of the (Leah) tribe of Judah, which later occupied the area mentioned in these verses; when the tribe of Judah (accompanied by Caleb, Othniel and others) achieved the successes reported in Judges 1:11–20, they were exploiting opportunities presented by the earlier victories of Joshua.[161]

It is also argued that the "Rachel first" theory is supported by certain traditions in the book of Numbers.[162] There seem to be two different traditions about the route followed by the Israelites from the Kadesh oasis to the southern Transjordan and thence into the land west of the Jordan River. One tradition, in Numbers 33, says that the Israelites marched *through* Edomite and Moabite territory; this tradition, it is argued, represents a situation in the fourteenth century. This earlier tradition is taken to be the record of the movements of the *Rachel* tribes because the itinerary of Numbers 33 is designed to proceed through the taking of Jericho, a town in the territory of the Rachel tribes.[163] The other tradition, represented in Numbers 21–25 (cf. Judg. 11:17–18), reflects a period somewhat later, after Edom and Moab had become strong enough to prevent a march through their territory.[164] This tradition is associated with the movement of the Leah tribes because it is here that we have the report of the capture of Transjordanian territories (Num. 21:21–35) which were subsequently allotted to the "Leah" tribe of Reuben and to the tribe of Gad (associated with Leah by her maid Zilpah [Gen. 30:9–11]).[165]

The "Rachel first" theory conflicts on several points with the biblical traditions. It conflicts with the tradition that the "sons" of Leah were older than the "sons" of Rachel. Also, since Joshua (an Ephraimite) is connected with the entry of the Rachel tribes, it reverses the biblical sequence of Moses (a Levite associated with Leah) and Joshua.[166] Some proponents of the "Rachel first" theory dissociate the Rachel tribes from a residence in and exodus from Egypt[167] (since in their reconstruction it is the *later* Leah group with the Levite leader Moses which experienced these events), yet of all the sons of Jacob/Israel, it is pre-eminently Joseph the son of Rachel who is associated with the sojourn in Egypt.

Finally, with regard to the dating of the two traditions about the itinerary from Kadesh to Transjordan, recent developments in the study of settlement in the Transjordan seem to rule out any thesis based on the assumption that Edom and Moab experienced a surge in sedentary occupation and fortifications in the thirteenth century. It now appears that the date for the surge may not have occurred until the first millennium.[168] On balance, the case for the "Leah first" theory seems to be the stronger.

The entry of the Rachel group into Canaan is represented principally in the stories of Joshua 2–10, which deal with operations in territory that was subsequently held by the tribe of Benjamin. Especially among the German scholars there has been a tendency to regard the stories in Joshua 2–10 as etiologies which grew up after the tribes had settled in the land by peaceful means to explain unusual topographical phenomena.[169] The degree to which an historian grants credibility to these stories usually depends on his evaluation of the archaeological evidence from the sites where the battles are said to have occurred.

The Old Testament reports very little of military engagements in the area settled by the tribes of Ephraim and Manasseh.[170] There is no archaeological evidence from the Late Bronze Age to indicate the exercise of force in the occupation of this area, so all scholars who believe the Israelite occupation occurred in the thirteenth century have concluded that this finding supports the inference drawn from the biblical narratives that the Israelites were able to settle most of that region peacefully. If, however, more historians begin to consider an earlier date for the conquest, the evidence of destruction at the end of the Middle Bronze Age from sites like Shechem and Shiloh[171] may force a reconsideration of the manner in which Israelites occupied central Canaan.

Later events in the history of the Rachel tribes are inferred from allusions in tribal poems and genealogical statements scattered throughout the early books of the Old Testament. From the story of the birth of Benjamin after Jacob/Israel had returned to Canaan (Gen. 35:16–20) and the fact that the original meaning of the name Benjamin was probably "son of the south," it has been inferred that this tribe broke off (was "born") as the southernmost element of the Rachel tribes after the settlement in Canaan.[172] The rise of Ephraim to superiority over Manasseh is reflected in the story of the blessing of the two sons of Joseph (Genesis 48).[173] The migration of the Machirite clan, which was part of Manasseh, to the east side of the Jordan River has been mentioned earlier.[174]

Pre-settlement association?

How did it happen that tribes of such disparate origins, settling in the land of Canaan under different circumstances and from different directions and backgrounds, became united in the worship of Yahweh and eventually developed into the nation of Israel? If we give up the tradition that the twelve tribes were descended from a common ancestor (Jacob) and therefore had an ethnic unity pre-dating their respective entries into Canaan in the Late Bronze Age, how do we explain the sense of unity among the tribes which is manifest shortly after the tribes were established in the land?[175]

As has been mentioned, the territories occupied by the Israelite tribes were cut in two places by belts of Canaanite cities which the Israelites were unable to capture at the time of their entry into the land.[176] These two belts effectively cut off the tribes in central Canaan (i.e., the Rachel tribes) on the one hand from the Galilean tribes and on the other hand from the "Leah" tribe of Judah (which had absorbed Simeon) in the south. The Jordan River separated all these tribes from those in the Transjordan. Given this factor of physical separation, how did it happen that tribes which had entered the land at different times developed a sense of commonality? Certainly by the time of the monarchy the belts of Canaanite cities had been conquered; did the unity of "Israel" develop only at that time? Did the union of these various tribes eventuate only with the rise of the Hebrew monarchy? There are some difficulties with this position. Already in the pre-monarchical period there seems to have been some sort of bond felt between the Leah tribes and the Rachel tribes, as expressed, for example, in the very ancient Song of Deborah (Judges 5) and also in the stories of Judges 17–21.[177] The acceptance of the Benjaminite Saul as king by all tribes, including Judah, presupposes a prior feeling of unity.[178]

Noth sought to explain this unity with his theory of the *Israelite amphictyony*. He theorized that, in the period following the settlement, the twelve tribes were confederated in an amphictyonic organization focused upon a central sanctuary where the worship of Yahweh was celebrated by all the tribes. It was Noth's belief that the six Leah tribes had been allied in a six-tribe amphictyony prior to their entry into Palestine, but the association of these tribes with the other six came about only in the period of the judges. Only with the establishment of the twelve-tribe confederacy, he argued, was there laid the basis for the sense of oneness which constituted the people "Israel." Noth's theory has recently come under widespread attack; his theory has not, in the opinion of a growing number of scholars, satisfactorily explained the unity of the tribes.[179]

It is suggested by a number of scholars that many of the people who entered Palestine by different routes had, prior to their entry into the land, shared in a cult of Yahweh in the vicinity of Kadesh (even if not all the tribal groups were at Kadesh at the same time). The Kadesh holy place and the worship conducted there provided a bond of union among the groups, even if the groups were not simultaneously present at the sanctuary.[180]

The biblical traditions of the wilderness wanderings after the exodus assign a considerable block of material to the site of Kadesh.[181] Some historians believe that Kadesh was the desert sanctuary toward which Moses' group headed directly after the departure from Egypt;[182] others believe that the Moses group came to Kadesh after a journey to Sinai.[183]

Kadesh is the starting point for the attempted invasion of Canaan which is reported in Numbers 13–14, which account may be related somehow to the invasion of the land by the Leah tribes.[184] Kadesh is also a major point on the migration route of those tribes which found their way into the southern Transjordan before entering Canaan from the east.[185] It seems quite possible that tribal groups which entered

Canaan independently of each other had in common their participation in the religion celebrated at Kadesh.

The Internal Revolt Alternative

In all the views summarized in the preceding discussion there has been the presumption that the settlement of the Israelites in Canaan was a movement—whether warlike or peaceful or mixed—of various (semi)nomadic kinship groups from outside the land into Canaan, where they entered into a process of sedentarization. The virtually unanimous testimony of the Old Testament traditions is that the Israelites were not native to the land of Canaan. The organization of the Israelites in tribes has frequently been regarded as an indication of their nomadic origins.[186] And, as has been shown, archaeological evidence from the end of the Late Bronze Age and the beginning of the Early Iron Age has usually been interpreted as attesting the influx of new cultural groups into Canaan.[187]

More recently, a quite different understanding of the origins of Israel has been put forward, challenging these widely held invasion/immigration conceptions of Israel's origins. According to this newer thesis, which has been expounded principally by George E. Mendenhall and Norman K. Gottwald,[188] "Israel" grew up in Late Bronze-Early Iron Age Canaan as the result of a social revolt *within* Canaanite society.

The principal model for this social revolt concept, developed especially by Mendenhall, is the activity of *apiru* elements in Canaan who are referred to frequently in the diplomatic correspondence between the Egyptian court of the early fourteenth century B.C. and its vassal kings in Syria and Palestine (the so-called "Amarna letters").[189] The *apiru* have been described as "uprooted individuals of varied origins, without tribal or family ties, who joined in bands which could be hired as soldiers by organized states, or acted on their own.'"[190] They are mentioned in texts from all parts of the ancient Near East, primarily during the period from the eighteenth through the thirteenth centuries. A number of the kinglets in Syria-Palestine appealed (in the Amarna letters) to the Egyptian court for reinforcements against the harassing activities of the *apiru*. Mendenhall gives the term a more specialized meaning, namely, someone who has withdrawn from or rebelled against the existing political regime, someone who "has renounced any obligation to the society in which he formerly had some standing (if not status), and has in turn deprived himself of its protection.'"[191] He interprets the *ᶜapiru* activity in Canaan to have been the reaction of disaffected peasants to oppressive policies of the rulers and the continual vying for power among these ambitious dynasts. Mendenhall identifies the biblical Hebrews as late thirteenth-early twelfth century *ᶜapiru* and traces the origins of "Israel" to such movements of withdrawal from Canaanite society, unified about 1200 B.C. under the aegis of the Yahweh faith.[192]

There is, according to this theory, no need to imagine a substantial influx of new population into Canaan to account for the birth of Israel.[193] What occurred was a change in living conditions and political structure for an essentially constant population. Disenchanted elements in Canaanite society revolted against that society, withdrew from it, and established an alternative society. The Old Testament is correct (it is argued) in suggesting that the exodus group was a small group of about seventy families[194] and also in describing the nation of Israel in the post-Settlement period as a large group (Mendenhall uses a calculation of a quarter million which he attributes to Albright). Such rapid growth can be explained only if the exodus group was augmented by a large number of indigenous Canaanite peoples.[195]

The proponents of this theory have suggested that the peasants of Canaan, chafing under the increasingly exploitative administration of their kings, were galvanized into action by the ideology introduced into their country by a small band of former slaves escaped from Egypt, who had entered into a covenant with the god Yahweh.[196] The oppressed peasants of Canaan could identify with the traditions of bondage to Egyptian taskmasters; as the exodus group had sought relief from Egyptian power, so these Canaanite farmers and shepherds sought it from their Canaanite rulers.[197]

The politics of the rulers in Canaan had become ideologically and ethically bankrupt;[198] and the religions of Canaan served only to legitimate and guarantee the position of the rulers. The state was more concerned with enhancing its own power than with serving the interests of those whom it ruled. This preoccupation with power which characterized Canaanite rule carried the seeds of the state's destruction, as it fragmented society and stirred up discontent. In contrast, the ideology of the Yahweh covenant gave precedence to ethical concerns instead of economic or political.[199]

> Common loyalty to a single Overlord, and obligation to a common and simple group of norms created the community, a solidarity which was attractive to all persons suffering under the burden of subjection to a mo-

nopoly of power which they had no part in creating, and from which they received virtually nothing but tax-collectors.[200]

This theory fits better, its proponents argue, with archaeological and anthropological evidence than does any theory of invasion or immigration by nomadic outsiders, and it finds support (they argue) in the Old Testament traditions.

As pointed out earlier in this chapter, there is no archaeological evidence to prove the arrival of new peoples in Canaan shortly before or after 1200 B.C. The agents of the destruction wrought at various cities at that time cannot be identified with certainty. Mendenhall prefers to see this destruction as the effect of citizen unrest which preceded the arrival of the exodus group and the formation of Israel.[201] The cultural artifacts do not reveal influences which can be attributed to newly arrived Israelites. There are, as a matter of fact, clear signs of *continuity* with the Canaanite culture of the Late Bronze period. Gottwald speaks of "Israel's fundamental cultural continuity with Canaan over a very wide repertory,"[202] including, in addition to archaeological artifacts, language and forms of cultic practice.[203] The culture of Early Iron Age Palestine, while continuous with that of the Late Bronze period, was materially poorer, and this is interpreted as the consequence of the peasant revolt, which played havoc with the modes of production. Without an integrated society, maintenance of the former levels of technology and art was no longer possible.[204]

Housing in the Early Iron Age shows less contrast than does that of the Late Bronze period. Mendenhall interprets this as a reflection of the egalitarianism introduced into Canaanite society by the exodus-covenant group.[205] The spread of new Early Iron settlements in the hill country is attributed to the peasants' clearing of forest land for agriculture so they can establish autonomy vis-à-vis the deteriorating cities.[206]

Recent studies in the organization and evolution of primitive societies have concluded that the concept of a unilinear evolution of those societies from nomadism to sedentary existence to urbanization is untenable. There was a much closer relationship between pastoral nomads and the settled population than the old contrast between "the desert and the sown" was able to conceive.[207] The image of nomads coveting land and seizing it at the first opportunity simply does not accord with what anthropologists have found in the study of primitive cultures. Furthermore, the organization of the Israelites in tribes cannot be taken as a sign of nomadic origins, as was formerly thought;[208] tribalism was found among urban and agricultural peoples as well as among nomads.[209] Grouping into tribes was not based on kinship,[210] but was commonly a development among settled peoples to deal with crises. Tribes tend to emerge among people in a given vicinity when a specific problem arises.[211] The tribes of Israel, it is argued, developed in reaction to the oppressive Canaanite rule. The tribes were social organizations which grew up among those who accepted the rule of Yahweh instead of the rule of their erstwhile Canaanite masters.[212]

Various Old Testament materials are interpreted as congruent with this theory of Israel's origins. A close reading of the exodus and conquest narratives does not support the notion that the Israelites who entered Canaan under Joshua's leadership came from a nomadic background. Those Israelites who suffered under and escaped from Egyptian bondage are depicted as stockbreeders, fishermen, and small gardeners (e.g., Exod. 10:24; 12:38; Num. 11:5, 22; 20:4) who find it difficult to subsist in the wilderness.[213] Miracles were needed to sustain them during their wilderness trek, which, it will be noted, is not depicted as nomadic change of pasture, but as a migration undertaken from quite different motives. Therefore, the theory of Israel's nomadic origins finds as little support from the Bible itself as it does from anthropological studies.

The victory of Israel over Sihon (Num. 21:21–30) was made possible, according to Mendenhall, by the defection of "a very large part" of that kingdom's population to the religious community of Moses.[214] Similar groups followed suit, with the consequence that "a very considerable military potential was thus created practically overnight."[215] Battles on the west side of the Jordan followed, as kings organized coalitions in an effort to stem the revolt, which was enhanced by the addition of more and more disaffected groups. Joshua 12 contains lists of kings whose holdings were appropriated by the revolutionaries.[216] Passages which explicitly refer to Canaanite "converts" to Israel are adduced as further support for the theory: the story of Rahab and her family from Jericho (Josh. 2:1–14; 6:22–25), the informer and his family from Bethel (Judg. 1:22–26), the alliance with the Gibeonites (Joshua 9), and the assembly at Shechem (Joshua 24).[217]

As yet there has been no systematic presentation of arguments by proponents of the "revolt" thesis as to why the "revolt" is *dated* when it is. It appears that they have taken over much of the argumentation developed by the Albright school, whose concept of the origins of Israel they have challenged as erroneous! The Albright school arrived at a Late Bronze Age dating for the settlement of Israel in Canaan primarily on the basis of extra-biblical data which seemed to them to attest an exodus and an invasion in the thirteenth century. Since almost all of the arguments for that thirteenth century dating have been disputed,[218] and since the Mendenhall-Gottwald alternative denies the conquest model, it would seem that the supporters of the "revolt" model need to develop a fresh argumentation for dating the origins of Israel. Why, for example, is this revolt not associated with the *capiru* activity of the fourteenth century which is reflected in the Amarna letters?

Part of the rationale for the dating which is suggested is apparently the archaeological evidence of destruction at the end of the Late Bronze Age (attributed to the widespread dissatisfaction which swept through the Mediterranean civilizations and prepared the way for the revolt), the new settlements which sprang up in Palestine (attributed to peasants clearing new land to establish their autonomy from the cities), and the "democratization" of housing in the Early Iron Age (attributed to the influence of the newly emergent egalitarian ethic of the covenant). As we have had occasion to note in several previous instances, archaeo-logical data such as these are ambiguous, however. The destruction of Canaanite cities could have been caused by any of several attackers from without, or from inter-city warfare. The new settlements could be credited to improved agricultural techniques made possible by the de-velopment of iron implements, better cisterns, and terracing meth-ods.[219] The lesser contrast in housing could be owing to the general economic crisis which beset the whole Mediterranean region. The case for the chosen date needs to be made more substantial.

The most obvious criticism of the "internal revolt" theory as a comprehensive model for the origins of Israel, and ultimately the most damaging, is the persistent tradition in the Old Testament that Israel was not indigenous to the land of Canaan.[220] The biblical traditions, of course, witness to the assimilation by Israel of some indigenous Canaanite peoples, but Canaan is consistently depicted as a land not originally Israel's, but given to the Israelites by Yahweh, who brought them into it from other places. The traditions of the settlement show no consciousness of the Israelites' taking over a land already known to them. When one takes also into account the stories of the patriarchal migrations into Canaan, we have a *double* tradition of the Israelites having origins outside of the land.

Mendenhall's version of the theory, especially, rests heavily on the hypothesis that the covenant between Israel and Yahweh was estab-lished in the time of Moses.[221] Pervading Mendenhall's entire treatment of the origins of Israel is the theme that the covenant ethic provided the

ideological foundation for this new society, and that without this foundation there would be no way to explain the unity which grew up
among the (quite small) exodus group and the various peasant groups
of Canaan. The paganistic states of the Late Bronze Age exploited the
peasantry and undergirded their exercise of power with religious systems which confirmed the rulers' right to rule.[222] Such religious systems contained no room for self-criticism; it is precisely this which the
covenant supplied, by introducing an authority higher than any human
rule. The creative break with the value systems of the past which is
represented in Israel cannot be understood, argues Mendenhall, apart
from the Sinai covenant, which establishes the ethical obligation of
those in power to attend to the needs of all the citizenry. "The Sinai
event and the covenant established there are the only reasonable
sources for those aspects of Old Testament thought which constitute its
amazing contrast to the tired old political theologies of ancient
paganism."[223]

Mendenhall's thesis about the contrast between the value system
embodied in the Israelite covenant and the various "Baalistic" value
systems of the Late Bronze Age grows homiletical at points[224] and will
certainly "preach," but whether it is the only possible historical explanation for the appearance of the Israelite community in the late second
millennium is highly debatable. We saw in the last chapter how uncertain, if not dubious, is the hypothesis that the covenant dates from the
Mosaic era. If the evidence compels us to posit a later dating for the
covenant, we quite simply *have to* find another explanation for the
emergence of Israel in the late second millennium.

It has been argued by several writers, including Gottwald, that
Mendenhall has oversimplified and exaggerated the role of the ideolog-
ical/ethical factor in social revolution. As Alan Hauser has put it, Mendenhall "has too easily assumed that the 'ethically strong' society will
stand, while destruction is unavoidable for the 'ethically weak' society."[225] Mendenhall describes the Israelite ideology as one which dis-
avows the use of power;[226] in contrast, Gottwald writes, "Without a
central concern for marshalling and employing power Israel could never have come into existence."[227] The role of religious ideology in social movements should not be underestimated,[228] especially in the case
of Israel,[229] but it is easy to let the biblical traditions, with their emphasis on the religious factor, skew our perception of the forces at work in
the origination of the Israelite community, since these biblical traditions constitute virtually our only written record of the origins of Israel.
Gottwald's work shows promise of incorporating a broader perspective

into this general thesis of Israel's beginnings.[230]

Mendenhall's easy identification of the $^c apiru$ and the Israelites has been frequently challenged. It is pointed out by critics that the direct equation, $^c apiru$ = "Hebrews" = "Israelites" (so that whenever the Old Testament speaks of Hebrews, or even Israelites, one can read into these texts the $^c apiru$ traits) is untenable.[231] Although it is possible that there is a philological connection between the Egyptian term $^c apiru$ and the biblical term "Hebrew" ($^c ibrî$),[232] it is not at all clear that the biblical term connotes the same as the Egyptian, nor is it certain that the biblical words "Hebrew" and "Israelite" can be taken as synonymous.[233] 1 Samuel 14:21 seems to distinguish "Hebrews" from "Israelites." The law in Exodus 21:2–6 may refer to a particular type of slave who has bound himself voluntarily for a term, in which case the reader should not suppose that the term "Hebrew slave" is synonymous with "Israelite slave." There are some instances where the context might support Mendenhall's understanding of "Hebrew" as a rebel against the established authority (e.g., where it occurs as a term of contempt in the mouth of Israel's enemies, such as 1 Sam. 4:6, 9; 13:19), but it is unlikely that this meaning can be attached to all uses of the term, much less to uses of the term "Israelite." Significantly, the term "Hebrew" does not occur in the narratives of the settlement in Canaan in the time of Joshua and the judges, which is the period in which Mendenhall posits the $^c apiru$-like activity which gave birth to the nation of Israel.[234]

Other questions might be raised concerning this thesis. If the tribes of Israel were formed in reaction to governmental oppression and under the inspiration of the newly arrived exodus group, why do tribes like Reuben, Simeon, and Levi (depicted as the eldest "sons" of Jacob/Israel) not show up in the traditions of the post-"revolt" period? Their listing as the eldest sons would imply that the tribes bearing these names were among the leaders in the formative period of Israel's life. They are grouped with Judah as sons of Leah, and Mendenhall believes the tribe of Judah to have been formed out of the indigenous population elements south of Jerusalem;[235] should we not expect that the other "sons of Leah" originated about the same time? Or were they perhaps tribal groups formed in response to some *earlier* crisis, whose memory was preserved among those people who eventually entered the Israelite community around 1200?[236] This point needs to be clarified.

If the bulk of the Israelite community was composed of indigenous Canaanites, it has been queried, "why completely destroy towns which had been liberated from a city-state ruling establishment—especially if many of those who once lived in that town were now among the victors and might very well want to return to their homes? And why is there . . . a difference in architectural layout and in range of artifacts" in the settlements supposedly peopled by the revolutionaries?[237]

As an historical hypothesis is published and analyzed and criticized by others, refinements are often made to meet some of the criticisms. Certain modifications in or elaborations of the "internal revolt" hypothesis have been put forward both by the original proponents and by others.

As we saw above, Mendenhall originally depicted the revolutionary movement as one which coalesced overnight, with essentially two elements: the exodus group, which provided the ideology, and the peasants of Canaan, who provided the manpower. It was pointed out by Hauser that the power of the Canaanite rulers can hardly have been as fragile as Mendenhall's scenario suggests and that, moreover, the biblical traditions, such as Judges 1, reflect a more drawn-out undertaking than Mendenhall would have us believe.[238] Gottwald has observed, in commenting on this point, that the revolution was more likely a protracted enterprise extending over several decades and involving a number of diverse population elements which had in common their resentment of government policies.[239]

> In my judgment, the rebellious and revolutionary forces in Canaan had been at work for decades, at first divided from one another by city-state and regional boundaries and by socio-economic types (separate strategies by ᶜapiru, Shosu, pastoralists and peasants).[240]

The criticism has been made that in the period after 1200 we find the Israelites settled, not in the heart of Canaanite city-state territory, but in the hill country, and the Bible acknowledges the inability of the Israelites to drive the Canaanites out of their strongholds. This evidence militates against the theory that the masses of Canaanite society rose up and revolted successfully.[241] Gottwald responds that peasant wars of revolution and liberation commonly seek to gain first those regions where resistance will be lowest and move from there to regions where the enemy is more firmly entrenched.[242]

The model of the internal revolt has been adopted by several historians, not as a comprehensive understanding of the origins or settlement of Israel, but as a useful explanation for *some* of the Israelite settlement. R. de Vaux and A. H. J. Gunneweg, for instance, interpret the settlement of the northern tribes along the lines of a social revolt.[243] John Bright, in the second edition of his history of Israel, accepts Mendenhall's thesis to some extent. Unlike Mendenhall, Bright prefers to speak of the "conquest," and he attributes the destruction of the Late Bronze Age cities of Canaan to the activity of Joshua's army in concert with the indigenous revolutionaries.[244] Bright gives a qualified endorsement to Mendenhall's views and he acknowledges that "the *conquest* was to some degree (to how great a degree we shall perhaps never know) an 'inside job'!"[245] In Bright's reconstruction the extent to which the body of people who formed Israel was composed of autochthonous peoples is more limited than in Mendenhall's presentation. According to Bright, the elements who rallied to the cause of the exodus group shortly before 1200 included, among others, (a) descendants of the patriarchs (= "Amorites" who came originally from Mesopotamia) who never migrated to Egypt as did Jacob's family,[246] and (b) some of the "Leah tribes" who were active in the land prior to the exodus and possibly connected with the ^{c}apiru of the Amarna period.[247] Apparently Bright considers the tribe of Judah, along with the various clans related to that tribe,[248] to have entered Canaan from the south independently of the Joshua contingent.[249]

The discussion in this chapter bears out the judgment of de Vaux quoted on the opening page and illustrates well the challenges and frustrations of historical study. In wrestling with the problem of the Israelite settlement in Canaan, the historian has a rather extensive body of testimony from the Old Testament and a constantly expanding store of evidence from other disciplines. But the ambiguity of biblical texts and external evidence make it impossible for one to be categorical in his judgments or interpretations. At least three substantially different ways of conceiving the settlement have been developed. The dating of the Israelite beginnings in the land is difficult to pin down. And there continues the teasing thought that at least some of our reports of tribal settlements are but fictional stories designed to do something quite other than convey precise information about the past.

The historian does not operate under the illusion that unquestionable certainty is attainable. But he persists because the past is there, and he is always convinced that he can know it better than he does at the present.

CHAPTER

5

Historical Research: Literary Study and "External Evidence"

In the effort to determine the historical value of the biblical stories, some scholars have given priority to literary analysis of the stories, while others have tried to determine the reliability of the stories principally by testing them against independent, extra-biblical evidence. It is clear that each approach has merit, and the practice of either to the neglect of the other has generally produced distorted results. If one or the other of these approaches is to be assigned priority, the careful scrutiny of the "internal evidence," meaning literary study of the biblical text, should be attended to first.

Literary Study

Through the application of source criticism, form criticism, literary criticism, and tradition criticism,[1] scholars try to determine what the text of a given story originally looked like, what the author was trying to accomplish, and how the text has been modified in the process which culminated in its present form.

Attention to these tasks of literary study can sometimes save the historian from futile efforts to extract historical information from a narrative that has been substantially revised and supplemented in the course of its transmission (e.g., the Sinai narrative comes to mind as an apt example[2]), or which was never intended to give information of an historical nature.

Frequently stories from the Old Testament have been utilized in various historical reconstructions without adequate consideration of the nature or intention of the stories. Usually it is assumed that the author was transmitting information about events that actually happened, and little consideration is given to the possibility that the narrative is a fiction.

The Joseph story (Genesis 37, 39–50) is an account which has frequently been mined for historical details; for example, clues have been sought in this tale which can enable us to locate Joseph and his family chronologically. But a literary analysis of this tale reveals that it develops several popular folk motifs—"rags to riches," the wise courtier, the spurned seductress, the success of the younger brother, the Israelite who makes good in a foreign land[3]—seemingly with the intent of entertaining, not with the purpose of writing history. Certain sections of the Joseph story might have been composed as didactic narratives in a wisdom tradition.[4] There is a theological motive perceptible in the final version of the story (cf. Gen. 45:5–8; 50:20), but the dominating motive is that of story-telling; this is a romance, or a *novella*. It is not the kind of story from which one should expect evidence about the history of a people. Details and twists in the plot are designed to enhance the appeal of the story, not to provide information for the historian. Recent studies have concluded that the story of Joseph is likely a product of the first millennium B.C., inserted in its present literary location to serve as a bridge between the patriarchal narratives in Genesis and the story of the exodus from Egypt.[5]

Details in the legend of Moses' birth have similarly been used by some writers to reconstruct history. H. H. Rowley dated Moses during the Ramesside era by the fact that the pharaohs at that time had a palace close to the residence of the Hebrews, "so that at the time of the birth of Moses Pharaoh's daughter might find herself in the vicinity of the Israelites when she went out for a walk."[6] In the same vein, S. Horn recently wrote that the lifetime of Moses can probably be located during the time of the Eighteenth Dynasty of Egypt (considerably earlier than Rowley's dating!) because a baby like Moses would be especially cherished among several sonless generations of that dynasty.[7] Even if one's literary sensitivity were inadequate to make him recognize the legendary character of the story in itself, one should have been alerted by the resemblance of the story to the common motif of the exposed child. The probability that the plot was not original to the Moses tradition should have put one on guard against treating the narrative as an historical report. Attention to the literary dimensions of the Moses story would further prompt one to question the historicity of the oppression which provides the context for the exposure of Moses. Why would the Egyptians pursue a policy which would weaken their labor force (a labor force which Pharaoh is so reluctant to give up in the succeeding stages of the story)? There is no mention elsewhere in the Old Testament of the genocide tradition.[8] These kinds of literary observations lead to the conclusion that the stories in Exodus 1:15–2:10 are literary fictions. The details in this section are of a literary origin; they are elements designed to move the plot along rather than efforts to represent historical facts.

All of this is not to rule out the possibility that there is some information of historical value in these stories. For the literary analyst to proceed with the assumption that there is absolutely no recollection of historical realities in these stories would be an error. Identification of a text's literary form does not finally determine the historical value of the text.[9] But when the principal features and developments in a story can be attributed to literary devices and motives, the burden of proof should be placed upon the person who maintains that the story contains historical reminiscences. To be sure, we need to refine our understanding of ancient literary styles and techniques, but we need also to pass beyond the stage of biblical study where the prevailing assumption is that a story is *history* until proof to the contrary is forthcoming. Before he launches a search among extra-biblical materials for data to "confirm" or "disprove" a biblical account, the historian should attempt to determine the degree to which the account is intended to yield historical information.

Use of External Evidence

Marc Bloch observed that at the heart of all historical work is the principle of comparison.[10] The historian may in a particular instance arrive at historical conclusions by comparing *one biblical narrative with another* (as in the case of conflicting accounts of the Hebrew conquest of Canaan), or by comparing *a biblical account with non-biblical literature,* or he may compare *the biblical record with archaeological findings,* or the comparison may be *between a biblical report and a simple commonsense generalization about the laws of nature or human behavior.* In the absence of proof, which the historian of ancient times seldom has, one must ask about a given hypothesis, "Where does the *balance of probability*[11] lie?" The process of comparison reveals similarities and differences which aid the historian in deciding where this balance lies. Without comparative data, historical work would be virtually impossible.

The principle of comparison is thus applied in numerous ways, but none has received so much attention in recent biblical scholarship as the comparison of biblical materials with extra-biblical materials provided by other disciplines, especially archaeology. Patriarchal customs have been compared with customs known from ancient Mesopotamian cultures. The form of the Israelites' covenant with Yahweh has been compared with suzerainty treaties from the ancient Near East. The stories of Joshua's conquest have been compared with archaeological findings from the Middle and Late Bronze Ages, or, by other scholars, with information about social movements (especially peasant movements) among ancient and modern primitives.

The principle of comparing the biblical accounts with "external evidence" is sound enough and has made possible considerable strides in reconstructing the history of the biblical people. But the historian should remain cognizant of what "external evidence" can do and what it cannot do. Evidence from archaeology or geography or comparative literature or anthropology can, on the one hand, sometimes show the unreliability of the biblical account as an historical record (in other words, "falsify" the biblical account), as when it shows that a particular city was not in existence at the time the biblical story purports to describe events occurring in that city. On the other hand, the "external evidence" can sometimes show that there are no known conditions or circumstances which exclude the possibility that the biblical stories could have occurred as they are told (in other words, provide "permissive" or "non-falsifying" evidence). It is not often that external evidence offers direct confirmation of a biblical story.[12] Anyone who intends to use "external evidence" to test the reliability of the biblical stories must be prepared to accept the testimony when it is negative as well as when it permits a judgment more favorable to the historical accuracy of the biblical account.

In the use of external evidence, the historian should guard against assuming what his investigations are designed to test: namely, that the biblical accounts are reliable in their reporting of historical happenings. The reliability of the Old Testament narrative is not a fixed, assured reference point. Especially if the extra-biblical evidence is to be used to test the reliability of the biblical stories, the latter cannot be used to establish what the extra-biblical material means. "When a written source has served as a determining factor in the interpretation of any given archaeological data, it is misleading to cite the interpreted archaeological data in turn as 'proof' of the accuracy of the written source."[13]

Just because the Old Testament contains the most extensive account extant of happenings in second millennium Palestine, this fact (which from one point of view could be considered an accident of preservation) does not establish any *a priori* probability that the Old Testament account will supply the best explanation for a given piece of archaeological evidence. The paucity of other historical sources does not enhance the reliability of the biblical record.[14] The biblical narrative has sometimes been used as if it were the only possible key to the interpretation of certain archaeological or epigraphic data from the second millennium. And then the extra-biblical data are cited as confirmation of the biblical narrative. For example, as described in chapter 2, documents from the Nuzi culture have been interpreted on the basis of episodes in the patriarchal stories of Genesis, and then the Nuzi material has been used as evidence of the antiquity of the patriarchal way of life![15]

Another example is found in the following remarks from a discussion of the archaeology of Palestine and the Old Testament: "Since Israel was already menacing the Canaanite towns in force before the following year, according to the famous Israel stele of Marniptah [Merneptah], we may safely date the fall of Canaanite Lachish in 1220 or shortly thereafter."[16] One would logically infer from these remarks that the Merneptah stele makes an explicit reference to a forceful invasion of Canaan by Israel. In fact, the stele (in a group of references to various enemies of Egypt) says simply, "Israel is laid waste, his seed is not."[17] To conclude from that statement that "Israel was already menacing the Canaanite towns in force" is a parade example of interpreting extra-biblical evidence by biblical accounts which have not been verified. The quoted statement assumes that the biblical narrative of the Israelite conquest of Canaan provides the only plausible explanation for the presence of "Israel" in Canaan in the time of Merneptah.[18] The stele supports the theory of a forceful invasion by Israel only if one has already decided that the Israelite foe of Merneptah must have arrived in Canaan in a manner like that described in the Bible. To hold that the stele alludes to an invasion by force because that is what the Bible reports, and then to verify (and date) the events in the biblical record by reference to the stele is circular reasoning.

The danger of imposing a "biblical" interpretation on the "external evidence" is compounded when the latter consists of non-epigraphic archaeological data, the testimony of which is often very ambiguous. For example, archaeological study cannot, in the absence of written materials, prove that changes in pottery techniques and repertoire or in burial customs or in house types were caused by the arrival of a new people. With regard to pottery, which has proved of great value in demarcating cultural changes and correlating strata from one site with those of other sites, there are various possibilities besides the arrival of a new population stock to account for changes: extension of the country's trade network, alteration of economic conditions (permitting more luxury ware and improved techniques, or, in the case of adverse conditions, the opposite of these), or internal developments by the country's craftsmen.

Destruction levels at a given site were not necessarily caused by events reported in the Bible. Palestine is subject to frequent earthquakes, and the destruction wrought by such a natural catastrophe could be heightened by fires started by the quake. Non-malevolent motives might also be considered (such as occasional renovation) in some instances. If it can be determined that the damage was caused by a human agent with malicious intent, the careful historian will remember that Palestine of the second millennium B.C. was ravaged by numerous wars which receive no mention in the pages of the Old Testament.

There is a certain heuristic value in comparing a biblical account with extra-biblical data in an effort to come up with a coherent interpretation of the data. One might tentatively ask, do the biblical references to "Amorites" in Canaan during the time of the Hebrew patriarchs help identify the bearers of the civilization of Palestinian Middle Bronze I or II with the "Amorites" known to us from Mesopotamian sources of the late third and early second millennia? Or, does the biblical story of the conquest of Jericho help make sense of the remains of that city? Or, do the activities of the ^{c}apiru attested in the Amarna letters coincide at any point with the settlement of the Israelites in Canaan? Such a procedure may possibly open up avenues of investigation which will disclose further information that can clarify either the biblical or the extra-biblical data, or both. But whenever this procedure is followed, the method must be recognized as potentially circular and the results hypothetical. It needs to be kept in mind that the reliability of the biblical witness for the period prior to the monarchy *is itself an hypothesis* which has not been proved. Moreover, as observed above, this procedure can claim cogency and relevance only if a literary study of the biblical material has indicated that there was an intent on the part of the writer to preserve information about actual events.

PART

THREE
Theological
Dimensions
of the Quest

6

If Jericho Was Not Razed, Is Our Faith in Vain?

In recent decades there have been theologians on both the right and left wings who argued that recovery of an historical underpinning was essential to the study of the biblical witness, and both types of theologians tried to use the methods and findings of historical research to undergird their theological programs. However, these efforts have proved to have limited success and effectiveness. Neither fundamentalist nor liberal theologians have been able to make much theological capital out of the results of the historical science. In this closing chapter we seek to point up the shortcomings and fallacies in these undertakings, and we shall also discuss some alternative lines of biblical interpretation which are not tied so closely to the findings of the historian.

Fundamentalists and Historical Verification

Historically, many fundamentalist theologians have agreed (along with those of other persuasions) that faith is self-authenticating and cannot be validated or demonstrated by empirical research.[1] But there has grown up in recent years a school of fundamentalist theology which argues that the theological claims of the Bible can and must be checked out and verified by historical methods. This school, represented by such writers as John Warwick Montgomery, Clark Pinnock, and Francis Schaeffer, has exercised some influence among college students, and it is my opinion that the inadequacies in the position argued by this school have not been exposed forcefully enough.

These fundamentalist theologians are obviously impressed by the arguments of philosophers who say that statements which cannot be verified are meaningless. They declare that the Christian faith should bring forward objective facts to support its theological claims, rather than affirming that faith is a "leap in the dark" which by its very nature is not subject to testing by scientific methods.[2]

Without objective proof, they argue, no one can tell theological truth from theological error. A person would be foolish, say these writers, to hold a conviction if there is no empirical evidence for the conviction. However, they mean to say more than simply, "There must be some concrete data which have the possibility of being interpreted as religious people do; there must at least be evidence which permits the theological interpretation that you hold." When these writers speak of evidence or "the testability of religious assertions," they mean something more than *permissive evidence*. They have in mind evidence which incontrovertibly proves the existence and activity of God. When illustrating the sort of empirical evidence required for faith, they nearly always refer to *miracles*—the signs given to Moses (Exod. 4:1–9), the signs given to Gideon (Judg. 6:36–40), the miraculous lighting of the sacrificial fire on Mount Carmel (1 Kings. 18:36–39), the "signs" wrought by Jesus according to the narrative in the Gospel of John.[3] "Verification," then, is provided by miraculous interruptions of the natural order of events. Such interruptions, according to the thinking of these writers, could have only one explanation (namely, divine intervention), and therefore a demonstration of their facticity would confirm the existence of God and supply verification for the Judeo-Christian faith claims.

Miracles, or what we might call "unlawful" occurrences (i.e., happenings contrary to the known laws of nature), constitute phenomena which cannot be explained by natural causes. So (the reasoning goes) the positing of a supernatural cause is the only means of explaining such occurrences. Miracles thereby become objective evidence of the activity of God. Confirmation of God's existence and activity comes through unlawful occurrences which cannot be accounted for by natural factors. It is necessary to invoke the God-hypothesis to explain the sequence of events.

Since, according to the thinking of these writers, verification is necessary to prevent religious conviction from being a "leap in the dark," and since miracles are the means by which God's existence and activity are most easily verified, the historicity of the miracle stories becomes the keystone of their theological system.

When an historian measures the credibility of biblical miracle stories by the criterion of the known laws of nature, these fundamentalist
theologians argue that he is biased from the start against the possibility
of miracles and other supernatural intervention in historical happenings.[4] Anyone who assumes the sufficiency of natural explanations for
what happens in this world excludes the possibility of verifying any
faith-affirmations about divine power in our experience.

Modern theology has abandoned the possibility of verifying its assertions about God, says Schaeffer, because it has accepted the presup-
positions of a uniformity of cause and effect in a closed system, which
rules out the possibility of intervention of any sort from an other-world-
ly (supernatural) source. Modern thinkers, including theologians, believe that what happens in this world is completely explainable, at least
in principle, by this-worldly causes, without resort to any kind of God-
hypothesis. Whenever modern theology affirms the reality of God, this
is done in a leap of faith, which cannot be justified by any empirical
demonstration or verification. Faith, in the modern view, is not to be
based on the findings of science or history. Indeed, says Schaeffer, in
modern theology there is a "total dichotomy" between the two. Dia-
grams like the following are scattered all through Schaeffer's works to
illustrate his concept of modern theology's separation of faith and
reason:[5]

Faith = No rationality, i.e., no contact with
the cosmos (science) or history

All rationality—including scientific evidence and history

To adopt this "two-storey" model which divorces faith from reason, says Schaeffer, and therewith to abandon the claim that faith is
historically verifiable, is to abandon the distinctive characteristic of the
Christian faith. Christian faith, says Schaeffer, "is not to be based on a
citadel mentality—sitting inside and saying, 'You cannot reach me
here.' " Apologetics, instead, "should be thought out and practised in
the rough and tumble of living contact with the present generation."[6]
Modern theologians renege on this obligation by talking of a faith
which is not based on or confirmable by the shifting findings of history
or science. Pinnock writes, "In this age of the non-rational existential
experience it is imperative to stress the fact that the gospel is about
God's acting in the *empirical realm*. For the validation of the Christian
claim we make our appeal to history."[7]

These men purport, then, to enter the lists with all the modern critical scholars in the verification process. They claim that, in contrast to the procedures of modern theology, "true Christianity" offers facts to prove its claims—facts which can be tested by any objective observer. Pinnock writes, "The basis on which we rest our defense of the gospel consists of evidence open to *all* investigators. The non-Christian has no right to disregard the gospel because it is a matter of 'faith' in the modern sense. On the contrary it is a matter of *fact*."[8] Schaeffer renders John 20:30–31, "Many *space-time proofs* did Jesus in the presence of his disciples which are not written in this book. But these are written that ye may believe that Jesus is the Christ, the Son of God."[9]

There is the desire to advance incontrovertible signs which can be explained only by the claims of the Bible concerning the existence and activity of God. "Faith is not believing what you know to be absurd. It is trusting what on *excellent testimony* appears to be true . . . Nowhere in the Bible is faith depicted as an unmotivated leap in the dark."[10]

Testability is crucial for any religious claim which would be respectable, they argue. "Only where objective verifiability is present can genuine faith be distinguished from blind faith."[11] Religious assertions are meaningless if removed from the realm of testability. In the words of Pinnock: "A religious claim without any way to test it out is as meaningless as a nuclear test ban treaty without adequate checks."[12]

As an illustration of the concern to test all claims carefully Schaeffer tells a parable. Imagine, he says, that a party of mountain climbers becomes lost in fog in the Alps, and the guide declares that they can expect to freeze to death before morning. One member of the party, with absolutely no knowledge or reason to support his action, drops into open space, in a "leap of faith," hoping to strike a ledge that will lead him to safety. Now imagine that the remaining members of the party hear a voice saying, "You cannot see me, but I know exactly where you are from your voices. I am on another ridge. I have lived in these mountains, man and boy, for over sixty years and I know every foot of them. I assure you that ten feet below you there is a ledge. If you hang and drop, you can make it through the night and I will get you in the morning." Schaeffer comments:

> I would not hang and drop at once, but would ask questions to try to ascertain if the man knew what he was talking about and if he was not my enemy . . . . In my desperate situation, even though time would be running out, I would ask him what to me would be the sufficient questions, and when I became convinced by his answers, then I would hang and drop.[13]

This sounds like a pledge to heed the canons of critical scientific and historical method in exercising careful, scrupulous analysis in the study of historical questions.

The first major complaint about this school of thought is its failure to carry out the discipline of critical procedure which is advocated in the statements of these writers. Before using the historicity of past events (such as miracles) as confirmatory evidence for anything, one must first of all establish as at least probable that the events *did take place* and that the reports of these events are not fictitious in nature. To speak of evidence which is "open to all investigators" and to speak of objective, empirical matters of *fact* is, when referring to past events, to speak of occurrences whose probability has been established by rigorous historical methods.

One of the methods involved in such historical study is a careful examination of the witnesses.[14] How credible is the witness? What do we know of circumstances which might affect his reporting in a distorting manner? Was he an eyewitness? If not, what is the chain of tradition linking the witness with the reported events? How critical an observer was our reporter? The disciplined, critical historian also asks about the internal consistency of the reporter's account, the agreement between his report and that of other evidence, the susceptibility of the reporter to commonly found exaggerative tendencies in folk tradition.

The careful historian examines all his witnesses with the same rigor. He plays no favorites. He grills all witnesses according to the same rules. If he is studying the events of Hittite history, he carefully weighs the reliability of the reporters. If he is attempting to reconstruct the life of the Buddha, he considers the bias which might have influenced the reporting, and likewise with the documents relating to the biblical history. The fundamentalist, in contrast, commonly lets the biblical witnesses off easy, not challenging their accounts,[15] because he believes that their reliability is guaranteed by divine inspiration. As the fundamentalist goes to the biblical records of past events, the answer to the question "What happened?" is too often a foregone conclusion: *whatever the biblical witnesses report*. Such an approach makes one simply a purveyor of tradition rather than an historian, and it hardly exhibits the rigor which Schaeffer, in his lost-in-the-fog parable, advocates. These fundamentalists should subject their biblical sources to the same sort of critical scrutiny that historical sources are commonly subjected to, or they should abandon the claim that they have unimpeachable, "excellent testimony" of the events in question. At virtually no point in the writings of this group is there found any effort to weigh the reliability or credibility of the "evidence" which is adduced to buttress the theological claims.

It turns out that what these writers really mean by "objective evidence" is frequently not evidence which has been critically weighed and proved out with sound methods, but evidence perceived only by eyes of faith. One cannot play so loose with the notion of "facts" or "objective evidence" as this and keep the respect of the "rough and tumble" world where they seek to get a hearing. A person with a certain kind of faith may be inclined to give more credence to a report which tells of an unlawful occurrence ("miracle") than someone else might. But acceptance of the supernaturalist viewpoint does not excuse the historian from cross-examining each such report, to ascertain if the *possibility* which he acknowledges did *in fact* occur. Even if a person acknowledges that miracles *can* happen, he will not automatically, as a good historian, assume that a miracle *did* happen on every occasion where someone has reported one. There is no indication in the writings of these fundamentalists of any willingness to question any biblical report of a miracle.

That which is publicly recognized and accepted by any observer has to be distinguished from that which is recognized only by a person with a certain faith. It is the professed intent of this fundamentalist school we are studying to demonstrate the truth of the biblical claims by reference to evidence which is available to *all* investigators. If the fundamentalist wants to engage in the discipline of critical historical research, he cannot rewrite the rules of admissible evidence and then pretend that he has demonstrated his claims according to the canons of the scientific historian. This is not to deny the reality of what only the believer perceives, but it is to remind ourselves that what the believer alone perceives does not fit within the common understanding of "objective evidence."

As noted above, the approach of these fundamentalists requires that there be occurrences for which no natural cause can be found, if "verification" is to be possible. Montgomery writes, "Gideon, realizing how easy it is to deceive oneself in matters of subjective religious assurance, asks an objective sign from God. . . . An objective test was the only way of ridding the situation of endless confusion and meaningless claims."[16] If God had not provided Gideon and Moses with some unlawful happenings, how could they have been sure that their perception of God's summons was not a subjective delusion? The possibility of verification, then, does not exist unless a "gap" occurs—an occurrence for which no natural explanation can be found. The fundamentalist principle of verification may be stated thus: *Confirmation (or verification) of God's existence and activity comes through the occurrence of unlawful happenings which cannot be accounted for by natural factors.*

The position and some of its ramifications can be seen in a passage where Schaeffer offers a personal testimony that this supernaturalistic view is to be utilized in understanding the present as well as when reading the Bible. He tells of an airplane flight over the Atlantic in which two engines on one wing stopped, and the agitated co-pilot instructed the passengers to put on their life jackets. As the plane began falling, Schaeffer began praying. He goes on:

> Then, while we could see the waves breaking beneath us and everybody was ready for the crash, suddenly the two motors started, and we went on into Gander. When we got down I found the pilot and asked what happened. "Well," he said, "it's a strange thing, something we can't explain. Only rarely do two motors stop on one wing, but you can make an absolute rule that when they do, they don't start again. We don't understand it." So I turned to him and I said, "I can explain it." He looked at me: "How?" And I said, "My Father in heaven started it because I was praying." That man got the strangest look on his face and he turned away.[17]

We can see in this account a tendency common to the fundamentalists which is seriously at odds with the sort of critical, objective methods of verification they profess to follow. If an individual, when confronted by a baffling, "unexplained" occurrence, attributes the occurrence to divine causation, this usually forecloses the search for any natural explanation. Schaeffer indicates no interest in pursuing any further the question of why the engines on the plane re-started, and he apparently believes there was no natural explanation. To equate the *inability of present understanding* to provide a satisfactory explanation with the *non-existence* of such an explanation is a fallacy into which religious people have too often slipped.

No practitioner of the scientific method[18] will ever make the assertion that "there is no natural cause." That is a determination that cannot be made this side of omniscience. All that one can conclude in a given instance is that there is no *known* natural cause for what transpired. When the fundamentalist proceeds to infer from this that the cause was divine intervention, this usually has the effect (as attested in the Schaeffer story) of terminating the search for a natural cause.[19]

Sometimes there are occurrences—in history, in nature, in medicine—where the critical examiner is at a loss for an explanation. Why did the army of Sennacherib depart from Jerusalem before conquering it? How did this or that animal species come about? Why did this disease suddenly go into remission? Why did the engines on Francis Schaeffer's plane start up again? The objective, scrupulous examiner continues to seek an answer which will commend itself to any unbiased judge. He seeks evidence which all investigators will acknowledge. If he cannot find satisfactory evidence and answers, he does not "close the book" on the case and conclude that there is no natural answer.

The fundamentalist resort to explaining the occurrence by direct divine intervention is the very "leap of faith" which they supposedly find so abhorrent. It is a leap into the "dark" of what scientific study does not yet know; it is a leap premised on the belief that scientific research will not in the future discover a natural cause. History is strewn with examples of "gaps" in human understanding which were "filled" with the explanation of divine causation, only to suffer embarrassment when further investigation into natural causation filled the gap with natural causative factors. To base the "verification" of God on "gaps" is to lay one's faith at the mercy of future research.

Not only is this fundamentalist approach inconsistent with scientific method; it also tends strongly to discourage theologizing about the commonplace. The fundamentalist approach encourages one to expect God in the unusual, the "miraculous," since this is the only place (according to their premises) where his presence can be verified. It would be idle, according to this viewpoint, to talk about God's activity in happenings which have natural causes. Affirmations about God's activity in natural events would be relegated to meaninglessness, since they are not subject to verification. To trace the activity of God in the birth of a child, or the recovery of a sick person, or the fall of Jerusalem is "meaningless" if these events can be given a natural or historical explanation.

This fundamentalist stance is in marked contrast to the prophetic theology of the Bible which perceives the hand of God in events which can also be explained by this-worldly factors. The prophet Isaiah, for example, recognizes that the accomplishments of the Assyrian war machine are explainable in human terms (Isa. 10:5–11), yet he declares that there is a hidden dimension to these events which the arrogant Assyrian ruler does not recognize or heed (Isa. 10:12–16). Likewise, the fall of Samaria and the fall of Jerusalem, while explainable in terms of military factors, are perceived by the prophetic interpreter as out-workings of the divine will. The interpretation of these happenings as the working of God is not resorted to because of a gap in the effort to give a "natural" explanation. It is not as if these events stood baffling and unexplained until the prophet delivers his analysis. Even when the prophet announces divine activity as a critical factor within historical developments, there is no suggestion that this activity is empirically demonstrable in the way the activity of a Sennacherib or a Nebuchad-nezzar is. The working of God is hidden. It is not objectively verifiable.

The fundamentalist position comes dangerously close to suggesting that natural causation and divine activity are mutually exclusive.[20] I suggest we should cease thinking of divine forces as forces which inter-rupt the sequence of natural causes, suspending the normal chain of cause-and-effect, replacing or overriding the natural causes. Rather, we need to see God at work through natural causes. To explain the birth of a child biologically does not preclude a believer from praising God for this event; God is at work in and through the biological process. One whose recovery from illness can be explained by the application of medical skills and drugs need not feel that these explanations leave no room for a theological interpretation of the recovery. We need more of the prophetic sensitivity to the presence of the transcendent in occur-rences which are quite explainable in natural, historical, this-worldly terms.

Historical, scientific methods cannot verify the workings of God. His activity is always "hidden." There are many happenings where we may, in faith, perceive his activity, but this faith-perception will al-ways be what the writer to the Hebrews said it was—the conviction of things not seen, not empirically demonstrable.

The "Revelation in History" Concept

One expects fundamentalist circles to contend for the historicity of all biblical stories. But the concern for an historical basis of the Old Testament stories also was prevalent in the middle decades of this cen-tury in the writings of what has been labelled the "biblical theology" movement.[21] Certain biblical theologians practiced critical biblical re-search and disavowed supernaturalistic understandings of Scripture which accepted miracle stories and references to direct divine causation at face value. Nevertheless, they believed that a truly biblical theology had to speak about God's acts in some objective way. While accepting the laws of natural causation and the principle of the uniformity of nature, they believed that it was nonetheless imperative to continue to speak of *God acting*. The biblical language could not simply be discarded as the Liberal theologians had done in recasting theological affirmations in human, natural terms; the Liberals had reduced theology and biblical narrative to statements about this-worldly phenomena.[22]

Because of the desire to recapture for theology the transcendent dimension which had been virtually eliminated by the humanistic and naturalistic thinking of the Liberal movement, it was frequently asserted that the God of the Bible had an objective reality because he revealed himself in actual events. "Christianity among the religions seems to be the only one that takes history seriously, for it assumed that the knowledge of God is associated with events that really happened in human life."[23]

They spoke of "the objectivity of God's historical acts" in contrast to "the subjectivity of inner, emotional, diffuse and mystical experience."[24] Two concerns were mingled together here which are shared by many believers who do not necessarily share all the aims and assumptions of this particular movement. There is, first, the desire to establish the *distinctiveness* of the biblical religions over against other religions.[25] Secondly, there is the apprehension—though not usually expressed so explicitly as in the writings of the fundamentalists discussed above—that a religion which cannot offer some *empirical, objective* verification for its claims will be unable to command the allegiance of modern, thinking people. The revelation of the biblical God in historical events was thought to offer both a distinctiveness vis-à-vis the gods of other religions and an objectivity which would appeal to the empirical orientation of modern thinkers. Because it was from actual events[26] that the biblical storytellers inferred the presence of God (which was supposed to be another way of saying that "God revealed himself in history"[27]), the biblical religions were thought to have an empirical anchor lacking in other religions.

The shortcomings in this notion of "revelation in history" have been rather clearly pointed out in recent years.[28] To hold that historical events were the essential medium of divine revelation is to invite the criticism that this is not the way the Bible itself usually represents God's people gaining knowledge of him. Knowledge of God is frequently received, according to the Bible, through direct verbal communication; it is not depicted as arising from retrospective contemplation of events. If we say that revelation came through inferences drawn from events, we are describing the process differently than the Bible does.[29]

Another problem with this position which holds that knowledge of God is imparted through historical events is that it does not adequately account for the knowledge of God attested in literature such as the wisdom writings or psalms, where there is often no reference to historical happenings. If "revelation is always given us through events,"[30] how are we to explain the sense of God manifested in these "non-historical" texts?[31]

Again, if it is *events* which mediated revelation, we are confronted with a complex situation in trying to comprehend such diverse "events" as the fall of Jerusalem, the exodus from Egypt, and the account of the great flood from which Noah was spared within the same rubric. Here are accounts about "God's acts" which most commentators would agree stand at varying distances from "historical facts."[32] To speak of God's being revealed through *history* and then to try and embrace such diverse episodes as these within that single framework is more confusing than helpful. All of these are stories about God and his dealings with his world which enlighten us about both God and the world, but it is awkward to treat all as instances of revelation mediated through real historical events.

Even apart from these deficiencies, the "revelation through history" program really cannot provide either the *distinctiveness* or the *objectivity* which its supporters hoped for.

The notion of the deity taking an active part in historical events was not so unusual in the ancient world as writers in the field of biblical theology at mid-century were inclined to think. The Hebrews were by no means the only people who conceived of their God effecting his will in the course of historical happenings. B. Albrektson has conveniently gathered together references ranging from the third millennium B.C. down to the first, and from peoples like the Sumerians, Assyrians, Babylonians, Hittites, and Moabites in which deities as diverse as Dagan, Era, Marduk, and the goddess of Arinna exercised an influence on the happenings of history.[33] "The Old Testament idea of historical events as divine revelation must be counted among the similarities, not among the distinctive traits: it is part of the common theology of the ancient Near East," wrote Albrektson.[34]

Without a verifiable event at the basis of a biblical story, it was apparently feared by many that the biblical witness lacked objectivity and might be suspected of propagating an illusory faith. But the emphasis on "historical events" behind the biblical stories does not assure the hoped-for objectivity any more than it assures the distinctiveness.

The "rootage" of a theological affirmation in an historical event does not guarantee that the theological affirmation is not illusory. Events are subject to various interpretations. A diversity of theological inferences can be drawn from a single, verified event. Two examples from biblical history will illustrate this. The success of Cyrus II ("the Great"), King of Persia, in overthrowing the Babylonian empire in ca. 539 B.C. would be accepted by any historian as an objective, historical event. The Israelite prophet of the exilic period, whom we call "Second Isaiah," attributes Cyrus's achievements to the leading of Yahweh, god of Israel (Isa. 45:1–6). But in his own description of the events, Cyrus assigns the credit to Marduk, god of Babylon, who was desirous of punishing his own people.[35] In the New Testament, the exorcisms of Jesus (the historicity of which may be debated by historians) are interpreted by the gospel writers as the work of "the finger of God" (Luke 11:20), yet some who witnessed these mighty works attributed them to Jesus' being in league with the prince of demons (Luke 11:15). The believer may well point to a verified event and say, "Behold the work of God!" But there is nothing in the event itself which confirms that it is the work of God.[36] The perception of the event *as an act of God* may still be an illusion. If historians should succeed in establishing, beyond a reasonable doubt, that sometime in the late second millennium B.C. a group of slaves escaped from Egypt under the leadership of a man named Moses and eventually made their way to the land of Canaan, this would not verify the biblical affirmation that this series of occurrences took place by the providence of God. The historian can investigate the question of Abraham's historicity and reach conclusions, via the historical method, about the probabilities of his having actually lived and migrated to Canaan, but the historian cannot apply his tools to the question of whether this migration—if it occurred—was directed by the God later worshipped by Israel.

The peculiar advantage of the biblical religion was supposed to lie in its interest in historical events.

> The Israelite knowledge of God . . . was not founded in the first instance on the numinous awareness of nature, as was the case of polytheism. It was based on historical event.[37]
>
> Israel's doctrine of God . . . was not derived from systematic or specu-

lative thought, but rather . . . from the attempt to explain the events which led to the establishment of the nation.[38]

A close scrutiny of the writings of these "biblical theologians," however, revealed that they were saying that what was objectively perceptible was not in fact the divine workings at all. It takes eyes of faith to see God's action "through" the objectively perceptible events. Real events are *interpreted* as God's activity. "The knowledge of God was an *inference* from what actually had happened in human history."[39] Ontologically, the presence of God in these historical events is of no different status than the presence of the pagan gods which was inferred from natural phenomena (or from different historical events).

Theological Value of Historical Substratum?

Because the theological claims of the Bible are claims or interpretations made in faith, they are unverifiable by objective, scientific means[40] (the same is true of the theological claims of other religious traditions, and the aesthetic claims of lovers of beauty, and the moral claims of ethicists, and all other value judgments), and the biblical theologian is unable finally to escape the possibility that the Bible's claims about God and his activity are in error. But we are not dealing with a matter of such pure subjectivism as some theological alarmists might suggest. One can argue that the community which has transmitted the biblical traditions and lived by them provides a certain measure of objectivity which ameliorates the likelihood that the faith of the storyteller, or my believing response to the storyteller's testimony, is simply subjective speculation. In the community of faith we have a corporate testimony, reaffirmed generation after generation, that "this tradition speaks truly about God, his people, and the world."

For many people, however, the question will no doubt continue to be a nagging one: "But what if these events did not happen . . . ?" Can we base our faith on Scriptures which tell of things which might never have happened? Although we acknowledge the power of myth and legend in other types of literature and recognize the capacity of these literary forms to convey meaning and truth, there is something about the nature of the Bible as "inspired," or as "revelation," or as "the word of God"[41] which makes us hesitant to categorize biblical stories as unhistorical and uncertain about the theological reliability of a story which is fictitious.

It was long ago acknowledged by many readers of the Bible that the power of the stories in Genesis 1–11 was not derived from any origin in happenings that corresponded to those described in the stories. That which gives these texts authority for the audience is their capacity to epitomize and focus—in story form—the beliefs of those who rehearse them. The stories in Genesis 12–50 and Joshua 1–12 (and, of course, others) have exhibited a similar capacity, irrespective of the question of their historicity. Even as regards traditions which grew out of actual events, it may be questioned whether it was the historical "rootage" of the traditions which made them meaningful for the audiences which heard them of old and acknowledged the "ring of truth" in them.

The Old Testament narrative that begins in Genesis 1 and runs through 2 Kings (or Ezra–Nehemiah) incorporates materials which we are now able to identify as standing at various distances from the historical "facts"—some dealing in a rather straightforward fashion with real persons and events, some based on real persons but imaginatively embellished, some having no basis at all in actual persons or happenings—all used by the biblical authors without any conscious distinction. Legendary narratives are used alongside historical reports without the slightest indication that the religious value of the respective stories is in any way proportional to the degree of correspondence with actual people or events.

Nevertheless, even among writers who are steeped in the critical methods of biblical study and who consciously aver no felt need to "prove the Bible true," there is frequently a tendency to hold on to the "historical" interpretation of a biblical story until this becomes demonstrably untenable. Fiction is the last alternative considered in studying the biblical narratives. It is assumed that a narrative is based on historical happenings until proof to the contrary is forthcoming. There seems to be a feeling that fiction is somehow a less appropriate or less honorable vehicle for saying whatever the biblical writers wanted to say.

We have been led to believe that the discovery of an historical substratum beneath a biblical narrative somehow enhances its apologetic value,[42] and that the religion of the Bible then stands on a firmer foundation than it would if the narrative were shown to be an historical fiction. R. de Vaux wrote, "If the historical faith of Israel is not in a certain way founded in *history*, this faith is erroneous and cannot command my assent."[43] Similarly, Alan Richardson has remarked, "The Christian faith . . . is bound up with certain happenings in the past, and if these happenings could be shown never to have occurred, or to have been quite different from the biblical-Christian account of them, then the whole edifice of Christian faith, life and worship would be found to have been built on sand.'"[44] G. Ernest Wright wrote, "In Biblical faith everything depends upon whether the central events actually occurred.'"[45] It would seem that if Jericho was not razed, then our faith is in vain.

As soon as the criterion of historicity is invoked as normative for the biblical traditions, a whole host of questions arise that call for treatment. Does the theological value of biblical stories vary according to their closeness to historical facts? If a basis in historical fact is as crucial as the quoted scholars suggest, shouldn't one specify the degree of deviation from the facts which is tolerable in a tradition?[46] Are there some stories for which an historical "core" is more important than it is for others?[47] If so, how does one recognize which is which?[48] By what criteria is it decided which stories must be based on actual occurrences and which others need not be so based? A more helpful exposition than has heretofore appeared is needed from those who deem it important theologically to establish a factual basis for the biblical narratives. Exactly when is an historical substratum essential, and why?

What is the presumed value of the "historical substratum" of the biblical narrative? How does the "rootage in history" of a biblical narrative function theologically? Is it supposed that a biblical story is more authoritative, and its power to evoke faith greater, if the story is based on actual events? The passion to demonstrate an historical "kernel" or "substratum" seems frequently to be out of proportion to the theological benefit which is derived if such a "kernel" can be recovered.

What is the theological gain, for example, if a patriarchal story can be traced back to some actual person who was an ancestor of some of the Israelites? It is not clear what is gained theologically and apologetically by demonstrating the "historicity" of Jacob, for example. It is widely conceded[49] that the figure of Jacob

(1) was not originally linked to Abraham and Isaac in a genealogical chain;

(2) was not originally associated with the twelve sons assigned to him in the present form of the Jacob narrative;

(3) was not really a brother of Edom's ancestor; and

(4) was originally a separate figure from "Israel."

To speak of an "historical Jacob" whose experiences lay behind the stories in the Jacob cycle, but to acknowledge that the associations mentioned above are all secondary developments in the growth of the Jacob cycle, is to speak of an "historical Jacob" who is so different from the Jacob we meet in the biblical traditions as to render theologically valueless the affirmation of Jacob's historicity.[50] The "historical Jacob" stands stripped of almost every feature which made him important to the communities which received and handed on the tradition. The fact that the stripped-down Jacob was an "actual historical person" would mean little. It is the *storied* Jacob which has served the Jewish and Christian communities through the years as a paradigmatic figure. What is lost, then, if the Jacob story is discovered—to consider another possibility—to be an out-and-out fiction, derived from *no* "actual person"? To look at the same point in a different way, what would be *gained,* theologically, if the story of Job or the Parable of the Prodigal Son were shown to be based on a "real" (i.e., historical) individual? How essential is it to theology-in-the-form-of-narrative that the narrative be historically accurate or at least based on actual persons or events? Is there a correlation between the degree of historical truth in a story and its theological value?

Consider the biblical story of Jericho's capture. If we should determine that there was a small unwalled city at Jericho which was conquered by a contingent of Benjaminite soldiers sometime in the Middle or Late Bronze Age, we would have recovered an "historical kernel" for Joshua 6–7. It would show that the story of the city's capture by an all-Israelite army under Joshua's command (the kind-hearted harlot, the procession around the city, the walls falling at the sound of the trumpets and all that) was, in the words of de Vaux quoted above, "in a certain way founded in history." What is the theological value that would attach to this? What if we were to determine, instead, that the event which gave birth to the biblical story was the capture of the city, accompanied by destruction of its walls, by pre-Israelite warriors in a period earlier than the Israelite settlement—a pre-Israelite people eventually assimilated (along with their conquest traditions) by the tribe of Benjamin when the latter arrived in the area? Would this discovery confirm the biblical record more, or less, than the discovery hypothesized at the beginning of this paragraph? And, again: how would this discovery be weighted in establishing the theological significance of Joshua 6–7?

Reading the Biblical Story as a *Story*

Biblical interpreters are now exploring afresh methods of interpretation which do not require or rely heavily on a recovery of the events lying behind the biblical stories. While the reconstruction of the history of biblical times will always be a legitimate and important historical undertaking, we seem to be witnessing in biblical studies the end of an era in which the settlement of the historical questions was thought to be of first importance and a sine qua non in the interpretation of the Bible. There is a serious effort in much recent biblical scholarship to come to grips with the biblical narrative as a *story*—which means listening to what it says about God and ourselves, *apart from the question of how accurately the narrative reflects the actual events of the past*.[51] Everyone readily acknowledges this principle when applied to non-biblical literature. A play like Hamlet, for example, can be enjoyed without reference to the historical circumstances which the play is supposed to reflect.[52] The play "works on" the audience or the reader quite apart from the possible relationship of the characters or events to actual people or happenings. Within the Bible the same can be observed about stories like Job or Ruth or the parables of Jesus.

The telling of a story does not in and of itself constitute a claim that the events narrated actually happened. The story has a world of its own, whether based on actual events or not. *As a story* it is not dependent on its correspondence with actual historical realities. The figure of Ruth moves us whether the figure in the story is based on an actual person or not. The character of the forgiving father in the story of "the prodigal son" is powerful and effective as an image of God even if he is not patterned after an actual historical father.

The use of story is the most characteristic feature of the biblical tradition,[53] and the extensive use of narrative distinguishes the biblical tradition from the Scriptures of the other major religions of the world. More so than any other major religious tradition, the Biblical testimonies utilize the narrative form of testimony.[54] The stories in the Old and New Testaments have had a sustaining and transforming power for Jews and Christians through the centuries. We understand who we are in the light of these stories. We comprehend by means of these stories—notably creation, the forbidden fruit, the wanderings of the patriarchs, the exodus from Egypt, the Sinai covenant, the gift of the promised land, the establishment of the kingship, the destruction of the kingdoms, exile, restoration, Jesus of Nazareth, the spread of the early church—what sort of God we have to do with, and how we stand in relation to this God. As Van Harvey has put it, these narratives "illumine our experience and our relationship to that upon which we are absolutely dependent."[55]

Faith can be and has been communicated and evoked by a variety of mediums, of which story is but one. Among stories, historical narrative is only one sub-type. It is difficult, if not impossible, to correlate the power and effectiveness (for faith) of a story with the degree of "historicity" in it.[56] There is a quality of being "true to life" which is more critical then being "accurate." Irrespective of their rootage in historical events or of their "historical accuracy," biblical stories cast up images which capture our imagination, illumine our contemporary situation, clarify what it means to live in the presence of God, and serve us as paradigms for the structuring of individual and corporate lifestyles.

The Jewish and Christian communities of faith through the centuries have lived off of these stories and in the light of these stories,[57] and it is within one or another of these communities of faith that these stories have exercised their claims upon each of us believers. We have no immediate access to the circumstances which gave birth to the biblical stories. It is not the inaugural events which claim and sustain us, but the *stories*. If historical research demonstrates them to be historically inaccurate, it nevertheless remains true that successive communities of believing peoples have accepted them. Generations have found in these stories (as they are, and not in some critically reconstructed history "behind" them) affirmations that shaped their understanding of what it meant to live in 900 B.C. or 500 B.C. or A.D. 1600 in the presence of the Lord God. For believers living at various points in history, the tradition "rang true." If we can demonstrate, with our research tools, that parts of that tradition tell of events or persons that never were, or at least never were like the tradition describes them, this does not alter the fact that the tradition has spoken to believers for generation after generation with power and expressed things which they believed to be true. The tradition "rang true" in their own experience and enabled them to develop a self-understanding and a lifestyle.[58] It was the tradition as received which accomplished this, not the past-as-it-actually-was.

ABBREVIATIONS

AHL   K. Kenyon, *Archaeology in the Holy Land* (New York: Praeger, 1960)

AHT   John Van Seters, *Abraham in History and Tradition* (New Haven: Yale Univ., 1975)

ANET   J. B. Pritchard, *Ancient Near Eastern Texts Relating to the Old Testament* (2d ed.; Princeton: Princeton Univ., 1955)

AOTS   D. Winton Thomas, ed., *Archaeology and Old Testament Study* (Oxford: Clarendon, 1967)

BA   *The Biblical Archaeologist* (Cambridge, Mass.: American Schools of Oriental Research)

BANE   G. Ernest Wright, ed., *The Bible and the Ancient Near East* (Garden City, N.Y.: Doubleday Anchor Books, 1965)

BAR   *Biblical Archaeology Review* (Washington: The Biblical Archaeology Society)

BASOR   *Bulletin of the American Schools of Oriental Research* (Cambridge, Mass.: American Schools of Oriental Research)

BAT   L. Perlitt, *Bundestheologie im Alten Testament* (Neukirchen-Vluyn: Neukirchener Verlag, 1969)

BHI   J. Bright, *A History of Israel* (2d ed.; Philadelphia: Westminster, 1972)

BP   W. F. Albright, *The Biblical Period from Abraham to Ezra* (2d ed.; New York: Harper Torchbooks, 1963)

CAH   I. E. S. Edwards et al., eds., *The Cambridge Ancient History* (3d ed.; Cambridge: University Press, 1971–)

CBQ   *The Catholic Biblical Quarterly* (Washington: Catholic Biblical Association)

CF   Klaus Baltzer, *The Covenant Formulary* (tr. D. E. Green; Philadelphia: Fortress, 1971)

DDS   Moshe Weinfeld, *Deuteronomy and the Deuteronomic School* (Oxford: Clarendon, 1972)

EAE   M. Avi-Yonah and E. Stern, eds., *Encyclopedia of Archaeological Excavations in the Holy Land* (Englewood Cliffs: Prentice-Hall, 1975–1978)

EHI   Roland de Vaux, *The Early History of Israel* (tr. D. Smith; Philadelphia: Westminster, 1978)

ESHT   E. W. Nicholson, *Exodus and Sinai in History and Tradition* (Richmond: John Knox, 1973)

FJJ   H. H. Rowley, *From Joseph to Joshua* (London: The British Academy, 1950)

HIOTT   S. Herrmann, *A History of Israel in Old Testament Times* (tr. J. Bowden; Philadelphia: Fortress, 1975)

HO   T. J. Meek, *Hebrew Origins* (New York: Harper Torchbooks, 1960)

HPN   Thomas L. Thompson, *The Historicity of the Patriarchal Narratives* (Berlin: de Gruyter, 1974)

HTR   *Harvard Theological Review* (Cambridge, Mass.: Harvard Divinity School)

IDB   G. A. Buttrick, ed., *The Interpreter's Dictionary of the Bible* (4 vols.; New York: Abingdon, 1962)

IJH   John H. Hayes and J. Maxwell Miller, eds., *Israelite and Judean History* (Philadelphia: Westminster, 1977)

IPJ   A. D. H. Mayes, *Israel in the Period of the Judges* (SBT II/29, 1974)

JBL   *Journal of Biblical Literature* (Missoula, Montana: Scholars Press)

JSOT   *Journal for the Study of the Old Testament* (Sheffield, Eng.: University of Sheffield)

LOB   Yohanan Aharoni, *The Land of the Bible: A Historical Geography* (tr. A. F. Rainey; Philadelphia: Westminster, 1967)

NHI   Martin Noth, *The History of Israel* (tr. P. R. Ackroyd; New York: Harper, 1960)

OHOST   Walter Beyerlin, *Origins and History of the Oldest Sinaitic Traditions* (tr. S. Rudman; Oxford: Blackwell, 1965)

OTC   D. J. McCarthy, *Old Testament Covenant* (Richmond: John Knox, 1972)

PC   Murray Newman, *The People of the Covenant* (New York: Abingdon, 1962)

POTT   D. J. Wiseman, ed., *Peoples of Old Testament Times* (Oxford: Clarendon, 1973)

REC   John J. Bimson, *Redating the Exodus and Conquest* (JSOT Supplement Series 2, 1978)

SBT   *Studies in Biblical Theology* (Naperville, Ill.: Alec R. Allenson)

SIDB   K. Crim, ed., Supplementary Volume to IDB (Nashville: Abingdon, 1976)

SITP   Manfred Weippert, *The Settlement of the Israelite Tribes in Palestine* (tr. J. D. Martin; SBT II/21, 1971)

T&C   Dennis J. McCarthy, *Treaty and Covenant* (2d ed.; Rome: Pontifical Biblical Institute, 1978)

TDOT   G. J. Botterweck and H. Ringgren, eds., *Theological Dictionary of the Old Testament* (tr. J. T. Willis; Grand Rapids: Eerdmans, 1974–)

TG   George E. Mendenhall, *The Tenth Generation* (Baltimore: Johns Hopkins, 1973)

TI   C. H. J. de Geus, *The Tribes of Israel* (tr. Mrs. G. E. van Baaren-Pape; Assen: Van Gorcum, 1976)

UOT   Bernhard W. Anderson, *Understanding the Old Testament* (3d ed.; Englewood Cliffs: Prentice-Hall, 1975)

VT   *Vetus Testamentum* (Leiden: E. J. Brill)

WHJP   B. Mazar, ed., *The World History of the Jewish People* (Israel: Jewish History Publications, 1970–)

NOTES

Chapter 1

1. Among handbooks one might consult for extensive discussion of the historian's methods, the work after which this chapter is entitled is especially recommended: Marc Bloch, *The Historian's Craft*, tr. P. Putnam (New York: Random House, 1953). Also recommended: Henry S. Commager, *The Nature and Study of History* (Columbus, Ohio: Merrill, 1965); J. Barzun and H. F. Graff, *The Modern Researcher* (2d ed.; New York: Harcourt, Brace and World, 1970); Allan J. Lichtmann and Valerie French, *Historians and the Living Past: The Theory and Practice of Historical Study* (Arlington Heights, Ill.: AHM Publishing, 1978). A delightful anthology of essays illustrating various problems and techniques of historical study is Robin W. Winks, ed., *The Historian as Detective: Essays on Evidence* (New York: Harper, 1968).

2. Winks, *The Historian as Detective;* Lichtmann and French, *Historians and the Living Past,* p. 27 and passim.

3. The image is used in Bloch, *The Historian's Craft,* p. 55, where it is credited to Francois Simiand.

4. "Everything that man says or writes, everything that he makes, everything he touches can and ought to teach us about him" (Bloch, ibid., p. 66).

5. For a discussion of whether they were organized in a tribal amphictyony, see the works listed in chap. 4, n. 100.

6. For problems and procedures of textual criticism, one may consult the following: Ralph W. Klein, *Textual Criticism of the Old Testament: From the LXX to Qumran* (Philadelphia: Fortress, 1974); D. R. Ap-Thomas, *A Primer of Old Testament Text Criticism* (2d ed.; Oxford: Blackwell, 1964); E. Würthwein, *The Text of the Old Testament* (Oxford: Blackwell, 1957); J. A. Thompson, "Textual criticism, OT," SIDB, pp. 886–891.

7. On form criticism, see Gene M. Tucker, *Form Criticism of the Old Testament* (Philadelphia: Fortress, 1971).

8. In biblical studies the term "literary criticism" has frequently been used in the past to denote *source criticism* (on which, see p. 8–9): cf. K. Grobel, "Biblical criticism," IDB, Vol. 1, p. 412; N. Habel, *Literary Criticism of the Old Testament* (Philadelphia: Fortress, 1971). It is important that the difference be recognized between source criticism, which

has to do with the process of a work's composition, and the " 'new' literary criticism," which seeks instead an appreciation of the literary features of a work.

9. For discussion of these questions of authorship and the reasons for the prevailing critical conclusions, see any of the standard introductions to the Old or New Testaments, such as O. Eissfeldt, *The Old Testament: An Introduction*, tr. P. R. Ackroyd (New York: Harper, 1965); E. Sellin-G. Fohrer, *Introduction to the Old Testament*, tr. D. E. Green (Nashville: Abingdon, 1968); W. G. Kümmel, *Introduction to the New Testament*, tr. A. J. Mattill, Jr. (London: SCM, 1966).

10. The frequently quoted words of Thucydides illustrate well the attitude of ancient historians:

As to the speeches that were made by different men . . . it has been difficult to recall with strict accuracy the words actually spoken, both for me as regards that which I myself heard, and for those who from various sources have brought me reports. Therefore the speeches are given in the language in which, as it seemed to me, the several speakers would express, on the subject under consideration, the sentiments most befitting the occasion, though at the same time I have adhered as closely as possible to the general sense of what was actually said. *(History,* I. 22; translation from H. J. Cadbury, *The Making of Luke-Acts* [2d ed.; Naperville, Ill.: Allenson, 1958], p. 185).

11. This is not to deny that a "spurious" document may contain valuable historical data. But if an historian determines that a document is not in fact the work of the person purported to be the author, this is a "red flag" which calls for more scrupulous examination of the information in the document.

12. On source criticism, cf. Habel, *Literary Criticism*; T. E. Fretheim, "Source criticism, OT," in SIDB, pp. 838–839. On tradition criticism, cf. W. E. Rast, *Tradition History and the Old Testament* (Philadelphia: Fortress, 1972); K. Koch, *The Growth of the Biblical Tradition*, tr. S. M. Cupitt (New York: Scribners, 1969); D. A. Knight, *Rediscovering the Traditions of Israel* (2d ed.; Missoula: Scholars Press, 1975).

13. "The truth is that the majority of minds are but mediocre recording-cameras of the surrounding world. Add that, since evidence, strictly speaking, is no more than the expression of remembrance, the first errors of perception run the constant risk of being entangled with the errors of memory." (Bloch, p. 101)

14. "What a witness thinks he sees is in large part filtered through the prism of his own individual mode of perception and conception which, in turn, is heavily influenced by the modes of thought of the culture of which he is a part. Men are historical creatures, and their judgments reflect the

'world' that they bring with them and to which they appeal in support of those judgments.'' (Van Harvey, *The Historian and the Believer* [New York: Macmillan, 1966], pp. 41–42)

15. Cf. Harvey, *The Historian and the Believer*, pp. 43–48, 77–89, 91–99.

16. G. E. Wright and F. V. Filson, eds., *Westminster Historical Atlas to the Bible* (Philadelphia: Westminster, 1956), p. 40.

17. See further below, concerning the variety of types of arguments an historian might use.

18. John E. Huesman, "Archaeology and Early Israel: The Scene Today," CBQ 37 (1975), p. 9.

19. Cf. the following example in Bloch, *The Historian's Craft*, pp. 53–54: "In the royal tombs of Ur in Chaldea, there have been found beads of necklaces made of amazonite. As the nearest deposits of this mineral are located either in the heart of India or in the neighborhood of Lake Baikal, it has seemed obvious to conclude that, as far back as the third millennium before Christ, the cities of the lower Euphrates maintained trading relations with some very distant lands."

20. R. G. Collingwood, *The Idea of History* (London: Oxford, 1946), pp. 257–261 and passim.

21. E. H. Carr, *What is History?* (New York: Knopf, 1961), p. 16.

22. Wood Gray et al., *Historian's Handbook: A Key to the Study and Writing of History* (revised ed.; Boston: Houghton Mifflin, 1959, 1964), p. 58.

23. See J. A. Wilson, *The Culture of Ancient Egypt* (Chicago: U. of Chicago Press, 1951), pp. 245–246.

24. See discussion in chapter 4, pp. 69 and 72–73.

25. See pp. 109–115 for discussion of fundamentalist objections to this.

26. J. Bright, BHI, p. 119.

27. Cf. M. Noth, *The Old Testament World*, tr. Victor I. Gruhn (Philadelphia: Fortress, 1966), pp. 360–361.

28. See note 25.

29. Cf. G. W. Ramsey, "Speech Forms in Hebrew Law and Prophetic Oracles," JBL 96 (1977), pp. 45–58.

30. See L. Sabourin, S. J., *The Psalms: Their Origin and Meaning* (New York: Alba House, 1974), pp. 48–62.

31. See chapter 3, pp. 53–58.

32. Cf. Robert R. Wilson, *Genealogy and History in the Biblical World* (New Haven: Yale, 1977).

33. Cf. R. C. Culley, *Studies in the Structure of Hebrew Narrative* (Missoula: Scholars Press, 1976), Part I; idem, *Oral Tradition and Old Testament Studies (Semeia* 5; Missoula: Scholars Press, 1976), esp. the articles by Culley and Long.

34. Cf. C. H. J. de Geus, *The Tribes of Israel* (Assen: Van Gorcum, 1976), esp. Chapter III.

35. The period of Hyksos rule in Egypt extended from about 1720 B.C. until about 1550 B.C. The "Amarna Age" was, roughly speaking, the second quarter of the fourteenth century B.C. For discussion of these periods, cf. Bright, BHI, pp. 60–62, 108–110.

36. Regarding many of these narratives, there is the additional—prior—question as to whether they are historical at all. If that question is answered in the negative, the whole issue of dating the events of course becomes moot, and one turns instead to the question of trying to date the composition of the narratives and determine what they meant to the Israelites at that date.

37. Sean M. Warner, "The Patriarchs and Extra-Biblical Sources," JSOT 2 (1977), pp. 52–53.

38. See chapter 2.

39. See chapter 3, pp. 53–58.

40. See chapter 4.

41. To assign a *relative* date to an object is simply to locate it in its proper place in a sequence; that is, it is determined to be later than this object and earlier than that object. To assign an *absolute* date to the object is to determine the calendar date to which it belongs, such as 1365 B.C. Obviously, an object whose relative date is later than one which can be dated absolutely at 1365 B.C. and earlier than one dated absolutely at 1250 B.C. can be assigned an approximate absolute date in this interim between 1365 and 1250.

42. See chapter 3, pp. 50–52, for discussion of this.

43. E.g., B. W. Anderson, UOT, p. 128.

44. T. A. Roberts, *History and Christian Apologetic* (London: S.P.C.K., 1968), p. 33, quoting L. Dickinson, who was expressing himself with special reference to the uncertainties of biblical history.

45. Roberts, *History and Christian Apologetic,* pp. 39–40.

46. Actually, judgments of an inferential sort, in which we lack absolutely certain knowledge, are made and acted upon by each of us rather routinely every day. Inference and hypothesis are not the tools only of the erudite expert. If I should see a student walk past my windowless office

carrying an umbrella dripping water, I infer that it has begun raining, and I take my spare umbrella with me when I depart. A woman comes across an undated newspaper article containing advice on the use of pesticides, and she would like to know how recent the article is. On the reverse side she discovers an article about an upcoming public appearance by President Gerald Ford; from this she is able to infer the approximate date, as well as the latest possible date (what scholars like to call the *terminus ad quem*) of the clipping. Most of our day-to-day inferences occasion no doubt or dispute; in many instances the inference you or I make is the only reasonable inference from the evidence, so we do not feel constrained to spend much time trying to defend our inferences to ourselves or to others.

47. Roberts, *History and Christian Apologetic*, p. 32, in discussing this point, observes that we should not expect our knowledge of the past to measure up to that perfect record which could be kept by some Recording Angel.

48. Harvey, *The Historian and the Believer*, p. 43. This obligation of the historian to make public and plain the reasons for his historical conclusions is one of the fundamental points in Harvey's book, which should be required reading for all historians, especially biblical historians.

49. Ibid., pp. 49–50.

50. Harvey, drawing on the work of the philosopher Stephen Toulmin (principally his work *The Uses of Argument* [New York: Cambridge U. Press, 1958]), speaks of differing "fields of argument" and refers to a discipline which uses arguments from several fields as a "field-encompassing field."

Chapter 2

1. J. Wellhausen, *Prolegomena to the History of Ancient Israel* (New York: Meridian edition, 1957), pp. 318–319. For a discussion of the source-critical movement and Wellhausen's role, see R. E. Clements, *One Hundred Years of Old Testament Interpretation* (Philadelphia: Westminster, 1976), chap. 1.

2. The development and techniques of form criticism are discussed in Tucker, *Form Criticism*; idem, "Form criticism, OT," in SIDB, pp. 342–345; Koch, *The Growth of the Biblical Tradition*. Tradition criticism is discussed in Rast, *Tradition History*; Knight, *Rediscovering the Traditions*; G. W. Coats, "Tradition criticism, OT, " in SIDB, pp. 912–914.

3. J. Bright, *Early Israel in Recent History Writing* (SBT 19, 1956), p. 55. Cf. also pp. 121–126.

4. Among others: W. F. Albright, *From the Stone Age to Christianity* (3d ed.; Baltimore: Johns Hopkins, 1957), pp. 236–243; G. Fohrer, *History of Israelite Religion*, tr. D. Green (Nashville: Abingdon, 1974), pp. 29–32; J. Holt, *The Patriarchs of Israel* (Nashville: Vanderbilt, 1964), pp. 91–126; J. Paterson, "The Old Testament World," in W. Barclay, ed., *The Bible and History* (Nashville: Abingdon, 1968), pp. 48–56; Anderson, UOT, pp. 23–34.

5. It is not uncommon that the historical value of the narratives is esteemed highly enough that writers are prompted to claim that Abraham, Isaac, and Jacob must have been real historical individuals: cf. Bright, BHI, pp. 44, 91; H. H. Rowley, *Worship in Ancient Israel* (Philadelphia: Fortress, 1967), chap. 1; R. Murphy, "A History of Israel," in R. E. Brown et al., eds., *The Jerome Bible Commentary* (Englewood Cliffs: Prentice-Hall, 1968), Vol. II, pp. 675–676.

6. See especially the following two books: T. L. Thompson, HPN; J. Van Seters, AHT. Van Seters' arguments are presented in much briefer form in his article, "Patriarchs," SIDB, pp. 645–648.

7. Many of these parallels were proposed in the works of E. A. Speiser and Cyrus Gordon. A full bibliography for these scholars may be found in Thompson, HPN. A sampling of Old Testament scholars who have adopted these arguments would include: Bright, BHI, pp. 78–79; Anderson, UOT, pp. 30–31; Albright, *From the Stone Age to Christianity*, p. 237; and N. M. Sarna, *Understanding Genesis* (New York: Schocken, 1970), pp. 90–91, 122–123, 128–129, and passim.

8. Gen. 16:1–4; 30:1–8

9. Gen. 12:10–20; 20:1–18; 26:1–11.

10. Genesis 29–31.

11. Genesis 23.

12. J. M. Miller aptly comments that arguments of this sort resemble the old "ham and eggs" line: "if we had some eggs, we could have some ham and eggs, if we had some ham." Cf. his "Archaeology and the Israelite Conquest of Canaan," *Palestine Exploration Quarterly* 109 (1977), p. 91.

13. Van Seters and others criticized, in articles during the 1960s, various of the alleged parallels: J. Van Seters, "The Problem of Childlessness in Near Eastern Law and the Patriarchs of Israel," JBL 87 (1968), pp. 401–408; idem, "Jacob's Marriages and Ancient Near Eastern Customs: A Reexamination," HTR 62 (1969), pp. 377–395; M. Greenberg, "Another Look at Rachel's Theft of the Teraphim," JBL 81 (1962), pp. 239–248; H. Donner, "Adoption oder Legitimation?" *Oriens Antiquus* 8

(1969), pp. 87–119; G. M. Tucker, "The Legal Background of Genesis 23," JBL 85 (1966), pp. 77–84. But only with the publication of Thompson's monograph in 1974 and Van Seters' in 1976 (see note 6 above) was the whole range of alleged parallels brought under a sustained critique; R. de Vaux, in the original French edition (1971) of his *History* (EHI) did comment on the weakness of the supposed Nuzi parallels.

14. Laws from the Old Babylonian and Old Assyrian periods provide for a priestess to secure a slave girl to provide children for the husband of the priestess (who was forbidden by law from having children). But this law does not represent a real parallel to the Genesis accounts, in which none of the childless wives were priestesses.

15. If the regulations reflected in the Nuzi texts represented a law or custom by which the families of the patriarchs lived, it is surprising that the brother of Abraham, Nahor, after having eight children by his first wife, takes a concubine, who bears him further children (Gen. 22:20–24), which contravenes the arrangement described above. Note also that when Leah arranges for Jacob to get children by her maid (Gen. 30:9–13) Leah already has children, so obviously her motive is different from that behind the cited Nuzi law.

16. See Thompson, HPN, pp. 261–269, for discussion of other texts which reveal the sorts of arrangements likely to be made, covering a time period from the late third millennium into the mid-first millennium B.C.

17. Gen. 12:10–20; 20:1–18; 26:1–11.

18. E. A. Speiser, "The Wife-Sister Motif in the Patriarchal Narratives," in *Oriental and Biblical Studies: Collected Writings of E. A. Speiser* (Philadelphia: University of Pennsylvania, 1967), pp. 62–82 (original publication of article, 1963); idem, *Genesis* (Garden City, N.Y.: Doubleday, 1964), pp. XL, 92; idem, "Nuzi," IDB, Vol. 3, p. 574.

19. *Genesis*, p. XL. Speiser believed that this custom was rooted in fratriarchal society, in which violations of sistership arrangements were punished more severely than breaches of marriage contracts; cf. *Genesis*, p. 92. Thompson argues that the responsibility of a brother for his sister, especially following the death of their father, is a normal part of *patriarchal* society; Thompson, HPN, pp. 236–237.

20. See Van Seters, AHT, pp. 73–74, and Thompson, HPN, pp. 238–240, for discussion of the Nuzi texts which led Speiser to his theory. There is a set of three texts in which the same three principals are involved and the woman is described in one text as a certain man's sister and in another as his wife, but the texts more likely reflect *consecutive* legal arrangements than simultaneous.

21. So Van Seters, AHT, pp. 75–76.

22. G. E. Wright, *Biblical Archaeology* (2d ed.; Philadelphia: Westminster, 1962), p. 44.

23. C. H. Gordon, "Biblical Customs and the Nuzi Tablets," *The BA Reader No. 2* (Garden City: Doubleday Anchor, 1964), pp. 24–25.

24. Cf. Van Seters, AHT, pp. 79–80.

25. E. A. Speiser, "The Patriarchs and their Social Background," WHJP, Vol. 2, pp. 166–167; Gordon, "Biblical Customs," p. 25; Rowley, *Worship in Ancient Israel*, p. 20.

26. M. Greenberg, "Another Look at Rachel's Theft of the Teraphim," JBL 81 (1962), pp. 239–248, was the first seriously to challenge this interpretation. Greenberg cites the case of the possession of Saul's coronet and armband (2 Samuel 1) to show that mere possession was insufficient to establish a claim to the office which the objects symbolized.

27. Ibid., p. 242, n. 16. Texts such as the Nuzi document cited above signify the importance of the *bequeathal* of the gods, not the mere possession. If the father died intestate, possession of the objects might work in favor of the possessor, but this is not the case in the Genesis story.

28. See discussion in Greenberg, "Another Look," pp. 246–248 (the translation is that of Louis H. Feldman, *Josephus, Jewish Antiquities* [Loeb Classical Library; Cambridge: Harvard Univ., 1965], Vol. 9, Book 18, section 344, p. 195); also, Thompson, HPN, p. 278.

29. M. R. Lehmann, "Abraham's Purchase of Machpelah and Hittite Law," BASOR 129 (1953), pp. 15–18; cf. A. v. R. Sauer, "The Meaning of Archaeology for the Exegetical Task," *Concordia Theological Monthly* 41 (1970), p. 527.

30. Lehmann's interpretation has been disputed by the following: H. Petschow, "Die neubabylonische Zwiegesprachsurkunde und Genesis 23," *Journal of Cuneiform Studies* 19 (1965), pp. 103–120; G. M. Tucker, "The Legal Background of Genesis 23," JBL 85 (1966), pp. 77–84; Thompson, HPN, p. 296; Van Seters, AHT, pp. 98–100.

31. Concerning the reference to the "Hittites," see Van Seters' discussion of group names in Genesis, especially AHT, pp. 45–46.

32. Concerning the supposed adoption of Eliezer by Abraham (Gen. 15:2–4), see Thompson, HPN, pp. 203–230; Van Seters, AHT, pp. 85–87. On the marriage of Rebekah, see HPN, pp. 248–252; AHT, pp. 76–78. On the covenant with Abraham (Genesis 15), see AHT, pp. 100–103. On the rights of inheritance (as in Isaac's blessing of Jacob), see HPN, pp. 285–293; AHT, pp. 87–92.

33. C. Westermann, *Genesis 12–50* (Darmstadt: Wissenschaftliche Buchgesellschaft, 1975), pp. 85–86, observes that Nuzi texts and patriarchal stories can be usefully compared since both reflect societies where family law has a significant status in public law.

34. Bright, BHI, p. 78: "The profusion of . . . evidence from contemporary documents shows clearly that their names fit perfectly in the nomenclature of the Amorite population of the early second millennium, rather than in that of any later day."

35. Thompson, HPN, p. 35. Cf. Van Seters, AHT, pp. 40–42; in AHT, Van Seters asserts that a similar span exists for the name "Abraham," but in his article in SIDB, p. 646, he says there is no second millennium occurrence of "Abraham," which is most likely an Aramaic dialectical variant of "Abram."

36. Thompson, HPN, p. 43.

37. De Vaux, EHI, pp. 195–196. Thompson, noting the use of the names in Genesis 11, takes this as evidence that the genealogy is purely fictitious, constructed to give the patriarchs, elsewhere provided with an Egyptian or Transjordanian background, a connection with North Mesopotamia; cf. HPN, pp. 304–308. See also Van Seters, AHT, pp. 58–59. De Vaux argues that the original meaning of the names Abram, Isaac, and Jacob seems to have been forgotten by the time the traditions were redacted, so that new etymologies were constructed: for instance, "Abram" originally meant something like "The father is exalted," and the variant "Abraham" similarly; but in Gen. 17:5 the name is taken to mean "father of a multitude." The name Jacob originally meant "May (the god) protect," but is associated with the meaning "supplant" in Gen. 25:26 (EHI, p. 199). From this de Vaux concludes that the traditions surrounding these figures date from a period long before their written form. In so arguing, however, de Vaux is conceding that at least part of the Patriarchal traditions—the part dealing with the meaning of the patriarchs' names—originated at a late date (cf. Thompson, HPN, p. 24).

38. BHI, p. 80. Similar statements are to be found in the following: Fohrer, *History of Israelite Religion*, pp. 30–33, 35–42; M. Noth, *A History of the Pentateuchal Traditions*, tr. B. W. Anderson (Englewood Cliffs: Prentice-Hall, 1972), p. 106, n. 306; Herrmann, HIOTT, pp. 46–48; M. Weippert, "Canaan, Conquest and Settlement of," SIDB, p. 129; plus about everyone else who has written recently on the patriarchs.

39. Ibid.

40. Cf. Bright, BHI, p. 81. Regarding the Beni-Hasan painting, see p. 38 and note 71.

41. Van Seters, AHT, pp. 13–20; N. K. Gottwald, "Were the Early

Israelites Pastoral Nomads?" *Rhetorical Criticism* (Pittsburgh: Pickwick, 1974), pp. 223–255; idem, "Were the Early Israelites Pastoral Nomads?" BAR IV/2 (June, 1978), pp. 2–7; idem, "Nomadism," SIDB, pp. 629–631.

42. Gottwald, in *Rhetorical Criticism,* pp. 231–234. Cf. also the paper by Johnson cited in the next note.

43. "Historically, pastoral nomadism is best described as a specialized offshoot of agriculture that developed along the dry margins of rainfall civilization" (C. H. J. de Geus, TI, p. 126, quoting D. L. Johnson, *The Nature of Nomadism* [Chicago: U. of Chicago Dept. of Geography Research Papers 118, 1969], p. 2).

44. G. E. Mendenhall, "The Hebrew Conquest of Palestine," *BA Reader No. 3* (Garden City: Doubleday Anchor, 1970), p. 102; W. G. Dever, "The Patriarchal Traditions," IJH, p. 105. This contrast led many scholars in the past to imagine that cultural changes attested in archaeological remains were best explained by recurring waves of nomads invading the settled land.

45. Gottwald, in BAR IV/2, p. 3; idem, *Rhetorical Criticism,* p. 228.

46. The use of tents by the patriarchs (e.g., Gen. 13:3; 18:1; 25:27) is no unambiguous attestation of nomadism, since others utilized tents: Gottwald, in *Rhetorical Criticism,* p. 230. Van Seters, AHT, p. 14, argues that tents were a more common feature of first millennium nomadism than of second millennium nomadism; while this might be a piece of evidence for a late composition of the patriarchal traditions, it certainly does not strengthen the case against the nomadic character of the patriarchs.

47. De Geus, TI, pp. 127–130, 133–156; Gottwald, in *Rhetorical Criticism,* p. 249.

48. Gottwald, in SIDB, pp. 629–630.

49. Gen. 16:12; 20:15; 21:20–21. Note also the Jacob-Esau contrast. There are few, if any, signs in the patriarchal traditions of belligerence toward the settled regions.

50. Van Seters, AHT, pp. 16–18; Gottwald, in *Rhetorical Criticism,* p. 243.

51. Van Seters, AHT, p. 18.

52. Gottwald, in *Rhetorical Criticism,* p. 237; he mentions Gen. 37:12–17 and 38:12–13 as possible references to spring and summer upland grazing.

53. M. B. Rowton, "The Physical Environment and the Problem of the Nomads," in J. R. Kupper, ed., *La Civilisation de Mari* (Paris: les

Belles lettres, 1967), pp. 109–121; De Vaux, EHI, 229–231; M. Liverani, "The Amorites," in POTT, p. 107; Herrmann, HIOTT, p. 53, note 27.

54. Gottwald, *Rhetorical Criticism,* pp. 242–244, acknowledges the presence of pastoral nomads in patriarchal communities, but these do not constitute the sole socio-economic mode within these communities, nor is there evidence that this represents a transitional stage.

55. The mention of camels is likely an anachronism in stories about the second millennium B.C. See Van Seters' comments on this debated point, AHT, p. 17. I do not agree with Van Seters' judgment that the camels are "quite integral" to the account in Genesis 31, but they do play a substantial role in Genesis 24 (and therefore can hardly be excised from the latter passage as merely late, secondary accretions to the story). Cf. Weippert, SITP, p. 107, note 18, who thinks the mention of camels in Genesis need not be anachronistic.

56. Especially important here are the numerous writings of W. F. Albright; see, for example, *From the Stone Age to Christianity* (Garden City: Doubleday Anchor edition, 1957), pp. 162–166. An extensive bibliography of Albright's writings can be found in Thompson, HPN, pp. 336–339. Other important works are K. Kenyon, *Amorites and Canaanites* (London: Oxford U. Press, 1966); idem, "Syria and Palestine, ca. 2160–1780 B.C.," in CAH I/2, pp. 592–594. The theory of the Amorite migration is accepted by most students of the Middle Bronze Age (including Van Seters, AHT, pp. 20–23). In addition to Thompson, who challenges the theory, others who have recently expressed skepticism include C. H. J. de Geus, "The Amorites in the archaeology of Palestine," *Ugaritische Forschungen* 3 (1971), pp. 41–60; and M. Liverani, in POTT, pp. 106–109.

57. See discussion by C. J. Gadd, "Babylonia, ca. 2120–1800 B.C.," in CAH I/2, pp. 625–628; Liverani, in POTT, pp. 102–114; B. Mazar, "Canaan in the Patriarchal Age," in WHJP, Vol. 2, pp. 171–173.

58. Thompson, HPN, p. 80, with references.

59. W. Dever, "The Peoples of Palestine in the Middle Bronze I Period," HTR 64 (1971), pp. 217–219; cf. also Gadd, in CAH I/2, pp. 625–628, and references there.

60. Most recently, de Vaux, EHI, pp. 187–192; N. M. Sarna, *Understanding Genesis* (New York: Schocken Books, 1970), pp. 98–100; J. Paterson, in Barclay, ed., *The Bible and History,* pp. 48–49.

61. Thompson, HPN, p. 87.

62. E.g., Bright, BHI, pp. 85–91.

63. See, for example, Albright, BP, p. 3. On the other hand, W. G. Dever, who has written extensively on the Middle Bronze I period and who defends the theory of Amorite movements into Palestine in both Middle Bronze I and Middle Bronze IIA, seeks to establish his theory in strict isolation from the question of patriarchal origins; see his "The Peoples of Palestine," p. 226, n. 66.

64. Dever, "The Peoples of Palestine"; W. H. Stiebing, Jr., "When Was the Age of the Patriarchs?" BAR I/2 (1975), p. 19.

65. This archaeological period is, confusingly, labeled "Intermediate Early Bronze-Middle Bronze" (or simply "Intermediate Bronze") by some and "Early Bronze IV/Middle Bronze I" by some. See W. G. Dever, "The EB IV-MB I Horizon in Transjordan and Southern Palestine," BASOR 210 (1973), pp. 38–41; Van Seters, AHT, p. 104, n. 1; Thompson, HPN, p. 98, n. 39.

66. K. Kenyon, "Jericho," in AOTS, pp. 267–269: idem, AHL, pp. 159–161; Y. Aharoni, LOB, pp. 125–126; and, tentatively, de Vaux, EHI, p. 265.

67. G. Ernest Wright, "The Archaeology of Palestine," in BANE, p. 104; Kenyon, AHL, chap. 6; de Vaux, EHI, pp. 55–58.

68. Paul W. Lapp, Biblical Archaeology and History (New York: World, 1969), pp. 102–105; de Vaux, EHI, pp. 66–71; Dever, in IJH, p. 86.

69. W. G. Dever associates both Middle Bronze I and Middle Bronze IIA cultures with the Amorites. He believes that the people of MB I were seminomadic Amorites from the fringes of the Syrian culture, whereas the people of MB IIA were a later wave of urbanized Amorites, who introduced the new culture peacefully; cf. his "The Beginning of the Middle Bronze Age in Syria-Palestine," in F. M. Cross et al., eds., Magnalia Dei (Garden City: Doubleday, 1976), p. 15; "The Peoples of Palestine," pp. 224–225; and IJH, p. 86.

70. "The Admonitions of Ipuwer" (in ANET, pp. 441–444), "Instructions to Merikare" (in ANET, pp. 414–418), "Prophecy of Nefer-rohu" (in ANET, pp. 444–446); for discussion, see G. Posener, "Syria and Palestine, c. 2160–1780 B.C.," CAH I/2, pp. 532–535 (with reservations about the identification with the Amorites), 592–594; and de Vaux, EHI, pp. 61–63.

71. For a reproduction of the painting, see J. B. Pritchard, The Ancient Near East: An Anthology of Texts and Pictures (Princeton: Princeton University Press, 1958), figure 2; D. J. Wiseman, Illustrations from Biblical Archaeology (London: Tyndale Press, 1963), pp. 28–29; B. W. Anderson, UOT, pp. 220–221. For the accompanying text, see ANET, p. 229.

72. W. F. Albright, *The Archaeology of Palestine* (Baltimore: Penguin Books, 1960), p. 207; B. Mazar, in WHJP, Vol. 2, p. 175.

73. It was a common practice in the Egyptian Middle Kingdom (ca. 2050–1800 B.C.) to inscribe the names of real or potential enemies on pottery bowls or figurines which were smashed in the course of a cursing, or execration, ceremony, with the intent of magically effecting the enemies' destruction. There are three sets of these texts, separated in date from each other by several decades; the range of dates was ca. 1875–1800 B.C. according to one scholar (de Vaux, EHI, p. 63), and ca. 1810–1770 B.C., in the judgment of another (Thompson, HPN, 113). For a useful discussion, see M. Noth, "Thebes," in AOTS, pp. 22–29; Aharoni, LOB, pp. 131–135.

74. De Vaux, EHI, p. 63; Bright, BHI, pp. 55, 84; M. Noth, in AOTS, p. 28. It appeared to some interpreters that the earlier texts in this material mention more than one prince in a given geographical area, whereas later texts indicate only a single prince in the same area. Also, the later texts contained more place names. From these observations it was inferred that a progressive settling down and urbanization had occurred. See Thompson's critical response, HPN, pp. 115–116.

75. E.g., Dever, in *Magnalia Dei*, p. 10.

76. Thompson, HPN, pp. 162–165, lists five examples of pottery features from the intermediate period which have Early Bronze antecedents and seven instances of continuity between the intermediate period and the following period, in pottery, burial techniques, and architecture.

77. See de Geus, "The Amorites," notes 64, 65, and 68.

78. Ibid., p. 51.

79. Thompson, HPN, pp. 163–165. Contrast Dever, in *Magnalia Dei*, p. 5.

80. Thompson, HPN, p. 163; W. Y. Adams, "Invasion, Diffusion, Evolution?" *Antiquity* 42 (1968), p. 201.

81. Thompson, HPN, pp. 123–143; Stiebing, "When Was the Age of the Patriarchs?" p. 18. But cf. the caveat of A. Cody, in *Biblica* 57, p. 263.

82. Thompson, HPN, pp. 92–97; de Geus, "The Amorites," p. 59; H. B. Huffmon, "Amorites," SIDB, p. 21.

83. Thompson, HPN, p. 92, mentions several indications of West Semitic influence on Egyptian grammar.

84. Most scholars who have expressed themselves on this matter support this position, with some locating the migration in MB I and some in MB IIA. As noted above, this is seriously contested by Thompson, de Geus, and Liverani, among others, so that it cannot be said today, as Dever wrote in

"The 'Middle Bronze I' Period in Syria and Palestine," in J. A. Sanders, ed., *Near Eastern Archaeology in the Twentieth Century* (Garden City: Doubleday, 1970), p. 140, that "few scholars any longer oppose the 'Amorite'-MB I equation."

85. E.g., Gen. 25:23; 27:27–29, 39–40.

86. Cf. 2 Sam. 8:13–14. So O. Eissfeldt, "Genesis," IDB, Vol. 2, p. 371. N. E. Wagner, "Abraham and David?" in J. W. Wevers and D. B. Redford, eds., *Studies on the Ancient Palestinian World* (Toronto: Univ. of Toronto Press, 1972), pp. 129–130, believes that the final clause in Gen. 27:40 points to a time *later* than the era of David and Solomon, since there is no evidence for an Edomite rebellion before 850 B.C., or perhaps 735 B.C.

87. Gen. 12:2; 18:18, et al. See also the promise that Abraham will be the father of a multitude of nations (17:5), with kings as his descendants (17:6, 16; cf. 35:11).

88. C. Westermann, "Promises to the Patriarchs," SIDB, p. 692; Thompson, HPN, p. 325.

89. See Anderson, UOT, pp. 218–219; Bright, BHI, pp. 73, 76; Rowley, *Worship in Ancient Israel*, chap. 1.

90. "What Abraham, Isaac, and Jacob were like in their oldest dress is difficult to say, in view of the complete reworking of the traditions over a period of many years. The evidence suggests that Abraham was connected with the sanctuary near Hebron; Isaac, with the shrine at Beer-sheba; and Jacob, with the 'house of God' (*beth 'El*) at Bethel. Each of these places was an old Canaanite shrine that had been taken over by the Israelites, and some of the stories about these three figures were probably Canaanite in origin" (Anderson, UOT, p. 218) Cf. de Vaux, EHI, p. 167.

91. See chapter 4.

92. At least the sense that there were *twelve* tribes in the group. Smaller groups from among the twelve perhaps developed associations prior to their entry into Canaan.

93. Some scholars believe that the entity Israel, with twelve tribes, first developed at the *end* of the period of the judges or in the early monarchical period; see, for example, O. Eissfeldt, "The Hebrew Kingdoms," CAH II/2, p. 306; R. Smend, *Yahweh War and Tribal Confederation*, tr. M. G. Rogers (Nashville: Abingdon, 1970).

94. E.g., Gen. 21:32; 26:1–22.

95. De Vaux, EHI, pp. 503–510; J. C. Greenfield, "Philistines," IDB, vol. 3, pp. 791–795; Van Seters, AHT, pp. 52–54.

96. B. Mazar, "The Historical Background of the Book of Genesis," *Journal of Near Eastern Studies* 28 (1969), p. 78; Van Seters, AHT, pp. 52–54; Y. Aharoni, "Nothing Early and Nothing Late: Re-Writing Israel's Conquest," BA 39 (1976), p. 71.

97. Van Seters, AHT, pp. 42–52; idem, in SIDB, p. 646.

98. E.g., Gen. 12:6; 15:20, 21; 23:3; 24:3. On this point cf. also the article by Van Seters, "The Terms 'Amorite' and 'Hittite' in the Old Testament," VT 22 (1972), pp. 64–81.

99. On this see Mazar, "Historical Background," pp. 78–80; Thompson, HPN, pp. 298–308; Van Seters, AHT, pp. 29–34, 36–37, 60–64.

100. Genesis 24.

101. Gen. 28:2, 5, and succeeding chapters.

102. Genesis 29–30. Note also the genealogical relationship mentioned in Gen. 22:21.

103. De Vaux, EHI, p. 201; Van Seters, AHT, pp. 29–34, contain discussions of the debate over the obscure origins of the Arameans, with further references.

104. Gen. 25:1–5, 13–16.

105. Gen. 16:11–12; 21:20–21.

106. Van Seters, AHT, pp. 35–37, 60–64; Thompson, HPN, p. 302.

107. Gen. 11:28–29, 31.

108. Cf. Dever, in IJH, pp. 99–101.

109. See de Vaux, EHI, pp. 259–260; Stiebing, "When Was the Age of the Patriarchs?" p. 20; Van Seters, AHT, p. 105.

110. AHT, pp. 125–312.

111. E.g., AHT, pp. 253–254, 267–268.

112. E.g., AHT, pp. 263–269, 272–278, 304–308.

113. Among important works on this topic are: A. Alt, "The God of the Fathers," in *Essays on Old Testament History and Religion*, tr. R. A. Wilson (Oxford: Blackwell, 1966), pp. 1–77; F. M. Cross, *Canaanite Myth and Hebrew Epic* (Cambridge, Mass.: Harvard Univ. Press, 1973), chaps. 1–3, with references to his own earlier works; Rowley, *Worship in Ancient Israel*, chap. 1; H. Ringgren, *Israelite Religion*, tr. D. E. Green (Philadelphia: Fortress, 1966), pp. 17–27; G. Fohrer, *History of Israelite Religion*, pp. 35–42, 60–65.

114. Exod. 3:13–17; 6:2–3. Cf. also the distinction made in Josh. 24:2, 14–15, between Yahweh and the gods of the fathers. Herrmann, HIOTT,

p. 48, comments: "The absence of any such title as 'the God of Moses' may already be taken as an indication that in the case of Yahweh we are dealing with a different type of deity from the God of the fathers."

115. See references in note 113.

116. As reflected in personal names like Eli-ab ("my god is father") or Ammi-el ("El is my kinsman"). Cf. Bright, BHI, p. 98, and de Vaux, EHI, pp. 272–273, where it is noted that this type of personal name becomes rarer after the tenth century B.C.

117. E.g., Gen. 16:13; 17:1; 21:33; 31:13; 46:3. (The English word "God" represents the Hebrew word " 'El," so that, for instance, Hagar's name for the deity in 16:13 is actually "El Roi," which is translated into English as "God of seeing.") The traditions never represent the patriarchs engaging in the worship of the El-manifestations outside of Canaan, so it has been concluded that this must be a form of religion which the transmitters of the tradition knew the forefathers to have adopted only after their arrival in Canaan. Alt, in his pioneering study (cf. note 113), mistakenly believed each of the *elim* to be a separate local deity, but subsequent study of the Canaanite religion has rendered it virtually certain that the various references do not allude to separate gods.

118. D. N. Freedman, "The Chronology of Israel and the Ancient Near East. Section A: Old Testament Chronology," in BANE, pp. 268–269; P. D. Miller, Jr., *The Divine Warrior in Early Israel* (Cambridge, Mass.: Harvard Univ. Press, 1973), p. 62; J. T. Luke, "Abraham and the Iron Age: Reflections on the New Patriarchal Studies," JSOT 4 (1977), pp. 43–44; de Vaux, EHI, pp. 278–279.

119. The marrying of sisters is forbidden in Lev. 18:18. Similarly, the tradition of Abraham marrying his sister (Gen. 20:12) contravenes the legislation of Lev. 18:9, 11; Deut. 27:22. Regarding the pillars which Jacob set up at Bethel and Gilead (Gen. 28:18, 22; 35:14), contrast the laws in Lev. 26:1 and Deut. 16:22. Cf. Sarna, *Understanding Genesis*, p. 87. But see also J. Van Seters, "Dating the Patriarchal Stories," BAR IV/4 (1978), pp. 7–8.

120. Van Seters, AHT, pp. 29–34; Thompson, HPN, pp. 298–308.

121. Van Seters recognizes this problem and ventures a tentative response (AHT, p. 34), which seems weak to me.

122. HPN, p. 317.

123. C. Westermann, "Arten der Erzählung in der Genesis," *Forschung am Alten Testament* (Munich: Chr. Kaiser Verlag, 1964), pp. 9–91.

124. By "paradigmatic figures" we mean characters who constituted for later generations illuminating analogies for understanding their own circum-

stances, inspirational models for emulation, or compelling precedents.
See R. Smend, "Tradition and History: A Complex Relation," in D. A.
Knight, ed., *Tradition and Theology in the Old Testament* (Philadelphia:
Fortress, 1977), pp. 56–60.

Chapter 3

1. On the authenticity of the slavery tradition, cf. Bright, BHI, p. 119; O.
Eissfeldt, "The Exodus and Wanderings," in CAH II/2, p. 321; J. J.
Bimson, REC, p. 15.

2. In his annotation in *The New Oxford Annotated Bible with the
Apocrypha* (New York: Oxford, 1973), p. 82, B. W. Anderson esti-
mates that the figure implies a total number of "at least two and a half
million." A body of people this size would be roughly equivalent in
number to the population of the state of South Carolina, according to
the 1970 census.

3. Josephus, *Against Apion*, I.14, claiming to base his report on the
Egyptian historian Manetho, identified the entry of the Hebrews with the
arrival of the Hyksos. Cf. Anderson, UOT, pp. 39–40; Meek, HO, pp.
17–18; Eissfeldt, in CAH II/2, p. 312; de Vaux, EHI, p. 318. Josephus
associated the exodus of the Hebrews with the expulsion of the Hyksos
(which occurred ca. 1570 B.C.).

4. M. Haran, "The Exodus," SIDB, p. 307, maintains that in the reference
to four generations in Gen. 15:16 one generation was probably figured as
a hundred years (in which case there would be no conflict between verses
13 and 16 of that chapter); but Haran also believes that the figure, like
many other chronological data, is typological and not to be used for historical calculations.

5. Meek, HO, p. 17; Albright, BP, p. 10.

6. Rowley, FJJ, p. 24, n. 5; Wright, *Biblical Archaeology*, pp. 54–58;
Anderson, UOT, p. 40. Contrast Bimson, REC, p. 251.

7. De Vaux, EHI, p. 303.

8. For a discussion of these and other biblical texts which suggest a three or
four generation sojourn, see Rowley, FJJ, pp. 71–72; S. J. De Vries,
"Chronology of the OT," IDB, Vol. I, p. 582.

9. Anderson, UOT, p. 41.

10. Rowley, FJJ, pp. 26, 77.

11. Rowley, FJJ, p. 24.

12. D. B. Redford, *A Study of the Biblical Story of Joseph* (Supplements to
VT 20, 1970); W. L. Humphreys, "The Joseph Story," SIDB, pp.

491–493; T. L. Thompson and D. Irvin, "The Joseph and Moses Narratives," in IJH, pp. 154–155, 180–191.

13. Bright, BHI, pp. 135–136; de Vaux, EHI, p. 320. Cf. also Kenyon, *The Bible and Recent Archaeology* (Atlanta: John Knox, 1978), p. 31.

14. This date has recently been espoused anew, in the face of nearly unanimous opinion favoring a thirteenth century date, by John J. Bimson, REC. We shall discuss his views below.

15. For discussion, see Rowley, FJJ, pp. 12–17.

16. For discussions, with differing conclusions, cf. Rowley, FJJ, pp. 37–45, 110–119; and Meek, HO, pp. 18–23.

17. B. Mazar, "The Exodus and the Conquest," WHJP, Vol. 3, pp. 81–82; S. Yeivin, *The Israelite Conquest of Canaan* (Istanbul: Nederlands Historisch-Archaeologisch Instituut, 1971), pp. 31–32, 71–72; Rowley, FJJ, pp. 33–35; de Vaux, EHI, p. 664.

18. De Vaux, EHI, p. 389; S. H. Horn, "What We Don't Know About Moses and the Exodus," BAR III/2 (June, 1977), p. 23; Bimson, REC, pp. 92–93.

19. See, for example, Haran, in SIDB, p. 305. On the relations between the Hapiru and the Hebrews, see M. C. Astour, "Habiru," SIDB, pp. 382–385; de Vaux, EHI, pp. 105–112.

20. Note, for example, the discrepancy alluded to above between Gen. 15:16 and Exod. 12:40–41. Cf. Miller, in IJH, p. 241. On the ideological nature of chronological data in the Old Testament, see Thompson, HPN, pp. 9–16; Haran, in SIDB, p. 307.

21. W. F. Albright, "From the Patriarchs to Moses: II. Moses Out of Egypt," BA 36 (1973), pp. 62–63, dates the exodus at about 1297 B.C. Anderson, UOT, p. 42, opts for a date of ca. 1290. Bright, BHI, p. 121, suggests a date in the first half of the century, although he acknowledges the possibility of a date in the third quarter. De Vaux, EHI, pp. 388–392, favors a date of about 1250. Rowley, FJJ, pp. 131–140, 164, dated the exodus about 1230 B.C., with only a two-year period between that event and the beginning of the entry of the Joseph tribes into Palestine. (Rowley associates the tradition of the long wandering with the group of Leah tribes, who, on Rowley's theory, entered Palestine ca. 1400.) Eissfeldt, in CAH II/2, p. 322, reckons the exodus to the second half of the 1200s. Herrmann, HIOTT, p. 62, believes that "we can begin from the fact that the exodus took place at the end of the thirteenth century B.C."

22. Noth, NHI, pp. 114, 120.

23. Cf. de Vaux, EHI, pp. 325, 389; Aharoni, LOB, p. 178; Haran, in SIDB, p. 305.

24. These findings were made by Nelson Glueck, whose work is briefly discussed, with documentation of his supporters and critics, in Rowley, FJJ, pp. 20–22. For further discussion of Glueck's work, see chapter 4, pp. 68 and 70.

25. Bright, BHI, pp. 127–130; Wright, *Biblical Archaeology*, chap. V. An extensive summation of this argument may be found in P. W. Lapp, "The Conquest of Palestine in the Light of Archaeology," *Concordia Theological Monthly* 38 (1967), pp. 282–300. See chapter 4, pp. 69–72, for a critical appraisal.

26. For text, see ANET, pp. 376–378. Cf. Bright, BHI, pp. 112–113; Anderson, UOT, p. 118.

27. W. F. Albright, *Yahweh and the Gods of Canaan* (New York: Doubleday, 1968), pp. 157–159; Aharoni, LOB, p. 178, n. 10; H. Reviv, "History," *Encyclopedia Judaica*, ed. C. Roth (Jerusalem: Keter, 1971), Vol. 8, cols. 576, 577.

28. M. L. Newman, PC, p. 23; Rowley, FJJ, pp. 116–123; Bright, BHI, p. 136; Eissfeldt, in CAH II/2, pp. 320, 323; R. Smend, *Yahweh War and Tribal Confederation,* tr. M. G. Rogers (Nashville: Abingdon, 1970), pp. 112–113.

29. Cf. Bright, BHI, p. 119; de Vaux, EHI, p. 329; Meek, HO, p. 32.

30. Bright, BHI, p. 136; Newman, PC, p. 23. Meek, HO, pp. 31–33, believes that *only* the Levites were in Egypt.

31. Rowley, FJJ, p. 123; de Vaux, EHI, p. 533.

32. Bright, BHI, pp. 136–137; Noth, NHI, p. 119.

33. For an extended discussion of the matters discussed in this section, see Nicholson, ESHT; also, de Vaux, EHI, pp. 401–425.

34. Cf. quotation from Wellhausen cited in G. von Rad, "The Form-Critical Problem of the Hexateuch," in *The Problem of the Hexateuch and Other Essays,* tr. E. W. Trueman Dicken (Edinburgh: Oliver & Boyd, 1965), pp. 13–14. Further arguments are presented by von Rad on pp. 14–15.

35. Ibid.

36. "Problem," pp. 3–13. Actually, even Psalm 106 mentions only the golden calf incident, and not the giving of the law.

37. "Problem," pp. 20–40.

38. "Problem," pp. 48–67.

39. Also M. Noth, *A History of Pentateuchal Traditions,* p. 141; Anderson, UOT, pp. 11–12; Bright, BHI, pp. 72, 120. The latter two writers do not, however, concur that the absence of any reference to Sinai in the credo passages arises from an original separateness of the traditions.

40. For critical discussion, with references to further literature, see Nicholson, ESHT; de Vaux, EHI, pp. 401–419; J. I. Durham, "Credo, Ancient Israelite," SIDB, pp. 197–199.

41. See Nicholson, ESHT, pp. 20–23; J. P. Hyatt, "Were There an Ancient Historical Credo in Israel and an Independent Sinai Tradition?" in H. T. Frank and W. L. Reed, eds., *Translating and Understanding the Old Testament* (Nashville: Abingdon, 1970), pp. 156–160.

42. Anderson, UOT, pp. 92, 128; Nicholson, ESHT, p. 23; A. Weiser, *The Old Testament: Its Formation and Development*, tr. D. M. Barton (New York: Association Press, 1961), pp. 86–87.

43. De Vaux, EHI, p. 405; Nicholson, ESHT, pp. 23–25; T. L. Thompson, "The Joseph and Moses Narratives," in IJH, p. 163; Hyatt, "Were There . . . ?" p. 166.

44. E. W. Nicholson, *Deuteronomy and Tradition* (Oxford: Blackwell, 1967), pp. 42–43; R. E. Clements, *Prophecy and Covenant* (SBT 43, 1965), p. 54; de Vaux, EHI, pp. 412–413.

45. Some scholars have argued for the unity of the exodus and Sinai traditions on the basis of the thesis that the Sinai covenant shows the influence of the Near Eastern treaty genre (especially Hittite), in which a summary of benevolent deeds performed by the suzerain for the vassal preceded the enumeration of obligations imposed on the vassal. With the treaty genre as a model for the Sinai covenant, it was argued, the laws set forth at Sinai by the suzerain Yahweh for the vassal Israel would have to be accompanied (i.e., prefaced) by a recital of Yahweh's benevolent deeds for Israel. So the association of Yahweh's deed of deliverance (the exodus) with the laws is virtually demanded by the treaty/covenant genre. The difficulties with this line of argument are discussed in the next section of this chapter.

46. Cf. D. N. Freedman, "Divine Names and Titles in Early Hebrew Poetry," in F. M. Cross et al., eds., *Magnalia Dei*, pp. 55–107. Whether Exod. 19:4–6 is early or late is debated; cf. B. S. Childs, *The Book of Exodus* (Philadelphia: Westminster, 1974), pp. 360–361.

47. Cross, *Canaanite Myth and Hebrew Epic*, pp. 100–101.

48. J. Wellhausen, *Prolegomena to the History of Ancient Israel* (New York, Meridian edition, 1957), pp. 417–419.

49. G. E. Mendenhall, "Law and Covenant in Israel and in the Ancient Near East," BA 17 (1954), pp. 26–46, 49–76 (=*BA Reader No. 3*, pp. 3–24, 25–53); idem, "Covenant," IDB, Vol. I., pp. 714–723; idem, "Covenant," *Encyclopedia Britannica* (Chicago: Encyclopedia Britannica, Inc., 1979), Macropedia Vol. 5, pp. 226–229.

50. E.g., Bright, BHI, pp. 145–149; Anderson, UOT, pp. 88–91, 131–133;

E. F. Campbell, "Moses and the Foundations of Israel," *Interpretation* 29 (1975), pp. 146–151; Newman, PC, pp. 21–22 (but contrast idem, "Moses," SIDB, p. 604); J. A. Thompson, *The Ancient Near Eastern Treaties and the Old Testament* (London: Tyndale, 1964); D. R. Hillers, *Covenant: The History of a Biblical Idea* (Baltimore: Johns Hopkins U., 1969), esp. chaps. 2 and 3; Beyerlin, OHOST.

51. M. Weinfeld, DDS, pp. 60–66; idem, *"berît,"* TDOT, Vol. 2, pp. 266–268; D. J. McCarthy, T&C, chaps. 9 and 10; idem, OTC, chap. 2; Nicholson, ESHT, pp. 47–52; L. Perlitt, BAT.

52. K. Baltzer, CF; McCarthy, T&C. A good selection of treaty texts can be found in the appendix to McCarthy's study.

53. This point was originally made by V. Korošec, on whose 1931 analysis, *Hethitische Staatsverträge*, Mendenhall had based his study. The point about the necessity of the oath is also made by Weinfeld, DDS, pp. 63, 66–67.

54. Hillers, *Covenant*, p. 53; Thompson, *Ancient Near Eastern Treaties*, p. 21.

55. Beyerlin, OHOST, p. 54.

56. Bright, BHI, p. 147; Hillers, *Covenant*, pp. 50–51.

57. Bright, BHI, p. 147.

58. Beyerlin, OHOST, pp. 54–55.

59. Cf. McCarthy, T&C, p. 301; Beyerlin, OHOST, p. 52.

60. G. Fohrer, "Altes Testament—'Amphiktyonie' und 'Bund'?" *Theologische Literaturzeitung* 91 (1966), col. 896; Perlitt, BAT, p. 95.

61. T&C, p. 251 (the text actually reads "21,2" but this is an obvious printing error); cf. de Vaux, EHI, p. 442; Perlitt, BAT, p. 95.

62. McCarthy, T&C, p. 251; Fohrer, " 'Amphiktyonie' und 'Bund'?" col. 896; Perlitt, BAT, p. 83.

63. McCarthy, T&C, p. 250.

64. M. Weinfeld, "The Origin of the Apodictic Law," VT 23 (1973), pp. 63–75; idem, in TDOT, pp. 273–274; H. Cazelles, "Ten Commandments," SIDB, p. 876; J. J. Stamm and M. E. Andrew, *The Ten Commandments in Recent Research* (SBT II/2, 1967), pp. 43, 68.

65. E. Nielsen, *The Ten Commandments in New Perspective*, tr. D. J. Bourke (SBT II/7, 1968), pp. 96–105.

66. McCarthy, T&C, p. 249; n. 9; cf. idem, OTC, p. 20.

67. Baltzer, CF, p. 28; Thompson, *Ancient Near Eastern Treaties*, p. 21; cf. Beyerlin, OHOST, pp. 67–77.

68. Thompson, *Ancient Near Eastern Treaties,* p. 22; Beyerlin, OHOST, p. 64.

69. Baltzer, CF, pp. 39–43; Beyerlin, OHOST, pp. 88–90; Thompson, *Ancient Near Eastern Treaties,* pp. 33–34.

70. Perlitt, BAT, pp. 169–181; de Vaux, EHI, p. 441. On the variety of opinions concerning the date of this text, see Childs, *The Book of Exodus,* pp. 360–361.

71. Perlitt, BAT, p. 179.

72. McCarthy, T&C, p. 254; idem, OTC, p. 31. Weinfeld, DDS, pp. 62–63, 102–103, gives a different interpretation of the evidence; he says that treaties of the third and second millennia were sealed by sacrificial rites, whereas the Hittite treaties and the first millennium treaties received their validity by the swearing of oaths. So the connection with the Hittite treaty genre would be weakened, but (on Weinfeld's argumentation) parallels with other early treaty types would exist.

73. De Vaux, EHI, pp. 442–443; McCarthy, T&C, pp. 259–262.

74. "Covenant Forms," in *BA Reader No. 3,* p. 31. This argument was picked up by Bright, BHI, pp. 146–147; Hillers, *Covenant,* pp. 69–70; cf. Campbell, "Moses and the Foundations," pp. 149–150.

75. McCarthy, T&C; idem, OTC, p. 28; Weinfeld, DDS, pp. 59–69; Stamm and Andrew, *The Ten Commandments,* p. 64.

76. Fohrer, " 'Amphiktyonie' und 'Bund'?" col. 896; de Vaux, EHI, p. 443.

77. Weinfeld, DDS, pp. 65–66; idem, in TDOT, pp. 266–269; McCarthy, OTC, pp. 69–72.

78. See note 70.

79. See the standard introductions to the Old Testament.

80. Nicholson, ESHT, pp. 74–75; Thompson, in IJH, p. 162. For a more conservative view, see Anderson, UOT, p. 93.

81. De Vaux, EHI, p. 448; Nicholson, ESHT, pp. 75–76.

82. M. Noth, *Exodus: A Commentary,* tr. J. S. Bowden (Philadelphia: Westminster, 1962), p. 154; Perlitt, BAT, pp. 90–92; E. Gerstenberger, *Wesen und Herkunft des "Apodiktischen Rechts"* (Neukirchen-Vluyn: Neukirchener Verlag, 1965), pp. 93–94. For a different opinion, see McCarthy, T&C, p. 248, n. 8.

83. Perlitt, BAT, pp. 86–90. The influential monograph by Gerstenberger (see preceding note) proposed tribal wisdom as the originating context; Gerstenberger's thesis was challenged by J. Bright, "The Apodictic Prohibition: Some Observations," JBL 92 (1973), pp. 185–204.

84. Nielsen, *The Ten Commandments,* pp. 96–112.

85. Some of the Deuteronomic language includes: "who brought you out of the land of Egypt, out of the house of bondage," "that your days may be long in the land which the Lord your God gives you." Cf. Nielsen, *The Ten Commandments,* pp. 35, 98–99, 100, 103–104; Fohrer, " 'Amphiktyonie' und 'Bund'?" col. 896; Perlitt, BAT, pp. 85–86.

86. H. H. Rowley, "Moses and the Decalogue," in idem, *Men of God* (London: Thos. Nelson & Sons, 1963), pp. 1–36; Bright, BHI, p. 142; Beyerlin, OHOST, pp. 145–151; Mendenhall, in *Encyclopedia Britannica,* pp. 227–228.

87. De Vaux, EHI, pp. 448–449, 464–472; Nielsen, *The Ten Commandments,* pp. 120, 139; implied by Cazelles, in SIDB, p. 876.

88. Stamm and Andrew, *The Ten Commandments,* p. 69; W. M. Clark, "Law," in J. H. Hayes, ed., *Old Testament Form Criticism* (San Antonio: Trinity University, 1974), p. 123; Nielsen, *The Ten Commandments,* pp. 132–138; Perlitt, BAT, pp. 82–102.

89. Exod. 19:20–25 is almost universally regarded as secondary. Cf. Childs, *The Book of Exodus,* pp. 361–364, 369–370.

90. Vss. 1b–2 are commonly regarded as secondary because of the inherent contradiction with 1a and 9–11; see Beyerlin, OHOST, p. 14; Noth, *Exodus,* pp. 196–197; de Vaux, EHI, p. 444.

91. Nicholson, ESHT, pp. 67–84; cf. Herrmann, HIOTT, p. 74.

92. Fohrer, *History of Israelite Religion,* pp. 80–81; Gerstenberger, *Wesen und Herkunft,* p. 95.

93. E.g., Anderson, UOT, p. 83; Noth, *Exodus,* p. 196.

94. Especially the reference to the performance of the sacrifice by the "young men" derives from a time prior to the establishment of an ordained priesthood; the sprinkling of blood is usually thought to be a primitive rite. Cf. Beyerlin, OHOST, pp. 38–39.

95. The reference to the twelve pillars symbolizing the tribes of Israel could not have entered the tradition until after the twelve-tribe league came into existence. As will become clear in chap. 4 below, this occurred after the settlement in Canaan.

96. So de Vaux, EHI, pp. 444–447; Weinfeld, DDS, pp. 151–152.

97. Even if vss. 3 and 7, which refer to the words and the book of the covenant, are deleted as secondary additions (they are similar to Exod. 19:7–8, which is widely held to be a Deuteronomic composition; cf. note 70), McCarthy observes that the phrase "blood of the covenant" (v. 8) does not have a Deuteronomic ring and the reference could be to a primitive type of covenant which was not based on any set of laws or covenant

"book"; cf. his remarks in his review of Perlitt, BAT, in *Biblica* 53 (1972), p. 117.

98. This utterance attributed to Elijah might be a composition of the Deuteronomistic historian. It would be a rather slender basis for postulating Elijah's knowledge of a Sinai covenant.

99. Perlitt, BAT, pp. 140–152, argues that these uses in the book of Hosea are late. Much of his argument is based on the work of E. Kutsch, whose studies on the concept of $b^e r\hat{\imath}t$ are collected in *Verheissung und Gesetz* (Berlin: de Gruyter, 1973). Kutsch maintains also that "Bund" or "covenant" is an inappropriate translation for the Hebrew $b^e r\hat{\imath}t$, which (according to him) always carries the connotation of either a *promise* made by one party or a *law* imposed on one party, rather than a two-sided agreement (as both *Bund* and "covenant" imply).

100. Anderson, UOT, pp. 273–274, 286–287, 316–318; Hillers, *Covenant*, chap. 6; Clements, *Prophecy and Covenant*, pp. 16–26 and passim (but contrast idem, *Prophecy and Tradition* [Atlanta: John Knox, 1975], chap. 2, and esp. pp. 22–23).

101. Mendenhall, "Covenant Forms," in *BA Reader No. 3*, pp. 47–49; Hillers, *Covenant*, pp. 141–142; J. Bright, *Covenant and Promise* (Philadelphia: Westminster, 1976), pp. 41–42.

102. Cf. McCarthy, OTC, pp. 78–79; Clements, *Prophecy and Tradition*, pp. 16–20; on the wisdom tradition, see Gerstenberger, *Wesen und Hurkunft*.

103. Principally the book of Deuteronomy, the "Deuteronomistic History" (Joshua through 2 Kings), and some editing of the prophetic books.

104. Horeb is the Deuteronomic term for Sinai.

105. BAT.

106. Cf. review of BAT by McCarthy in *Biblica* 53 (1972), pp. 110–121; also the review by M. J. Buss in JBL 90 (1971), pp. 210–212.

107. Bright, BHI, p. 145; Clements, *Prophecy and Tradition*, pp. 21–23.

108. See pp. 56, 57 (cf. n. 70), 59 of this chapter.

109. See pp. 53–58 of this chapter.

110. E.g., the prophetic announcements of judgment have been traced to treaty curses (cf. esp. D. R. Hillers, *Treaty Curses and the Old Testament Prophets* [Rome: Pontifical Biblical Institute, 1964]); the prophetic lawsuit (or *rîb*) has been related to the treaty genre (cf. W. E. March, "Prophecy," in *Old Testament Form Criticism*, pp. 166–168; McCarthy, OTC, pp. 38–39, 78–79, for brief discussions and references); and various psalms have been related to liturgies based on the treaty/covenant motif (cf. E. Gerstenberger, "Psalms," in *Old Testament Form Criticism*, pp. 192–196, for discussion).

111. Cf. McCarthy, OTC, pp. 76–79; Clements, *Prophecy and Tradition*, pp. 16–21; Perlitt, BAT, p. 132.

112. See, most recently, Mendenhall, "Between Theology and Archaeology," JSOT 7 (1978), pp. 31–33.

Chapter 4

1. Cf. J. M. Miller, "The Israelite Occupation of Canaan," in IJH, pp. 213–245, for a survey.

2. Cf. ibid., pp. 245–252.

3. Cf. ibid., pp. 252–262; P. W. Lapp, "The Conquest of Palestine in the Light of Archaeology," *Concordia Theological Monthly* 38 (1967), pp. 283–300.

4. De Vaux, EHI, p. 475. As S. Herrmann remarks, "Tribes and tribal groups on the move do not usually keep careful annals" (HIOTT, p. 87).

5. Cf. Miller, in IJH, p. 216. G. Ernest Wright, "The Literary and Historical Problem of Joshua 10 and Judges 1," *Journal of Near Eastern Studies* 5 (1946), pp. 105–114, presents arguments attempting to show that there is no real conflict between these accounts, but that they depict differing stages of Israel's movement into Canaan.

6. See Miller, in IJH, pp. 222–225; A. D. H. Mayes, IPJ, pp. 100–101; Weippert, SITP, pp. 44–45.

7. Cf. Miller, in IJH, pp. 227–230.

8. J. A. Soggin, *Joshua*, tr. R. A. Wilson (London: SCM Press, 1972), pp. 9–10.

9. See de Vaux, EHI, pp. 422–423, 527.

10. E.g., H. H. Rowley, FJJ, pp. 111–112; Mayes, IPJ, pp. 100–101; Herrmann, HIOTT, p. 80.

11. For differing opinions as to whether this narrative goes back to an actual event in which the tribal league was organized, cf. Bright, BHI, pp. 139, 160; Noth, NHI, pp. 92–94; Herrmann, HIOTT, pp. 123–124; L. Perlitt, BAT, part V.

12. T. J. Meek, HO, p. 47; Herrmann, HIOTT, p. 104.

13. Cf. Gen. 25:23; 49:1–28. Note also the "roll call" of tribes in Judges 5, which speaks of the tribal groups as if they were individuals. Genealogies were frequently constructed by relating to one another—as if they were individuals linked by blood ties—places or groups which had some historical relationship with one another; cf. H. Reviv, "History," *Encyclopedia Judaica*, Vol. 8, cols. 581–582.

14. Albright, BP, p. 32; idem, *From the Stone Age to Christianity*, pp.

276–281; Weippert, SITP, p. 19; de Vaux, EHI, p. 746; Rowley, FJJ, p. 113; Bright, BHI, p. 132; M. Newman, PC, pp. 79, 81. O. Eissfeldt, in CAH II/2, p. 316, suggests that the story is a literary invention. Whether the tradition originally had to do with Simeon and Levi has been questioned: see de Vaux, EHI, pp. 532–533.

15. Noth, NHI, pp. 146–147.

16. J. Bright, *Early Israel in Recent History Writing* (SBT I/19, 1956), p. 118; de Vaux, EHI, p. 577. This point involves a double inference: (1) that the listing of the sons in fact says something about the *tribes* which bore these names, and (2) that the "sons" are listed in order of seniority (rather than according to some geographical pattern of their tribal areas, for example). The stories of the births of Jacob's children (Genesis 29–30) are based on the understanding that the appearance of Reuben, Simeon, and Levi at the beginning of the tribal lists is based on their seniority.

17. Noth, NHI, pp. 88–89; Bright, BHI, p. 132; Newman, PC, p. 79.

18. For discussion of Garstang's work, see Rowley, FJJ, pp. 10–17; K. Kenyon, *The Bible and Recent Archaeology*, p. 36.

19. For discussion of these letters, see Bright, BHI, p. 109, with references to other literature.

20. See Meek, HO, p. 30; Rowley, FJJ, pp. 33–35; Noth, NHI, p. 145. De Vaux, EHI, p. 664 is cautious on this point.

21. Represented, in addition to Albright's own works, most notably in John Bright's *A History of Israel* and G. Ernest Wright's *Biblical Archaeology*.

22. See Bright's remarks in *Early Israel,* pp. 87–89, 121–126.

23. N. Glueck, "Transjordan," in AOTS, p. 443. See further pp. 435–436, 445, 449. Other discussions of Glueck's work in the Transjordan can be found in Rowley, FJJ, pp. 20–22; Haran, in SIDB, p. 306 (note editorial parentheses, however); Bimson, REC, pp. 70–74.

24. Rowley, FJJ, pp. 31–33; Aharoni, LOB, p. 178; Haran, in SIDB, p. 305; de Vaux, EHI, pp. 325, 389.

25. The text of this stele appears in ANET, pp. 376–378. See Bright, BHI, p. 112; Anderson, UOT, p. 118; Reviv, in *Encyclopedia Judaica,* Vol. 8, col. 576.

26. Reviv, in *Encyclopedia Judaica,* Vol. 8, col. 578; Bright, BHI, p. 129; Wright, *Biblical Archaeology,* p. 90; Weippert, SITP, p. 135. Cf. Miller, in IJH, pp. 255, 261, 271.

27. See references in note 18. Also: K. Kenyon, AHL, pp. 210–211; idem, "Jericho," in AOTS, pp. 264–275.

28. Kenyon, in AOTS, p. 273. Some would explain the lack of remains from the Late Bronze period by postulating wind and rain erosion (e.g., Albright, BP, pp. 28–29; P. W. Lapp, "The Conquest of Palestine," p. 291), but compare the remarks of G. Landes, "Jericho," SIDB, p. 473.

29. Cf., conveniently, J. A. Callaway, "Ai," SIDB, pp. 14–16; also, idem, "Ai," EAE, pp. 36–52.

30. Efforts to identify Ai with other sites than et-Tell (which is the site that was uninhabited between the late third millennium and ca. 1200 B.C.) have not been widely accepted. See J. A. Callaway, "New Evidence on the Conquest of ᶜAi," JBL 87 (1968), pp. 314–315; Weippert, SITP, p. 24, note 52; J. M. Miller, "Archaeology and the Israelite Conquest of Canaan: Some Methodological Observations," Palestine Exploration Quarterly 109 (1977), p. 89. But see Bimson, REC, pp. 53, 215–225. Efforts to reconcile the biblical account with the archaeological data by various stratagems are discussed briefly by Miller, ibid., pp. 89–91.

31. J. B. Pritchard, "Gibeon," EAE, pp. 446–450.

32. S. H. Horn, "Heshbon," SIDB, pp. 410–411; idem, "Heshbon," EAE, pp. 510–514.

33. De Vaux, EHI, p. 538; Miller, in IJH, p. 261.

34. Y. Aharoni, "Nothing Early and Nothing Late: Re-writing Israel's Conquest," BA 39 (1976), pp. 55–76; cf. A. Kempinski, "Masos, Tel," EAE, pp. 816–819.

35. Y. Aharoni and R. Amiran, "Arad," EAE, pp. 74–89; Aharoni, "Nothing Early"; idem, "Arad," SIDB, pp. 38–39.

36. This observation made by Miller, in IJH, p. 256.

37. H. J. Franken and W. J. A. Power, "Glueck's Explorations in Eastern Palestine [New Haven: Annual of the American School of Oriental Research 14 (1934), 15 (1935), 18–19 (1939), 25–28 (1951)] in the light of recent evidence," VT 21 (1971), pp. 119–123; Miller, in IJH, pp. 258–259; C.-M. Bennett, "Edom," SIDB, pp. 251–252; Kenyon, The Bible and Recent Archaeology, p. 33.

38. Bimson, REC, p. 69; Kenyon, ibid.; de Vaux, EHI, pp. 392, 518–519.

39. Cf. Bimson, REC, pp. 53–56.

40. H. J. Franken, "Palestine in the Time of the Nineteenth Dynasty: (b) Archaeological Evidence," CAH II/2, p. 334; Callaway, "New Evidence," pp. 318–320.

41. Weippert, SITP, pp. 130–131; de Vaux, EHI, p. 484.

42. Wright, Biblical Archaeology, p. 70.

43. Kenyon, AHL, pp. 214–215; O. Tufnell, "Lachish," in AOTS, p. 302

(who cites ANET, p. 262, for evidence of such a scorched-earth policy); de Vaux, "On Right and Wrong Uses of Archaeology," in J. A. Sanders, ed., *Near Eastern Archaeology*, p. 77.

44. M. Kochavi, "Rabud, Khirbet," EAE, p. 995 (the older identification of Debir with Tell beit Mirsim is still espoused in the same encyclopedia [EAE] in Albright's article, "Beit Mirsim, Tell," p. 172); "Where Is Biblical Debir?" BAR I/1 (March, 1975), pp. 5–7; E. F. Campbell, Jr., "Moses and the Foundations of Israel," *Interpretation* 29 (1975), p. 152; Miller, in IJH, pp. 261, 273.

45. Bimson, REC, p. 55, calls attention to the fact that if Eglon should be identified with Tell en-Negileh (instead of with Tell el-Hesi) it would show little trace of occupation during the 1200s.

46. Bimson, REC, p. 56.

47. Map, Aharoni, LOB, p. 213.

48. Noth, NHI, p. 149; Weippert, SITP, pp. 33–34.

49. J. L. Kelso, "Bethel," IDB, Vol. 1, p. 391; cf. Wright, *Biblical Archaeology*, p. 81.

50. Weippert, SITP, p. 48, note 9; de Vaux, EHI, p. 617; Miller, in IJH, pp. 260–261.

51. De Vaux, "Right and Wrong Uses," p. 77. Callaway, "New Evidence," p. 318, speculates that Bethel might have fallen to *pre-Israelite* invaders.

52. "Such proof would be simple if the conquerors had left their victory steles behind on the ruins of the Late Bronze Age Canaanite cities." (Weippert, SITP, p. 128)

53. "Destruction by man is by no means a necessary indication of malicious intent. We know well that mud houses deteriorate very rapidly, and periodically have to be torn down and rebuilt. Moreover, anyone who has tried it will have discovered that there is usually no 'gentle' way of destroying a mud wall. . . . Even concurrent evidence of deliberate burning need not necessarily point to enemy activity, for vermin infestation is one of the most common reasons for the abandonment of houses in primitive communities. Admittedly, the best way to deal with it is to move to a new location, but if this is not possible then burning of the older house is the second-best solution." (Adams, "Invasion, Diffusion, Evolution?" pp. 207–208)

54. Weippert, SITP, p. 131.

55. De Vaux, "Right and Wrong Uses," pp. 72–75, cites an instructive parallel from the efforts to correlate Homer's account of the Trojan War with archaeological findings at the presumed site of Troy.

56. Cf. references in note 26 of this chapter.

57. Weippert, SITP, p. 133; G. E. Mendenhall, TG, pp. 22–23; cf. de Geus, "The Amorites," p. 52, note 69.

58. Bimson, REC, pp. 56–65; de Geus, TI, p. 167. Albright, *The Archaeology of Palestine*, p. 118, associated a type of pottery known as "Collared Rim Ware," which usually appeared in early Iron Age settlements in Palestine, as Israelite pottery; but see Weippert, SITP, pp. 133–135; Miller, in IJH, pp. 271–272, 274; Bimson, REC, p. 58.

59. Cf. references in note 24 plus these: Meek, HO, pp. 33–34; Anderson, UOT, p. 42; Eissfeldt, in CAH II/2, p. 322.

60. On this possibility, see D. B. Redford, "Exodus I: 11," VT 13 (1963), pp. 401–418; T. L. Thompson, "The Joseph and Moses Narratives," in IJH, pp. 153–154.

61. This is the position argued by Bimson, REC, pp. 35–48, where it is pointed out that recent writers on the subject are inclined to identify Raamses and Pithom with Qantir and Tell er-Retebah or Heliopolis, sites which were in existence long before the time of Seti I and Rameses II (which was believed not to be true of Tanis and Tell el-Maskouta, which formerly had been identified as Raamses and Pithom). Cf. S. H. Horn, in "Queries and Comments," BAR III/4 (Dec., 1977), p. 47.

62. See further, pp. 81–88.

63. See note 25, this chapter.

64. Weippert, SITP, p. 61, note 24; Mendenhall, TG, p. 23; de Vaux, EHI, p. 491.

65. In the initial publication (in fascicle form) of his chapter on "The Exodus and Wanderings" for the revised CAH, Eissfeldt suggested that the name on the stele might be read "Jezreel" instead of "Israel," but by the time of the final publication (CAH II/2, p. 318) this suggestion was deleted.

66. Noth, NHI, p. 3; de Vaux, EHI, pp. 390–391, 490–491; Reviv, in *Encyclopedia Judaica*, Vol. 8, col. 576; M. Weippert, "Canaan, conquest and settlement of," SIDB, p. 128; Miller, in IJH, p. 267.

67. Callaway, "New Evidence."

68. Ai is commonly identified with the site et-Tell. Albright, BP, p. 29, even says "there is no other possible site for Ai than et-Tell." But that identification is challenged by some writers; see, most recently, Bimson, REC, pp. 215–225.

69. So Bimson, REC, p. 64; de Vaux, EHI, p. 617.

70. See summaries of several of these in Bimson, REC, pp. 122–127, 189–191.

71. Bimson, REC.

72. See note 61, this chapter.

73. This assumes the usual identification of Bethel with the site Beitin. Bimson is uncertain whether to accept this identification or the alternative proposed by D. Livingston, that Bethel is to be located at Bireh. Accepting this alternate location for Bethel would necessitate finding a different location also for Ai (which was near Bethel, according to Josh. 7:2; 8:12; 12:9; cf. Gen. 12:8), and for some writers this at least opens up the possibility that a new "Ai" would reveal Late Bronze Age occupation and solve the "problem" which Ai poses for a dating of the conquest prior to 1200 B.C. See Bimson's discussion, REC, pp. 215–225.

74. This assumes the identification of Debir with Tell beit Mirsim, first proposed by Albright (cf. his article, "Debir," in AOTS, pp. 207–220). Recently scholars have tended to identify Debir with Khirbet Rabud (cf. note 44, this chapter). One wonders if Bimson's decision to stick with the Albright identification (REC, p. 211) is influenced by the fact that Tell beit Mirsim attests Middle Bronze Age occupation, whereas the first walled city at Khirbet Rabud was built during the Late Bronze Age.

75. See REC, pp. 110–111, 115.

76. "There is no evidence that the Egyptians continued their pursuit of the Hyksos beyond Sharuhen," (REC, 133) which it took them three years to defeat. Further in support of his argument that the destruction of Canaanite cities at the end of the Middle Bronze Age should not be attributed to the Egyptians he cites (REC, p. 233) a statement from Y. Aharoni about Egyptian policy: "The Egyptians were not interested in the destruction of the cities which they exploited so profitably, they had to punish them in cases of mutiny, but they did not destroy them" (Aharoni, in *Antiquity and Survival* 2 [1957], p. 145).

77. Identification of certain Palestinian cities as "Hyksos" has been based primarily on a type of defensive fortification associated with the Hyksos, but several recent studies have cast doubt upon the theory linking these fortifications to Hyksos influence. One writer (quoted by Bimson, REC, p. 137) notes that "no certain instance [of this fortification type] is known from Egypt, the only country where the actual Hyksos are established with certainty as a political factor!"

78. See Rowley, FJJ, p. 87; de Vaux, EHI, pp. 689–690.

79. For discussion of how figures for these might be calculated, see Bimson, REC, pp. 96–102; also Rowley, FJJ, pp. 87–88.

80. Rowley, FJJ, pp. 86–88; de Vaux, EHI, pp. 689–691.

81. *Contra Apion*, I, 16. See discussion in Rowley, FJJ, p. 130, note 2.

82. For a moderate view on this point, see A. Malamat, "The Period of the Judges," WHJP, Vol. 3, pp. 129–130. See also Anderson, UOT, pp. 147–149.

83. The material concerning the "minor judges" (Judg. 10:1–5; 12:8–15) is judged by most commentators to be a separate tradition from the stories of the major judges, and the combination of the two blocks of tradition into a single system of "judges" artificial and secondary. Cf. de Vaux, EHI, pp. 688–689. To use the resulting arrangement for historical chronological purposes would obviously be misguided.

84. Bimson, REC, pp. 93–95, 110.

85. The brief notice about Shamgar and his deliverance of Israel from the Philistines (Judg. 3:31) appears after the section on Ehud, and this is at least a minor embarrassment to Bimson's argument that the Philistines do not appear until the latter part of the book. We will concede, however, that the opening verse of the Deborah account (Judg. 4:1) implies that there has been no deliverer between Ehud and Deborah, and the verse about Shamgar may be a secondary intrusion. See Bimson, REC, pp. 94–95.

86. REC, p. 77. Bimson makes this remark to explain how it is that, if the Israelites resided in Canaan from ca. 1430, as he maintains, there is no mention whatsoever in the book of Judges of Egyptian activities in the land at a time when Egypt would have been in her Empire period and conducting numerous campaigns into Asia.

87. Bimson, REC, p. 96.

88. Rowley, FJJ, p. 78, makes this point in a discussion of the problematical issue of biblical chronology relating to the date of the exodus.

89. It should also be noted that, in the course of developing various aspects of his theory, Bimson shows an inclination to take at face value such items as the story of Rahab (REC, p. 129), the collapse of the walls of Jericho (p. 130), the opening of the earth to swallow those who rebelled against Moses (p. 131), the striking of Egypt by a plague of boils (p. 171), as well as many of the round numbers given in chronological notes (such as the forty-year figure for the wilderness wandering: p. 144). Such an uncritical approach to the biblical narrative will not commend itself to a lot of scholars and will detract from the real merits of the book.

90. A. Alt, "The Settlement of the Israelites in Palestine," in *Essays on Old Testament History and Religion*, pp. 135–169; idem, "Erwägungen über der Landnahme der Israeliten in Palästina," *Palästina Jahrbuch* 35 (1939), pp. 8–63.

91. Weippert, SITP; idem, "Canaan," SIDB, pp. 125–130; also represented in A. H. J. Gunneweg, *Geschichte Israels bis Bar Kochba*

(Stuttgart: Kohlhammer, 1972), pp. 32–39.

92. SITP, p. 18; cf. idem, in SIDB, p. 129; Alt, "Settlement," pp. 165–169; Noth, NHI, pp. 68–70.

93. Note the acknowledgment of this in Josh. 15:63; 16:10; 17:12; Judg. 1:21–36.

94. Noth, NHI, pp. 147–149; Weippert, SITP, p. 41. Weippert, SITP, p. 146, suggests that the impetus for this military phase came from the arrival of the Rachel tribes (with reference to R. Smend's thesis that the Rachel tribes brought with them the tradition of "Yahweh War").

95. M. Noth, *Josua* (2d. ed.; Tübingen: Mohr [Siebeck], 1953), pp. 43, 47; idem, NHI, p. 149, note 2.

96. Noth, *Josua*, p. 43.

97. Noth, *Josua*, pp. 60–61; Weippert, SITP, p. 31.

98. An etiology is a story which purports to give the origin of some phenomenon, custom, or institution which exists in the storyteller's time.

99. E.g., Noth, *Josua*, pp. 33, 43, 60.

100. For a discussion of the theory that early Israel was organized in a twelve-tribe "amphictyony," which theory was expounded especially by Noth, cf. NHI, pp. 85–109; also, Bright, BHI, pp. 156–166. Noth's theory has come under heavy criticism in recent years: cf. de Vaux, EHI, pp. 695–715; de Geus, TI; Mayes, IPJ; or, more briefly, Mayes, "The Period of the Judges and the Rise of the Monarchy," IJH, pp. 297–308; M. C. Astour, "Amphictyony," SIDB, pp. 23–25.

101. And perhaps Ephraimites, according to Noth, *Josua*, p. 61.

102. This is Noth's view: NHI, pp. 93–95; *Josua*, p. 106. Alt, "Josua," BZAW 66 (1936), pp. 24–25, believes that Joshua was also involved in the battle at Gibeon (Josh. 10:1–14). Cf. Weippert, SITP, pp. 37–41.

103. See especially J. Bright, *Early Israel*, Chapters II and IV.

104. Bright, *Early Israel*, p. 87; G. E. Wright, "Archaeology and Old Testament Studies," JBL 77 (1958), pp. 47–48.

105. Cf. Thompson, HPN, p. 6, note 19.

106. M. Noth, "Der Beitrag der Archäologie zur Geschichte Israels," *Supplements to VT* 7 (1960), pp. 262–263.

107. SITP, pp. 128–136.

108. H. J. Franken, in CAH II/2, pp. 331–337; de Vaux, "Right and Wrong Uses."

109. Albright, "The Israelite Conquest of Canaan in the Light of Archaeology," BASOR 74 (1939), pp. 11–23; Bright, *Early Israel*, pp. 89–110.

110. Bright, *Early Israel*, pp. 90, 91. Cf. Albright, "The Israelite Conquest," p. 12: "The ultimate historicity of a given datum is never established or disproved by the literary framework in which it is embedded: there must always be external evidence." Cf. C. Westermann, "Arten der Erzählung in der Genesis," in *Forschung am Alten Testament: Gesammelte Studien* (Munich: Chr. Kaiser Verlag, 1964), p. 44.

111. Bright, *Early Israel*, p. 91.

112. A demonstration that an etiology is a secondary motif in a tradition does not, of course, mean that the original story *is* derived from actual facts.

113. B. S. Childs, "A Study of the Formula 'Until This Day,' " JBL 82 (1963), pp. 279–292.

114. B. S. Childs, "The etiological tale re-examined," VT 24 (1974), pp. 387–397.

115. In his *Myth and Reality in the Old Testament* (SBT 27, 1960), p. 29, Childs defines "myth" in this way: "Myth . . . concerns itself with showing how an action of a deity, conceived of as occurring in the primeval age, determines a phase of contemporary world order. Existing world order is maintained through the actualization of the myth in the cult."

116. Westermann, "Arten der Erzählung."

117. Ibid., p. 40.

118. Cf. the remarks of de Vaux, "Method in the Study of Early Hebrew History," in J. P. Hyatt, ed., *The Bible in Modern Scholarship* (Nashville: Abingdon, 1965), pp. 18–20.

119. Genealogies in the ancient world functioned differently from modern family records, where the concern is to record individuals' kinship relationships accurately. Ancient genealogies were arranged differently, according to the function they were to serve. The possible purposes of a biblical genealogy are more numerous than one might expect. A genealogy might express (as today's genealogies) actual family lineage; it might reflect political relationships between groups; it might express the relative social, political, or religious status of individuals or groups represented in the listing; it might be used to enhance the political, social, or religious claims of an individual or group by demonstrating descent from some prominent person. Different purposes or functions might necessitate different (i.e., literally contradictory) "genealogies" for the same person or group. Cf. R. R. Wilson, *Genealogy and History in the Biblical World* (New Haven: Yale, 1977); idem, "Between 'Azel' and 'Azel': Interpreting the Biblical Genealogies," BA 42 (1979), pp. 11–22.

120. See discussion in de Vaux, EHI, p. 542.

121. Cf. ibid., pp. 586–587, 651; Aharoni, LOB, p. 222; Mayes, IPJ, pp. 28–29.

122. Other examples in Aharoni, LOB, pp. 222–223.

123. Noth, NHI, pp. 78–80, 145. Since the known tribal dwelling-places of Zebulun were not near the sea, Noth infers from Gen. 49:13 that Zebulun performed hired service in the harbors in payment to the Canaanites for land in the Galilean mountains.

124. Aharoni, in WHJP, Vol. 3, p. 116; idem, LOB, p. 175. Contrast Herrmann, HIOTT, p. 107, note 28.

125. ANET, p. 484; cf. Herrmann, HIOTT, pp. 93–94; Aharoni, in WHJP, Vol. 3, pp. 116–117; Eissfeldt, in CAH II/2, p. 317. One of the Canaanite princes, Baridiya, writes to the Egyptian court, whose interests he is charged with guarding, that he is using corvée workers to plow in the area of Shunem (a city assigned to Issachar, according to Josh. 19:18), which had been destroyed by Labaya, prince of Shechem. Another text, from the time of Seti I (cf. ANET, p. 255), mentions Hapiru in territory which the Old Testament assigns to Issachar, and some take this as evidence that the tribe of Issachar was there in Seti's time; cf. Aharoni, WHJP, Vol. 3, p. 116; Reviv, in *Encyclopedia Judaica*, Vol. 8, col. 579.

126. Meek, HO, p. 30; Rowley, FJJ, pp. 33–35, 113 (where evidence from Ras Shamra is also mentioned); Aharoni, LOB, pp. 175, 200; see ANET, pp. 475–479, and note 42.

127. Herrmann, HIOTT, p. 93.

128. Meek, HO, pp. 30, 42–43; Newman, PC, p. 110, note 21. By "concubine tribes" we mean Dan, Naphtali, Gad, and Asher, whose eponymous ancestors were born to the maids of Jacob's wives, according to the tradition in Genesis 30. Miller, in IJH, pp. 243, 282, speculates that several of the northern tribes were originally settled along the Mediterranean coast and were forced inland by the Sea Peoples or were perhaps themselves Sea Peoples.

129. According to this interpretation, the Song passes to the Transjordan only in vs. 17. Cf. Noth, NHI, pp. 64, 70; Eissfeldt, in CAH II/2, p. 548. Several other pieces of evidence seeming to point in this direction are discussed by these writers. Herrmann, HIOTT, pp. 101–103, thinks the whole settlement of Transjordan took place from the west.

130. Newman, PC, pp. 81–83. Cf. also the allusion to this in Deut. 33:6.

131. So Aharoni, in WHJP, Vol. 3, p. 123; and de Vaux, EHI, pp. 578–581.

132. De Vaux, EHI, pp. 266, 591. In contrast, Mayes, IPJ, pp. 30–31, infers from the absence of any reference to Gad in Judges 5 that Gad was not

formed by the time of the battle described therein.

133. Aharoni, in WHJP, Vol. 3, p. 123.

134. Miller, in IJH, pp. 229, 283.

135. Mentioned as a possibility by Aharoni, in WHJP, Vol. 3, pp. 123–124; de Vaux, EHI, p. 788. Contrast Noth, NHI, p. 60.

136. Aharoni, LOB, p. 223. Contrast de Vaux, EHI, p. 788.

137. Usually dated ca. 1125 B.C.: cf. Bright, BHI, p. 172. For a later dating see Mayes, IPJ, pp. 92–96; idem, in IJH, p. 314. For an earlier dating, see Bimson, REC, pp. 104–108, 194–200.

138. De Vaux, EHI, pp. 586–587; Aharoni, LOB, p. 222.

139. Because Issachar and Zebulun are grouped with the children of Leah among the offspring of Jacob, and are yet separate in a way from the other four sons of Leah (cf. Gen. 29:31–35; 30:14–20), several different hypotheses have grown up about how they were originally associated with the other four Leah tribes. For differing treatments of these other two "Leah tribes," see Noth, NHI, p. 78; Newman, PC, pp. 78–83, 110 and note 21 there; Eissfeldt, in CAH II/2, pp. 316–317; de Vaux, EHI, pp. 745–746.

140. Bright, BHI, p. 132; Noth, NHI, pp. 70–71.

141. Noth, NHI, pp. 71, 76 (note 1); Weippert, SITP, p. 19; Rowley, FJJ, pp. 112–114. The association of Simeon and Levi with this incident has, however, been challenged: cf. de Vaux, EHI, pp. 529, 532–533. In any case, Gen. 49:5–7 attests some sort of catastrophe which befell these tribes.

142. See p. 83.

143. Aharoni, LOB, p. 200; Meek, HO, p. 41; Rowley, FJJ, p. 141. De Vaux believes that the episode is wrongly located in the patriarchal period (EHI, pp. 266, 542).

144. Rowley, FJJ, pp. 112–114, believes that references in the Amarna letters (cf. ANET, pp. 483–490) to activity around Shechem by Hapiru might be associated with the Genesis 34 incident; similarly, Bright, BHI, p. 132.

145. Rowley, FJJ, pp. 111–112; Bright, BHI, p. 133; de Vaux, EHI, pp. 523–550 (esp. pp. 533–534, 538–540); Herrmann, HIOTT, p. 80; Mayes, IPJ, p. 100. Newman posits an original entry from the Transjordan in the Amarna period, at which time the Leah tribes constituted a six-tribe amphictyony. He believes that the catastrophes alluded to in Genesis 34 and 49:3–7 subsequently caused the Leah tribes of Simeon, Levi, and Judah to retire to the Negeb (whereas Issachar and Zebulun held their ground and remained friendly with the Shechemites, and Reu-

ben moved to the Transjordan), whence, after an association at Kadesh in the early 1200s with the Moses group which had escaped from Egypt (i.e., the Rachel tribes), the Leah tribes penetrated Canaan a second time from the *south* (as in Judges 1). See Newman, PC, pp. 78–83, 107–108.

146. =Judg. 1:17?

147. There is some evidence that the "city of palms" referred to in Judg. 1:16 is not Jericho (as in Deut. 34:3; Judg. 3:13), but the site of Zoar south of the Dead Sea. Cf. Miller, in IJH, p. 239; Aharoni, LOB, p. 198.

148. Noth, NHI, p. 77; Mazar, in WHJP, Vol. 3, pp. 88–89. If one assumes that all the Leah tribes entered Canaan together, and that some of them (at least Simeon and Levi) pushed into central Canaan, an entry from the east is more reasonable because the way into central Cisjordan from the south would have been obstructed by the chain of Canaanite cities (cf. p. 77 of this chapter and note 93). Newman, PC, p. 79, thinks an entry from the east may be reflected in Gen. 33:18–20, which speaks of Jacob's journey to Shechem from the direction of Paddan-aram.

149. Cf. above and notes 141, 144 of this chapter.

150. Whether the tribe of Levi should be connected with the priestly Levites is a disputed question. Among those who believe that the secular tribe of Levi, following upon the unfortunate experiences which crippled it (Gen. 34; 49:5–7), undertook priestly functions are Rowley, FIJ, p. 8 and note 5; de Vaux, EHI, p. 529; Newman, PC, chap. 3. Disagreeing with this theory are Noth, NHI, p. 88, note 2; Weippert, SITP, p. 43, note 139.

151. Cf. Deut. 33:6. De Vaux, EHI, pp. 576–581, thinks that these texts refer to incidents during the period of the judges when Reuben, settled in the Transjordan, was attacked by Moabites (cf. also Bright, BHI, p. 172) or Gadites, or both. De Vaux believes that Reuben arrived in Transjordan with the Moses group (so he does not envisage an earlier, pre-exodus history for the tribe), took the lead in the battle with Sihon (Num. 21:21–30)—which earned the tribe a reputation for eminence—and settled east of the Jordan without ever setting foot on the west bank of the river. A primary difficulty in de Vaux' thesis is that it leaves unexplained why Reuben is linked in the genealogies with the Leah tribes, with whom (according to his reconstruction) Reuben historically had nothing in common.

152. See p. 83.

153. Newman, PC, p. 83, disputes this; see note 145.

154. Eissfeldt, in CAH, II/2, p. 545, suggests that the archaeological evidence of the destruction of Lachish (cf. pp. 70–71) might be owing to some *warlike* expansion by Judah in this period.

155. W. F. Albright, "Archaeology and the Date of the Hebrew Conquest of

Palestine," BASOR 58 (1935), pp. 10–18; Meek, HO, pp. 42–48. Mazar, in WHJP, Vol. 3, pp. 77–78, 84–93, dates the entry of the Rachelites earlier, but he brings the two entries much closer together in time than does either Albright or Meek.

156. In whose territory the bulk of the conquest tradition, including the capture of Jericho, is located. Joshua is said to be an Ephraimite (Num. 13:8, 16; cf. Josh. 24:29–30).

157. Somewhat more broadly it has been argued that the name of Joshua is "engraved" as the first leader of the conquest of the territory west of the River Jordan: Mazar, in WHJP, Vol. 3, p. 85.

158. Glueck's findings regarding Transjordan; archaeological finds attesting thirteenth century destruction at Lachish, Debir, Hazor, etc. See pp. 68–69.

159. Meek, HO, pp. viii, 18–23. The contrary opinion is argued in Rowley, FJJ, pp. 40–45. Rowley ties the settlement of the *Leah* tribes in with Hapiru activity reported in the Amarna letters (cf. n. 144 above). Rowley argues that the pattern of Hapiru attacks reported in those letters does not at all coincide with the stories of Joshua's conquest. He interprets the letters as showing Hapiru activity in the fourteenth century only in the north and in the south of Canaan, not in the center; he bases on this his hypothesis that in the Amarna period the four senior Leah tribes were entering from the south, and tribes like Asher, Zebulun, and Dan were entering in the north. The one town in central Canaan where Hapiru activity is reported is Shechem; Rowley relates this to Genesis 34 and uses it as evidence for the priority of the Leah group, whereas Meek (HO, pp. 25–28) relates it to Joshua 24 as evidence for the priority of the Rachel group.

160. HO, pp. 46–47.

161. Newman, PC, pp. 106–108 (who, however, brings the two movements very close together chronologically); cf. also G. E. Wright, "The Literary and Historical Problem," (see note 5) who sees Judges 1 as an account of a re-conquest, by individual tribal groups, of areas which Joshua had originally taken.

162. Mazar, in WHJP, Vol. 3, pp. 77–78, 84–85; Aharoni, LOB, pp. 184–192 (with map, p. 186); Reviv, in *Encyclopedia Judaica*, Vol. 8, cols. 577–578.

163. Reviv, ibid.

164. Aharoni, LOB, p. 189. Meek, HO, p. 42, takes this to be the route of Reuben's migration to his eventual homeland.

165. Mazar, in WHJP, Vol. 3, pp. 78, 88.

166. Meek argues that the precedence which is accorded Moses in the final form of the narrative is "the result of a prejudiced Judean interpretation of the events," which made Joshua appear subordinate to Moses (HO, pp. 27, 45–46 [quotation from p. 27]).

167. So Meek, HO, pp. 31–33; Albright, in BASOR 58, pp. 10–18, holds that the Joseph tribes entered Canaan first, and that it was the Leah tribes whom Moses led, but he wants to maintain the association of Joseph with Egypt and so posits that the Joseph tribes had come out of Egypt in a separate exodus, though he admits that "the circumstances and date of the first exodus are obscure" and unattested in the biblical traditions ("Historical and Mythical Elements in the Story of Joseph," JBL 37 [1918], p. 138).

168. Cf. references in n. 37 of this chapter.

169. See pp. 77–80.

170. Mendenhall, "The Hebrew Conquest of Palestine," BA Reader No. 3, p. 115, disputes this, on the basis of the list of defeated kings in Josh. 12:7–24, which mentions several places which elsewhere are associated with Manasseh. For a different opinion, cf. Wright, Biblical Archaeology, p. 76, n. 8; de Vaux, EHI, p. 637.

171. Cf. the respective entries in SIDB or EAE.

172. So de Vaux, EHI, pp. 641–642; Eissfeldt, in CAH II/2, pp. 318, 547, 550; Mayes, IPJ, p. 82; Miller, in IJH, p. 283. A differing opinion is held by Noth, NHI, p. 74, n. 4.

173. Newman, PC, p. 122, n. 60; de Vaux, EHI, pp. 650–653. Mayes, IPJ, p. 19, argues that Manasseh was never superior, and that the motif of Ephraim's being the younger son is simply a literary device to enhance the significance of his success.

174. See p. 84.

175. Cf. Miller, in IJH, p. 267.

176. See map in Aharoni, LOB, p. 213.

177. Cf. Rowley, FJJ, p. 103; G. W. Anderson, "Israel: Amphictyony: ᶜAM; Ḵ ĀHĀL; ᶜĒDÂH," in H. T. Frank and W. L. Reed, eds., Translating and Understanding the Old Testament (Nashville: Abingdon, 1970), p. 149, n. 40.

178. Eissfeldt, in CAH II/2, p. 552; Mayes, IPJ, pp. 3–4.

179. Cf. note 100 of this chapter.

180. Newman, PC, pp. 72–90; Herrmann, HIOTT, pp. 77–78; de Vaux, EHI, pp. 423–425; Aharoni, LOB, p. 184; Eissfeldt, in CAH II/2, pp. 325–327.

181. Generally, Exod. 15:22–18:27; Num. 11:1–20:21. Cf. Eissfeldt, CAH II/2, p. 325; Newman, PC, pp. 73–75; cautiously, de Vaux, EHI, pp. 419–423.

182. Eissfeldt, CAH II/2, p. 321; Rowley, FJJ, pp. 105–108; Beyerlin, OHOST, pp. 145–151. Cf. Judg. 11:16.

183. Newman, PC, pp. 75–76. De Vaux, EHI, pp. 424–425, believes that there were two exodi from Egypt, with one group going straight to Kadesh, and the other to Sinai.

184. See p. 85.

185. See M. Haran, "Exodus, The," SIDB, pp. 308–310, for a discussion, with maps, of the various traditions relating to this route.

186. E.g., R. de Vaux, *Ancient Israel*, tr. J. McHugh (New York: McGraw-Hill, 1961), pp. 4–12; cf. M. C. Astour, "Habiru," SIDB, p. 384.

187. See pp. 68–69.

188. Mendenhall, "Hebrew Conquest"; idem, TG; idem, "Social Organization in Early Israel," in Cross et al., eds., *Magnalia Dei*, pp. 132–151; idem, " 'Change and Decay in All Around I See': Conquest, Covenant and *The Tenth Generation*," BA 39 (1976), pp. 152–157; N. K. Gottwald, "Were the Early Israelites Pastoral Nomads?" in *Rhetorical Criticism*, pp. 223–255; idem, "Domain assumptions and societal models in the study of Pre-monarchic Israel," *Supplements to VT* 28 (1975), pp. 89–100; idem, "The Hypothesis of the Revolutionary Origins of Ancient Israel: A Response to Hauser and Thompson," JSOT 7 (1978), pp. 37–52. A recent work of Gottwald's is *The Tribes of Yahweh: A Sociology of the Religion of Liberated Israel, 1250–1000 B.C.* (Maryknoll, N.Y.: Orbis, 1979).

189. On these texts, see W. F. Albright, "The Amarna Letters from Palestine," CAH II/2, pp. 98–116; E. F. Campbell, "The Amarna Letters and the Amarna Period," *BA Reader No. 3*, pp. 54–75; T. O. Lambdin, "Tell el-Amarna," IDB, Vol. 4, pp. 529–533; A. F. Rainey, "Tell el-Amarna," SIDB, p. 869.

190. Astour, "Habiru," SIDB, p. 383, with reference to the views of B. Landsberger.

191. "Hebrew Conquest," p. 105.

192. Ibid., pp. 105–107; TG, pp. 133–138; " 'Change and Decay,' " p. 154.

193. Mendenhall, "Hebrew Conquest," p. 107. In earlier decades it was thought that the $^{c}apiru$ of the Amarna letters were groups which invaded Canaan from without, and scholars often identified them with the invading army of Joshua; but more recent studies of the Amarna texts have determined that the $^{c}apiru$ were not outsiders; cf. Campbell,

"The Amarna Letters," p. 68; Weippert, SITP, p. 71; de Geus, TI, p. 187.

194. Mendenhall, "Hebrew Conquest," p. 113; cf. p. 46 of this book.

195. "Hebrew Conquest," p. 113; TG, p. 25; " 'Change and Decay,' " p. 155; also cf. Bright, BHI, p. 134.

196. Cf. pp. 53–58, for discussion of Mendenhall's thesis concerning the Mosaic date of the covenant.

197. Mendenhall, "Hebrew Conquest," p. 108.

198. Mendenhall, TG, p. 22.

199. Mendenhall, TG, pp. 18, 21–22, 28, 65, 225–226.

200. Mendenhall, "Hebrew Conquest," p. 108.

201. TG, p. 23; "Social Organization," p. 147; cf. also his review of the original German edition of SITP, in Biblica 50 (1969), p. 435.

202. "Domain Assumptions," p. 92.

203. Cf. Mendenhall, " 'Change and Decay,' " p. 156. In addition to similarities in language and cult practices, Mendenhall here refers to the Bible's use of pre-Mosaic traditions such as the "Song of Heshbon" (Num. 21:27–30) as another indicator that the Israelite people incorporated indigenous peoples into their religious community. He proposes that the story of Jericho might also be just such a tradition, deriving from pre-Mosaic times and preserved in memory by some of the people who joined up with the exodus group. He proposes a similar theory regarding the patriarchal stories.

204. Mendenhall, TG, pp. 186–187. De Geus, TI, p. 167, points out, however, that this degeneration had begun already in the Late Bronze period.

205. TG, p. 23.

206. "Social Organization," pp. 138, 141.

207. See chap. 2, p. 35. Cf. Mendenhall, TG, p. 164; de Geus, TI, pp. 124–127, 177.

208. See note 186 of this chapter.

209. Mendenhall, "Tribe," SIDB, pp. 919–920; idem, TG, pp. 184–185; Gottwald, "Nomadism," SIDB, p. 629; de Geus, TI, pp. 150–156.

210. Although tribal genealogies might be fabricated to band the tribal members more closely together. Cf. de Geus, TI, pp. 147–150.

211. Mendenhall, in SIDB, pp. 919–920; de Geus, TI, p. 131.

212. Mendenhall, "Social Organization," p. 147; Gottwald, in Rhetorical Criticism, p. 254.

213. Gottwald, in *Rhetorical Criticism*, pp. 244–246; idem, in SIDB, p. 630. Note that the Israelites ask, concerning the bread which they find in the wilderness, "What is it?" (Heb. $m\bar{a}n$ $h\hat{u}$' = "manna," Exod. 16:14–15).

214. "Hebrew Conquest," p. 115; cf. Bright, BHI, pp. 137–138.

215. "Hebrew Conquest," p. 115.

216. Ibid.; TG, p. 26.

217. Gottwald, "Hypothesis of the Revolutionary Origins," p. 42.

218. See pp. 69–73.

219. Cf. de Geus, TI, pp. 167–168.

220. Miller, in IJH, p. 279; de Vaux, EHI, p. 486; A. J. Hauser, "Israel's Conquest of Palestine: A Peasants' Rebellion?" JSOT 7 (1978), pp. 10–11; Bimson, REC, pp. 62–63.

221. See the programmatic statement in TG, pp. x–xi. Also cf. pp. 14–16, 21–22, and passim.

222. E.g., TG, pp. 188–197.

223. TG, p. 64.

224. E.g., TG, pp. 16–18, 65–66, 195–197, 225–226.

225. "Israel's Conquest," p. 6. Cf. Gottwald, "Hypothesis of the Revolutionary Origins," p. 45.

226. TG, p. 196; "Social Organization," p. 136.

227. "Domain Assumptions," p. 94.

228. As de Geus does (TI, p. 186, n. 260).

229. Note also the early history of Islam.

230. Cf. his remarks in "Hypothesis of the Revolutionary Origins," with references to his recently published book.

231. Weippert, SITP, pp. 63–102; Miller, in IJH, p. 279; Hauser, "Israel's Conquest," pp. 12–13.

232. On this possibility, cf. Weippert, SITP, pp. 74–82; de Vaux, EHI,. 213–216; H. Cazelles, "The Hebrews," POTT, pp. 4–6.

233. On the following, cf. Weippert, SITP, pp. 82–101; de Vaux, EHI, pp. 209–216.

234. It also should be noted that Mendenhall's interpretation of the $^c apiru$ of the Amarna letters as social revolutionaries is challenged by various other scholars. De Geus, for example, writes, "To speak, with Mendenhall, of social revolt, is going too far" (TI, p. 184). Cazelles, in POTT, pp. 6–21, identifies the Hapiru as military aristocracy. Cf. also T. L.

Thompson, "Historical Notes on 'Israel's Conquest of Palestine: A Peasants' Rebellion?'" JSOT 7 (1978), p. 24. De Vaux, EHI, pp. 105–112, and Herrmann, HIOTT, p. 60, think that the term had an ethnic meaning.

235. "Social Organization," p. 147.

236. Perhaps Mendenhall is suggesting this in "'Change and Decay,'" p. 156.

237. E. F. Campbell, "Moses and the Foundations of Israel," p. 152; Campbell is generally sympathetic to Mendenhall's thesis.

238. Hauser, "Israel's Conquest," pp. 11–12.

239. Gottwald, "Hypothesis of the Revolutionary Origins," pp. 42–46.

240. Ibid., p. 45; cf. idem, SIDB, p. 465.

241. Hauser, "Israel's Conquest," pp. 10–11.

242. "Hypothesis of the Revolutionary Origins," pp. 43–44. Gottwald cites the modern examples of the Viet Cong seizing the remote areas of Viet Nam, where the Saigon regime was least represented.

243. De Vaux, EHI, p. 666; Gunneweg, *Geschichte Israels*, pp. 38–39.

244. BHI, pp. 138–139; cf. references to Mendenhall in n. 201 above.

245. BHI, p. 134 (my italics). See the whole discussion, pp. 133–139.

246. BHI, pp. 90–91, 134. In his recent article, "'Change and Decay,'" Mendenhall might be hinting at something of the same thing when he refers, p. 156, to pre-Mosaic stories about Jacob which were incorporated into the Israelite tradition.

247. BHI, pp. 109, 132, 135. It is not clear whether Bright considers these to have been indigenous Canaanite peoples or not.

248. Such as the Kenites, Kenizzites, and Jerahmeelites.

249. Mendenhall, "Social Organization," p. 147, thinks of Judah as a tribe formed out of indigenous peoples south of Jerusalem, in the wake of the revolt ca. 1200 B.C.

Chapter 5

1. See discussion of these in chapter 1.

2. See discussion in chapter 3, pp. 58–60.

3. Cf. D. Irvin, "The Joseph and Moses stories as narrative in the light of ancient Near Eastern narrative," in IJH, esp. pp. 180–191.

4. G. von Rad, *Genesis: A Commentary,* tr. J. H. Marks (Philadelphia: Westminster, 1961), pp. 428–434; idem, "The Joseph Narrative and Ancient Wisdom," in *The Problem of the Hexateuch*, pp. 292–300.

5. M. Noth, *A History of Pentateuchal Traditions,* pp. 208–213; G. W. Coats, *From Canaan to Egypt* (CBQ Monograph Series 4, 1976), pp. 77–79.

6. Rowley, FJJ, p. 24.

7. S. H. Horn, "What We Don't Know About Moses and the Exodus," BAR III/2 (June, 1977), pp. 23–24. Horn goes so far as to say that Moses might have been adopted by Hatshepsut and loved by her more than the illegitimate child who eventually became Thutmosis III, thereby explaining the hostility of Thutmosis III toward Hatshepsut.

8. These latter points have been made by B. S. Childs, *The Book of Exodus,* p. 11.

9. Cf. the discussion in chapter 4, pp. 77–80, as to whether etiologies contain information of historical value.

10. Bloch, *The Historian's Craft,* p. 110.

11. This concept is stressed especially by J. Bright; cf. his *Early Israel in Recent History Writing,* pp. 88, 123–126.

12. As in the case of the Moabite Stone's confirmation of 2 Kgs. 3:4–5. For the text, cf. ANET, pp. 320–321. For discussion, text, and photograph, see D. W. Thomas, ed., *Documents from Old Testament Times* (New York: Harper Torchbooks, 1958), pp. 195–199.

13. J. M. Miller, *The Old Testament and the Historian* (Philadelphia: Fortress, 1976), p. 47.

14. Cf. S. M. Warner, "The Patriarchs and Extra-Biblical Sources," JSOT 2 (1977), p. 59, on the question of whether the "patriarchal period" should be posited as a distinct era separate from and prior to the period of the exodus: "Data does exist which links the patriarchal period to another biblical period, namely the Exodus. . . . However suspect, inaccurate, or contradictory this information might be, it should still nonetheless be used. There is no other information at our disposal." J. M. Miller comments aptly in the same issue of JSOT, p. 65, "An historian is never obliged to draw conclusions from suspicious, inaccurate, or contradictory information simply because it is all he has at hand."

15. See chapter 2, pp. 29–33.

16. W. F. Albright, "The Old Testament and the Archaeology of Palestine," in H. H. Rowley, ed., *The Old Testament and Modern Study* (Oxford: Clarendon, 1951), p. 11.

17. ANET, p. 378.

18. Cf. chap. 4, pp. 77–81, for discussion of the "peaceful entry alternative" which posits the arrival of Israelites by peaceful transhumance, and pp. 90–98, for discussion of the "social revolt alternative"

which hypothesizes that "Israel" was essentially an indigenous Canaanite peasants' movement.

Chapter 6

1. For discussion of this "fideist" approach, see Clark H. Pinnock, *Biblical Revelation* (Chicago: Moody Press, 1971), pp. 38–44, where this approach is criticized as inadequate, flimsy, and subject to delusion.

2. Cf., for example, J. W. Montgomery, *The Suicide of Christian Theology* (Minneapolis: Bethany Fellowship, 1970), pp. 325–327. It is not my purpose here to argue with those who claim that statements which are not empirically verifiable are meaningless; for that, the reader is referred to works such as Frederick Ferré, *Language, Logic and God* (New York: Harper Torchbooks, 1969); John Hick, *Faith and Knowledge* (Ithaca: Cornell U. Press, 1957); J. W. McClendon, Jr., "How Is Religious Talk Justifiable?" in M. Novak, ed., *American Philosophy and the Future* (New York: Scribner's, 1968), pp. 324–347. My purpose in this discussion is to show that the efforts of the fundamentalist "verificationist" school to verify theological statements by historical methods cannot achieve this end.

3. Cf. Montgomery, *Suicide*, p. 343; Clark H. Pinnock, *Set Forth Your Case* (Nutley, N. J.: Craig Press, 1968), p. 41.

4. E.g., Pinnock, ibid., pp. 43–44.

5. Francis A. Schaeffer, *The God Who Is There* (Chicago: InterVarsity Press, 1968), p. 78; cf. also Schaeffer's book *Escape from Reason* (Chicago: InterVarsity Press, 1968).

6. Both quotations from *God Who Is There*, p. 140.

7. Pinnock, *Set Forth Your Case*, p. 43.

8. Ibid., p. 44.

9. *God Who Is There*, p. 141.

10. Pinnock, *Set Forth Your Case*, p. 49 (italics mine).

11. Montgomery, *Suicide*, p. 355, n. 64.

12. *Set Forth Your Case*, p. 44.

13. F. A. Schaeffer, *He Is There and He Is Not Silent* (Wheaton, Ill.: Tyndale House, 1972), pp. 99–100.

14. See chap. 1 of this book, pp. 7–10.

15. Cf. Pinnock, *Set Forth Your Case*, p. 41; Montgomery, *Suicide*, p. 343; Schaeffer, *Escape from Reason*, pp. 89–90.

16. *Suicide*, p. 343.

17. F. A. Schaeffer, *Death in the City* (Chicago: InterVarsity Press, 1969), pp. 132–133.

18. We should emphasize that the "scientific method" is just that—a careful, critical *method* of studying phenomena, and not a given set of theories and laws.

19. Logically, before one could jump from the discovery that there is no known natural cause for an event to the conclusion that there was a supernatural (divine) cause, one would have to establish that the event was not *uncaused*. The fundamentalists' rejection of the concept of a uniformity of causes would seem to militate against the assumption that there *has* to be a cause!

20. I have the same difficulty with those who, in the midst of the recently awakened interest in the demonic and exorcisms looked for a "supernatural" explanation (i.e., demonic influence) only after all efforts at natural explanations for untoward happenings or aberrant behavior seemed to have been exhausted. It is bad theology to suppose that divine or demonic forces operate only or primarily apart from natural causes.

21. For discussion of this movement and some of the attendant problems, cf. the following: L. Gilkey, "Cosmology, Ontology, and the Travail of Biblical Language," *Journal of Religion* 41 (1961), pp. 194–205; W. L. King, "Some Ambiguities in Biblical Theology," *Religion in Life* 27 (1957–58), pp. 95–104; Brevard S. Childs, *Biblical Theology in Crisis* (Philadelphia: Westminster, 1970); and the works of James Barr listed in notes 28, 41 and 51, this chapter. James D. Smart, in a recent book, *The Past, Present, and Future of Biblical Theology* (Philadelphia: Westminster, 1979), has argued that "biblical theology" is not such a unified movement as most of the aforementioned critiques have suggested and that the announcement of the demise of biblical theology is premature. A number of Smart's points are well-taken, but the criticisms of the "revelation in history" approach made by such writers as Barr, Childs, and Gilkey remain valid.

22. So that, for example, "revelation" was reinterpreted as human insight, and "creation" was reinterpreted as the evolutionary process of natural development. The reference here to "Liberals" is to the school of theology which flourished at the end of the nineteenth and the beginning of the twentieth century and was known by that name. A convenient discussion of Liberalism may be found in W. E. Hordern, *A Layman's Guide to Protestant Theology* (revised ed.; New York: Macmillan, 1968), chap. 4.

23. G. E. Wright and R. H. Fuller, *The Book of the Acts of God* (Garden City, N.Y.: Doubleday Anchor, 1960), p. 7.

24. G. E. Wright, *God Who Acts* (SBT 8, 1952), p. 55.

25. See expressions of this aim in G. E. Wright, *The Old Testament Against Its Environment* (SBT 2, 1950), pp. 20–29; idem, *God Who Acts*, pp. 38–46.

26. Many of which could be attested by findings from archaeology, which played an important supporting role in the program of this movement. There is no better example of this juxtaposition of theology and archaeology than in the works of Wright himself, whose reputation in the field of archaeology was very good.

27. Cf. Wright, *God Who Acts*, p. 44.

28. Especially in the writings of James Barr; see his "Revelation Through History in the Old Testament and in Modern Theology," *Interpretation* 17 (1963), pp. 193–205; and "Revelation in History," in SIDB, pp. 746–749; plus the works listed in notes 41 and 51 below.

29. "We may argue, of course, from a critical viewpoint that the stories of such dialogues [as, for example, the burning bush episode] arose in fact as inference from a divine act already known and believed, and for this there may be good reasons. All I want to say is that if we do this we do it on critical grounds and not on biblical grounds, for this is not how the biblical narrative represents the events" (J. Barr, "Revelation Through History," p. 197).

30. So J. Baillie, *The Idea of Revelation in Recent Thought* (New York: Columbia U. Press, 1956), p. 78.

31. J. Barr, *Old and New in Interpretation* (London: SCM, 1966), pp. 72–73.

32. Cf. p. 120 below, and Barr, "Revelation Through History," pp. 198–199.

33. B. Albrektson, *History and the Gods* (Lund: CWK Gleerup, 1967).

34. Ibid., p. 114.

35. Text in ANET, pp. 315–316.

36. Conceded in Wright and Fuller, *Book of the Acts of God*, p. 11: "Historical and archaeological research can uncover the factual background in ancient history. But the meaning, the interpretation, the faith which in the Bible is an integral part of the event itself—this no one can prove."

37. Wright, *The Old Testament Against Its Environment*, p. 22.

38. Wright, *God Who Acts*, p. 44.

39. Ibid.

40. Cf. J. Macquarrie, *The Scope of Demythologizing* (New York: Harper

Torchbooks, 1966), pp. 70–71; G. Hasel, *Old Testament Theology: Basic Issues in the Current Debate* (revised ed.; Grand Rapids: Eerdmans, 1975), p. 66, quoting E. Osswald.

41. Cf. Barr's discussion of these concepts in *The Bible in the Modern World* (New York: Harper & Row, 1973), chap. 2; and in *Old and New in Interpretation*, pp. 82–102.

42. "Apologetic" is used here, of course, in the sense of "having to do with the defense of one's faith."

43. R. de Vaux, "Method in the Study of Early Hebrew History," in J. P. Hyatt, ed., *The Bible in Modern Scholarship* (Nashville: Abingdon, 1965), p. 16.

44. A. Richardson, *Christian Apologetics* (London: SCM, 1947), p. 91.

45. Wright, *God Who Acts*, p. 126.

46. Note especially the quotation above from Richardson.

47. The "central events" referred to in the quotation from Wright?

48. Would one say, for example, that it is less important that the story of Moses' birth be factual than that the account of the ten plagues be factual and that for both of these it is less important than for the story of the escape of the slaves from Egypt?

49. Cf. the work of de Vaux himself, EHI, esp. pp. 169–177.

50. Note again the quotation from Richardson above.

51. Cf. James Barr, *The Bible in the Modern World*, Chap. IV, "The Bible as Literature"; idem, "Story and History in Biblical Theology," *Journal of Religion* 56 (1976), pp. 1–17; Robert Alter, "A Literary Approach to the Bible," *Commentary* 60 (Dec., 1975), pp. 70–77; idem, "Biblical Narrative," *Commentary* 61 (May, 1976), pp. 61–67; J. J. Collins, "The 'Historical Character' of the Old Testament in Recent Biblical Theology," CBQ 41 (1979), pp. 185–204. For a brief discussion of the study of the Bible as literature, see D. Robertson, "The Bible as Literature," SIDB, pp. 547–551, with discussion and bibliography on structuralist and other methods of study. The April, 1974 issue of *Interpretation* was devoted to the topic of structuralism in biblical studies. The approach known as "rhetorical criticism" took its cue from the work of James Muilenberg; see especially his article, "Form criticism and beyond," JBL 88 (1969), pp. 1–18, and the volume honoring Muilenberg: J. J. Jackson and M. Kessler, ; eds., *Rhetorical Criticism* (Pittsburgh: Pickwick, 1974).

52. Cf. K. R. R. Gros Louis, "Introduction," in Gros Louis et al., eds., *Literary Interpretations of Biblical Narratives* (Nashville: Abingdon, 1974), p. 11; Collins, "The 'Historical Character,' " p. 195.

53. This is not to ignore or relegate to a secondary status the other types of literature in the biblical tradition—psalms, wisdom sayings, prophetic oracles, letters, and the like.

54. Some of the other types of biblical literature—such as some of the psalms, prophetic oracles, or the letters of Paul—make reference to the basic story and are frequently located chronologically by reference to the story.

55. Harvey, *The Historian and the Believer*, p. 282.

56. An example from our own experience may offer a useful analogy. The value and perceptiveness of editorial cartoons are recognized daily. If one acknowledges as valid the "distortions" of historical reality which editorial cartoonists create, it is nonetheless difficult to enunciate precise guidelines as to how much distortion is permissible before the cartoonist becomes a deceiver or a fraud. The judgment that a given cartoonist is not to be trusted will in fact be made on the basis of factors quite other than how far he departs from an "accurate" portrayal of "facts."

57. See the studies of James A. Sanders, especially *Torah and Canon* (Philadelphia: Fortress, 1972); "Reopening Old Questions About Scripture," *Interpretation* 28 (1974), pp. 321–330.

58. Sanders speaks of *muthos* and *ethos*; e.g., his "Torah and Christ," *Interpretation* 29 (1975), pp. 372–390.

SELECTED BIBLIOGRAPHY

General Works on the History of Israel

J. Bright. *A History of Israel.* 2d edition. Philadelphia: Westminster, 1972. Represents the school of OT historical research stemming from W. F. Albright. Maintains the view that archaeology has to a considerable degree vindicated a core of historicity in the traditions relating to early Israel.

S. Herrmann. *A History of Israel in Old Testament Times.* Translated by J. Bowden. Philadelphia: Fortress, 1975. A German work which occupies a middle ground between the conservative work of Bright and the more radical work of Noth.

J. H. Hayes and J. M. Miller, eds. *Israelite and Judean History.* Philadelphia: Westminster, 1977. A volume of critical articles summarizing and evaluating research into the various periods of Israelite history. Full bibliographies on each period.

M. Noth. *The History of Israel.* Translated by P. R. Ackroyd. Oxford: Blackwell, 1960. Represents the school of OT research stemming from A. Alt. Skeptical about the historical value in many narratives relating to the early period of Israel's history.

R. de Vaux. *The Early History of Israel.* Translated by D. Smith. Philadelphia: Westminster, 1978. This is the magnum opus of a noted French historian-archaeologist who adopted a moderate view concerning the value of archaeological data in substantiating OT narratives. A generally high regard for the likelihood that OT narratives contain genuine historical reminiscences. An extensive discussion of the major questions in historical research into Israel's earliest history.

G. E. Wright. *Biblical Archaeology.* 2d edition. Philadelphia: Westminster, 1962. A study of how the findings of archaeology shed light on the stories of the Bible. Written by another member of "the Albright school," this volume represents the viewpoint that many stories about early Israel find support from archaeological discoveries.

PART ONE

Chapter 1: The Historian's Craft

M. Bloch. *The Historian's Craft.* Translated by P. Putnam. New York: Random House, 1953. Written by a French historian whose specialty was medieval history, this is probably the best handbook on the principles of historical research.

J. Barzun and H. F. Graff. *The Modern Researcher.* 2d edition. New York: Harcourt, Brace and World, 1970. An engagingly written, widely used handbook on the methods and principles of research and writing history.

H. S. Commager. *The Nature and Study of History.* Columbus, Ohio: Merrill, 1965. A handbook dealing with what history is, how to go about studying history, the kinds of problems an historian faces, the interpretations and judgments an historian has to make, and some thoughts on a philosophy of history.

V. Harvey. *The Historian and the Believer.* New York: Macmillan, 1966. An exploration of the problems which faith and the scientific study of history pose for each other. An important work for anyone working on religious history.

J. M. Miller. *The Old Testament and the Historian.* Philadelphia: Fortress, 1976. Treats the problems and methods of the Old Testament historian. Especially concerned with the problem of relating archaeological evidence to evidence from ancient written sources (such as the OT).

PART TWO

Chapter 2: The "Patriarchal Period"

(See the relevant sections in the "General Works" listed above.)

J. Bright. *Early Israel in Recent History Writing.* Naperville, Ill.: Allenson, 1956. A methodological essay reviewing the major approaches to the reconstruction of early Israelite history in the first half of this century. Expresses the viewpoint that archaeological evidence needs to be more seriously taken into account in weighing the "balance of probability" concerning the reliability of OT narratives.

T. L. Thompson. *The Historicity of the Patriarchal Narratives.* Berlin: de Gruyter, 1974. A critical exposure of the weaknesses in numerous lines of argument used in recent decades to support the thesis that the patriarchal narratives originated in the period of which they purport to tell and therefore contain a kernel of historical reminiscence.

J. Van Seters. *Abraham in History and Tradition.* New Haven: Yale, 1975. Similar to Thompson in criticisms of the arguments for the historicity of the patriarchs. Part II of the book develops a literary study of the Abraham material, leading to the conclusion that the patriarchal narratives are essentially products of the exilic period and later.

Chapter 3: The Exodus and Sinai

(See the relevant sections in the "General Works" listed above.)

K. Baltzer. *The Covenant Formulary*. Translated by D. E. Green. Philadelphia: Fortress, 1971. A study of the covenant concept and outline as they are found throughout the OT in various contexts and genres.

D. R. Hillers. *Covenant: The History of a Biblical Idea*. Baltimore: Johns Hopkins, 1969. A semi-popular presentation of the thesis that the covenant concept and form were basic to Hebrew religion from the late second millennium onwards and were modelled on the Near Eastern vassal treaties.

G. E. Mendenhall. "Ancient Oriental and Biblical Law," in *The Biblical Archaeologist*, Vol. 17 (1954), pp. 26–46; idem, "Covenant Forms in Israelite Tradition," in *The Biblical Archaeologist*, Vol. 17 (1954), pp. 49–76. The first study clearly suggesting a parallel between the structure of the Sinai covenant and certain vassal treaties of the ancient Near East (esp. Hittite treaties). Concludes that the Sinai covenant tradition, because of the signs of its influence by the treaty form, can be dated to the second millennium B.C.

D. J. McCarthy. *Treaty and Covenant*. 2d edition. Rome: Pontifical Biblical Institute, 1978. A study similar to those of Baltzer and Mendenhall, but encompassing comparative materials from a broader geographical area and a lengthier chronological period. Disputes the thesis that the Sinai narrative in Exodus reflects influence of the vassal treaty form.

E. W. Nicholson. *Exodus and Sinai in History and Tradition*. Richmond: John Knox, 1973. A review of theories regarding the original unity or separateness of the exodus and Sinai traditions, with the conclusions that the exodus and Sinai traditions originally belonged together, but that the Sinai tradition did not in the beginning contain the covenant motif.

L. Perlitt. *Bundestheologie im Alten Testament*. Neukirchen-Vluyn: Neukirchener Verlag, 1969. Perlitt is the preeminent representative among recent scholars who maintain the thesis that the covenant concept was an innovation introduced into Hebrew religion by the Deuteronomist school (seventh century B.C.).

G. von Rad. "The Form-Critical Problem of the Hexateuch," in idem, *The Problem of the Hexateuch and Other Essays*. Translated by E. W. Trueman Dicken. Edinburgh: Oliver & Boyd, 1965. Pp. 1–78. Originally published in 1938, this essay constitutes an important and influential study of the exodus and Sinai traditions and their relationship to each other. Von Rad concludes that these blocks of tradition originated among different groups of Israelite ancestors and were originally celebrated in separate religious festivals.

H. H. Rowley. *From Joseph to Joshua*. London: The British Academy, 1950. A careful attempt from the 1940s (1948 Schweich Lectures) to interpret all data from biblical and archaeological sources into a synthetic picture of the origins of Israel. Rowley assumes that virtually all of the narratives of the Hexateuch embodied a historiographical concern.

Chapter 4: The Settlement in Canaan

(See the relevant sections in the "General Works" listed above.)

J. J. Bimson. *Redating the Exodus and Conquest*. Sheffield, Eng.: University of Sheffield, 1978. A challenge to the dating of the exodus and settlement in the thirteenth century B.C., which has been the prevailing view in recent years. Bimson cites the inconclusiveness of arguments based on archaeological data, but he bases his own proposal for a fifteenth century date on a rather uncritical interpretation of selected chronological data in the OT.

N. K. Gottwald. *The Tribes of Yahweh*. Maryknoll, N.Y.: Orbis, 1979. An enormous work which attempts to utilize sociological methods and models, in addition to the conventional tools of the biblical critic, to reconstruct the origins of the Israelite nation. Gottwald adopts as a starting point Mendenhall's thesis that the Israelite tribes were composed essentially of Canaanites who had withdrawn from the society of their former overlords. This volume appeared too late for any substantial consideration in the text of this present book.

G. E. Mendenhall. *The Tenth Generation*. Baltimore: Johns Hopkins, 1973. An extended presentation of Mendenhall's theses that (1) the Hebrew covenant with Yahweh originated in the second millennium B.C., under the influence of Hittite treaty forms, and (2) "Israel" was an entity which developed, not so much from tribal groups invading Canaan from without, but from disaffected peasant elements in Canaan who withdrew from (or revolted against) their erstwhile masters, challenging the rulers' ethic of power with the egalitarian ethic of the Yahweh covenant.

M. Newman. *People of the Covenant*. New York: Abingdon, 1962. An attempt, along the lines of Rowley's work, to reconstruct the origin of the Israelite league from the histories of various tribal groups entering Canaan at different periods between 1500 and 1200 B.C.

M. Weippert. *The Settlement of the Israelite Tribes in Palestine*. Translated by J. D. Martin. Naperville: Allenson, 1971. A critical review of three major approaches to or models of the Israelite settlement: (1) conquest

(Albright, Bright); (2) peaceful migration (Alt, Noth); (3) peasants' revolt (Mendenhall). Weippert defends the second of these.

PART THREE

Chapter 6: Faith and History

J. Barr. *The Bible in the Modern World.* New York: Harper & Row, 1973. A representative work by one of the writers who have challenged theologians to turn from a preoccupation with the "history" imbedded in biblical stories to an appreciation of the biblical stories as literature.

D. A. Knight, ed. *Tradition and Theology in the Old Testament.* Philadelphia: Fortress, 1977. A group of articles treating the function and the fate of OT traditions as they are transmitted, as distinct from a concern to reconstruct the historical events which first gave birth to the tradition.

J. W. Montgomery. *The Suicide of Christian Theology.* Minneapolis: Bethany Fellowship, 1970. A collection of articles by one of the representatives of the fundamentalist thesis that the events reported in the biblical stories can be verified by objective means.

C. H. Pinnock. *Biblical Revelation.* Chicago: Moody, 1971. An effort to defend the position that divine action and revelation can be verified, and that this position is more desirable apologetically than the fundamentalist position (the "fideist" position) which holds otherwise.

J. A. Sanders. *Torah and Canon.* Philadelphia: Fortress, 1972. Shows Sanders' interest, exhibited in many of his shorter writings, in the ways biblical traditions functioned (and experienced reshaping and reinterpretation) in the communities which received and transmitted them.

F. A. Schaeffer. *The God Who Is There.* Chicago: InterVarsity, 1968. One book among numerous writings of Schaeffer which expound a fundamentalist view of Scripture and a claim that evidence for biblical stories, including miracles, is such that objective historians can investigate it.

G. E. Wright. *God Who Acts.* Naperville, Ill.: Allenson, 1952. The most frequently-cited example of the theology of "revelation in history."

SCRIPTURE INDEX

Genesis

1-11	80, 120
11	136
11:10-26	34
11:28-29, 31	142
11:31	37
12	36
12-50	28, 33, 120
12:1-9	37
12:2	141
12:6	142
12:8	157
12:10-20	133, 134
13:3	137
15	135
15:2-4	135
15:7	16
15:13	46, 144
15:16	47, 144, 145
15:20, 21	142
16:1-4	133
16:2	30
16:11-12	142
16:12	137
16:13	143
17:1	143
17:5	136, 141
17:6	141
17:16	141
18:1	137
18:18	141
20:1-18	133, 134
20:12	143
20:15	137
21:10	30
21:20-21	137, 142
21:33	143
22:20-24	134
22:21	142
23	33, 133
23:3	142
23:11	33
24	36, 138, 142
24:3	142
25:1-5, 13-16	142
25:23	141, 152
25:26	136
25:27	137
26:1-11	133, 134
27:27-29, 39-40	141
27:40	141
28-33	36
28:2, 5	142
28:18, 22	143
29-30	30, 142, 153
29-31	133
29:31-35	84, 162
29:31-30:24	84
30	161
30:1-8	133
30:9-11	87
30:9-13	134
30:14-20	162
30:25	32
30:25-28	32
31	138
31:4-13	32
31:13	143
31:18	32
31:19, 30-35	31
31:43	31, 32
31:43-54	60, 83
31:50	31
33:18-20	163
34	67, 85, 162, 163, 164
35:11	141
35:14	143
35:16-18	84
35:16-20	88
35:22	83
35:23-26	84
36:31	15
37	100
37:12-17	137
38	67, 82, 85, 86
38:12-13	137
39-50	100
41:45	47
42:24	49
45:5-8	100
45:10	47
46:3	143
46:9	82
46:26-27	45

46:27... 46
46:28–29 47
46:34.............................. 15, 47
48 88
49:1–28....................................152
49:3–4 85
49:3–7 162
49:4 83
49:5–7 .... 85, 162, 163
49:13..161
49:15... 83
50:20..100

Exodus
1... 72
1:1–5.. 45
1:8, 9 47
1:11 ....48, 69, 72, 73
1:15–2:10 101
3:8.. 52
3:13–17....................................142
4:1–9..108
6:2–3............................... 16, 142
6:6–8.. 52
6:16–20............................. 46, 47
6:21–24.................................... 76
7–12 xiv
10:24.. 93
12:37.. 46
12:38.. 93
12:40–41 .... 46, 145
13:17.. 15
15:13, 17................................. 52
15:22–18:27 166
16:14–15 168
18:12.. 60
19–24 57
19:3–8 ....56, 57, 58–59
19:4–6 ....52, 147
19:5 45
19:7–8 150
19:9–19.................................... 60
19:20–25 150
20:1 55
20:2–17.........................54–56, 59
20:18–21 60
20:22–23:19 59
21:2–6 96
23:12–19 59
24 57
24:1a, 9–11 ....60, 150
24:1b–2....................................150
24:3 150

24:3–8 60
24:7 ....45, 150
24:12–15a................................. 59
24:15b–31:18............................ 59
32 .... 55, 59
33 59
34 .... 55, 57, 59
34:10.. 45
34:10–28 57
34:27.. 45
35–40....................................... 59

Leviticus
18:9, 11 143
18:18..143
26:1 143

Numbers
1–10 59
1:7.. 76
11:1–20:21...............................166
11:5, 22 93
13–14 ....45, 66, 67, 85, 89
13:8, 16 164
13:22–24 66
14:24.. 66
20 45
20:4 93
20:14–21 .... 48, 69
21 66
21–25 86
21:1–3 .... 67, 85
21:3 70
21:21–30 ....93, 163
21:21–31 75
21:21–35 87
21:27–30 167
22–24 .... 48, 69
22:28–30 15
26:5–6 82
26:19–22 82
26:29.............................. 82, 84
32 .... 66, 83
32:2–5 66
32:39–40 84
33 86

Deuteronomy
1:46 45
6:1.. 51
6:20–25.................................... 51
6:21–23.................................... 50
10:1–5 55

10:22...................................... 46
16:22...................................... 143
26:5–9 .... 50, 51
27:22...................................... 143
31:9–13.................................... 55
33:2 .... 52, 61
33:6 .... 161, 163
34:3 163

Joshua
1–12 .... 65, 66, 67, 78, 81, 120
2–10 .... 66, 87
2–11 78
2:1–14 93
4:6... 78
4:9... 78
4:21 78
5:9... 78
6–7 122
6:20–26.................................... 70
6:22–25.................................... 93
7–8 .... 12, 78
7:2.. 157
7:18 82
7:26 78
8.. 73
8:12 157
8:18–28.................................... 70
8:28 73
8:28, 29 78
9.. 93
10:1–14.................................... 159
10:1–15.................................... 78
10:16–27 78
10:27.. 78
10:28–39 .... 66, 86
10:36.. 66
11:1–15.............................. 67, 70, 78
11:16–23 66
12:7–24................................66, 165
12:9 157
14:6–15.................................... 66
15:6 83
15:13–14 66
15:63.................................. 66, 159
16:10.................................. 66, 159
17:1 .... 82, 84
17:3 84
17:11–12 71
17:11–13 66
17:12....................................... 159
17:14–18 78
18:17.. 83

19:1–9 85
19:18...................................... 161
19:47–48 67
21:43–45 66
24 ....20, 67, 93, 164
24:1–28.................................... 78
24:2–13............................... 50, 51
24:2, 14–15 142
24:27....................................... 57
24:29–30 164

Judges
1 ....85, 97, 164
1:1–20 .... 67, 85
1:11–20............................. 66, 67, 86
1:16 163
1:17 .... 70, 163
1:21–36................................... 159
1:22–26......................... 67, 71, 93
1:27 71
1:27–28, 30–33 66
1:29 66
3:7–11 75
3:13 163
3:31 158
4–5.. xiv
4:1.. 158
5................................. 152, 161
5:4–5 52
5:5... 61
5:14 84
5:14–16.................................... 83
5:17 161
6:36–40.................................... 108
9:7–15 15
10:1–5 158
11:16....................................45, 166
11:17 69
11:17–18 86
11:26 .... 48, 75, 83
12:1–6 83
12:8–15.................................... 158
15:20.. 75
16:31.. 75
17–18 67
17–21 89
21:1–14.................................... 84

Ruth
4:20–22.................................... 76

1 Samuel
4:6, 9 96

11 84
12:8 50
13:19 96
14:21 96
31:11–13 84

2 Samuel
1 135
8:13–14 141
18:6 84
21:12 84

1 Kings
6:1 .... 48, 74, 75, 76
18:36–39 108
19:10, 14 61

2 Kings
3:4–5 170

1 Chronicles
2:21, 23 84
6:33–37 76
29:22 60

Nehemiah
9 .... 50, 52

Psalms
68:9 61
78 50
105 50

106 .... 50, 146
135 50
136 50

Song of Songs
5:1–2 31

Isaiah
1:2–3 62
10:5–11 114
10:12–16 114
45:1–6 118

Hosea
1–3 62
6:7 61
8:1 61
11:1–9 62

Amos
3:1–2 62

Luke
11:15 118
11:20 118

John
20:30–31 110

Tobit
8:4 31

NAME INDEX

Ackroyd, P. R., 129
Adams, W. Y., 140, 155
Aharoni, Y., 139, 140, 142, 145, 146, 153, 154, 155, 157, 161, 162, 163, 164, 165
Albrektson, B., 117, 173
Albright, W. F., 68, 78, 79, 80, 81, 91, 93, 133, 138, 139, 140, 144, 145, 146, 152, 153, 154, 155, 156, 157, 159, 160, 163, 165, 166, 170
Alt, A., 77, 78, 79, 80, 81, 142, 143, 158, 159
Alter, R., 174
Amiran, R., 154
Anderson, B. W., 131, 133, 136, 139, 141, 144, 145, 146, 147, 149, 150, 151, 153, 156, 158
Anderson, G. W., 165
Andrew, M. E., 148, 149, 150
Ap–Thomas, D. R., 128
Astour, M. C., 145, 159, 166
Baillie, J., 173
Baltzer, K., 54, 148, 149
Barclay, W., 133, 138
Barr, J., 172, 173, 174
Barzun, J., 128
Bennett, C. -M., 154
Beyerlin, W., 55, 56, 148, 149, 150, 166
Bimson, J. J., 73, 74, 75, 76, 77, 144, 145, 153, 154, 155, 156, 157, 158, 162, 168
Bloch, M., 101, 128, 129, 130, 170
Bourke, D. J., 148
Bowden, J. S., 149
Bright, J., 28, 34, 49, 79, 97, 98, 130, 131, 132, 133, 136, 138, 140, 141, 143, 144, 145, 146, 147, 148, 149, 150, 151, 152, 153, 159, 160, 162, 163, 167, 168, 169, 170
Brown, R. E., 133
Buss, M. J., 151
Cadbury, H. J., 129
Callaway, J. A., 73, 154, 155, 156
Campbell, E. F., 148, 149, 155, 166, 169
Carr, E. H., 130
Cazelles, H., 148, 150, 168
Childs, B. S., 79, 147, 149, 150, 160, 170, 172
Clark, W. M., 150
Clements, R. E., 132, 147, 151, 152
Coats, G. W., 170
Cody, A., 140
Collingwood, R. G., 14, 130
Collins, J. J., 174
Commager, H. S., 128
Cross, F. M., 139, 142, 147, 166
Culley, R. C., 131
Cupitt, S. M., 129

Dever, W. G., 137, 138, 139, 140, 142
Dicken, E. W. T., 146
Dickinson, L., 131
Donner, H., 133
Durham, J. I., 147
Eissfeldt, O., 129, 141, 144, 145, 146, 153, 156, 161, 162, 163, 165, 166
Feldman, L. H., 135
Ferré, F., 171
Filson, F. V., 130
Fohrer, G., 129, 133, 136, 142, 148, 149, 150
Frank, H. T., 147, 165
Franken, H. J., 79, 154, 159
Freedman, D. N., 143, 147
French, V., 128
Fretheim, T. E., 129
Fuller, R. H., 172, 173
Gadd, C. J., 138
Garstang, J., 47, 68, 69, 153
Gerstenberger, E., 149, 150, 151
de Geus, C. H. J., 131, 137, 138, 140, 156, 159, 167, 168
Gilkey, L., 172
Glueck, N., 68, 70, 146, 153, 164
Gordon, C. H., 133, 135
Gottwald, N. K., 90, 92, 94, 95, 97, 136, 137, 138, 166, 167, 168, 169
Graff, H. F., 128
Gray, W., 130
Green, D. E., 129, 133, 142
Greenberg, M., 133, 135
Greenfield, J. C., 141
Grobel, K., 128
Gros Louis, K. R. R., 174
Gruhn, V. I., 130
Gunkel, H., 80
Gunneweg, A. H. J., 97, 158, 169
Habel, N., 128, 129
Haran, M., 144, 145, 153, 166
Harvey, V., 22, 124, 130, 132, 175
Hasel, G., 174
Hauser, A. J., 95, 166, 168, 169
Hayes, J. H., 150
Herrmann, S., 136, 138, 142, 145, 150, 152, 161, 162, 165, 169
Hick, J., 171
Hillers, D. R., 148, 149, 151
Holt, J., 133
Hordern, W. E., 172
Horn, S. H., 100, 145, 154, 156, 170
Huesman, J. E., 130
Huffmon, H. B., 140
Humphreys, W. L., 144
Hyatt, J. P., 147, 160, 174
Irvin, D., 145, 169
Jackson, J. J., 174
Johnson, D. L., 137

Josephus, Flavius, 32, 75, 135, 144, 157
Kelso, J. L., 155
Kempinski, A., 154
Kenyon, K., 138, 139, 145, 153, 154
Kessler, M., 174
King, W. L., 172
Klein, R. W., 128
Knight, D. A., 129, 132, 144
Koch, K., 129, 132
Kochavi, M., 155
Korošec, V., 148
Kümmel, W. G., 129
Kupper, J. R., 137
Kutsch, E., 151
Lambdin, T. O., 166
Landes, G., 154
Landsberger, B., 166
Lapp, P. W., 139, 146, 152, 154
Lehmann, M. R., 135
Lichtmann, A. J., 128
Liverani, M., 138, 140
Livingston, D., 157
Long, B. O., 131
Luke, J. T., 143
McCarthy, D. J., 54, 56, 57, 148, 149, 150, 151, 152
McClendon, J. W., Jr., 171
MacQuarrie, J., 173
Malamat, A., 158
March, W. E., 151
Marks, J. H., 169
Mattill, A. J., Jr., 129
Mayes, A. D. H., 152, 159, 161, 162, 165
Mazar, B., 138, 140, 142, 163, 164
Meek, T. J., 86, 144, 145, 146, 152, 153, 156, 161, 162, 164, 165
Mendenhall, G. E., 53, 54, 55, 57, 62, 63, 92, 93, 94, 95, 96, 97, 98, 137, 147, 148,
    149, 150, 151, 152, 156, 165, 166, 167, 168, 169
Miller, J. M., 133, 145, 152, 153, 154, 155, 156, 161, 162, 163, 165, 168, 170
Miller, P. D., Jr., 143
Montgomery, J. W., 107, 112, 171
Muilenberg, J., 174
Murphy, R., 133
Newman, M. L., 146, 148, 153, 161, 162, 163, 164, 165, 166
Nicholson, E. W., 146, 147, 148, 149, 150
Nielsen, E., 148, 150
Noth, M., 48, 49, 77, 78, 79, 81, 89, 130, 136, 140, 145, 146, 149, 150, 152, 153,
    155, 156, 159, 161, 162, 163, 165, 170
Novak, M., 171
Osswald, E., 174
Paterson, J., 133, 138
Perlitt, L., 148, 149, 150, 151, 152
Petschow, H., 135
Pinnock, C. H., 107, 109, 110, 171
Posener, G., 139

Power, W. J. A., 154
Pritchard, J. B., 139, 154
von Rad, G., 20, 50, 51, 146, 169
Rainey, A. F., 166
Ramsey, G. W., 130
Rast, W. E., 129, 132
Redford, D. B., 141, 144, 156
Reed, W. L., 147, 165
Reviv, H., 146, 152, 153, 156, 161, 164
Richardson, A., 120, 174
Ringgren, H., 142
Roberts, T. A., 131, 132
Robertson, D., 174
Rogers, M. G., 141
Rowley, H. H., 100, 133, 135, 141, 142, 144, 145, 146, 150, 152, 153, 157, 158,
    161, 162, 163, 164, 165, 166, 170
Rowton, M. B., 137
Sabourin, L., 130
Sanders, J. A., 141, 155, 175
Sarna, N. M., 133, 138
Sauer, A. v. R., 135
Schaeffer, F. A., 107, 109, 110, 113, 114, 171, 172
Sellin, E., 129
Simiand, F., 128
Smart, J. D., 172
Smend, R., 141, 144, 146, 159
Soggin, J. A., 152
Speiser, E. A., 30, 133, 134, 135
Stamm, J. J., 148, 149, 150
Stiebing, W. H., Jr., 139, 140, 142
Thomas, D. W., 170
Thompson, J. A., 128, 148, 149
Thompson, T. L., 44, 133, 134, 135, 136, 138, 139, 140, 141, 142, 143, 145, 147,
    149, 156, 159, 166, 169
Thucydides, 129
Toulmin, S., 132
Tucker, G. M., 128, 132, 134, 135
Tufnell, O., 154
Van Seters, J., 41, 42, 44, 133, 134, 135, 136, 137, 138, 139, 141, 142, 143
de Vaux, R., 46, 65, 79, 97, 98, 120, 122, 134, 136, 138, 139, 140, 141, 142, 143,
    144, 145, 146, 147, 148, 149, 150, 152, 153, 154, 155, 156, 157, 158, 159, 160,
    161, 162, 163, 165, 166, 168, 169, 174
de Vries, S. J., 144
Wagner, N. E., 141
Warner, S. M., 131, 170
Weinfeld, M., 148, 149, 150
Weippert, M., 77, 78, 136, 138, 152, 153, 154, 155, 156, 158, 159, 162, 163, 167,
    168
Weiser, A., 147
Wellhausen, J., 27, 52, 132, 146, 147
Westermann, C., 80, 136, 141, 143, 160
Wevers, J. W., 141
Wilson, J. A., 130

Wilson, R. A., 142, 152
Wilson, R. R., 130, 160
Winks, R. W., 128
Wiseman, D. J., 139
Wright, G. E., 121, 130, 135, 139, 144, 146, 152, 153, 154, 155, 159, 164, 165, 172, 173, 174
Würthwein, E., 128
Yeivin, S., 145

SUBJECT INDEX

Abraham (Abram), 33, 34, 37, 40, 44, 133, 135, 136, 141
Ai, 12, 69, 70, 73, 78, 154, 156
Amarna Age/Letters, 48, 82, 85, 90, 94, 104, 131, 162, 164, 166, 168
Amorites, 12, 36–40, 98, 104, 138, 139
Amphictyony, 89, 159
Amu, 38, 39
ᶜapiru, see Hapiru
Arad, 70, 74
Arameans, 41–42, 43–44, 142
Archaeological ages:
  Middle Bronze, 73–76, 88, 157
  MB I, 38, 39, 42, 139, 140–141
  MB IIA, 38, 39, 139, 140
  Late Bronze, 70, 72, 73, 74, 87, 90, 92, 93, 94, 95, 98, 154, 167
  Early Iron, 73, 90, 92, 94, 156
Archaeological findings:
  alternative explanations, 70–72, 104, 155
  limitations, 68–72, 78–79, 81, 92, 94, 102–104, 155
Asaru (Asharu), 48, 68, 83
Balance of probability, 101
Beersheba, 42
Beni-Hasan painting, 34, 38, 136
bᵉrît, 61
Bethel, 42, 69, 71, 74, 93, 155, 157
Certainty in historical study, degrees of, 20–22
"Congenial context," 17–19, 33, 34, 40, 53, 57–58, 62
Covenant, 17, 19, 52–63, 91–92, 94–95, 102
Credo, Israelite, 50–52
Dates, relative and absolute, 19–20, 131
Debir, 69, 71, 74, 155, 157
Decalogue, 54–56, 59–60, 61–62
Deuteronomy and Deuteronomic school, 51, 53, 56, 58, 59, 61, 62, 150, 151
Dimorphic society, 36
Eglon, 69, 71, 74, 155
Entry into Egypt, date of, 46–47
Etiologies, 78, 79–80, 81, 87, 159, 160, 170
Evidence:
  Collecting, 4–5
  "External evidence," 5, 27–28, 40, 68, 81–82, 101–104, 160
  "Genuine"/"Inauthentic," 7
  Intentional and unintentional, 4–5
  "Non-falsifying," 34–35, 102
  Sifting, 6–10
Execration Texts, 38, 39, 140
Exodus from Egypt, date of, 47–49, 145
Form criticism, see Genre analysis
Galilee, 66, 82–83

Genealogies, 82, 152, 160, 167
Genre analysis, 6, 13, 16–17, 27, 99, 101
Gezer, 66
Gibeon, 70, 73
Gideon, 112
Hapiru (ᶜapiru), 48, 68, 85, 86, 90–91, 94, 96, 97, 98, 104, 145, 161, 162, 164, 166,
    168–169
Hazor, 69, 70, 71, 74
Hebron, 42, 66, 67, 70, 73
Heshbon, 70, 75
"Historical substratum," 70, 118–122
Hittites, 17, 19, 29, 33, 53–58, 111, 135, 147
Hormah, 67, 70, 73
Hyksos, 46–47, 74, 75, 131, 144, 157
Inference, 13–20, 131–132
Jacob, 31–32, 33, 40, 41, 43, 44, 121–122, 141
Jephthah, 48, 75, 83
Jericho, 68, 69, 70, 73, 74, 86, 93, 122, 163, 164, 167
Jerusalem, 66
Joseph, 46, 47, 87, 100, 165
Kadesh, 49–50, 89–90, 162–163, 166
Lachish, 69, 70, 74, 103, 163
Laws of nature, 109
"Leap of faith," 108, 109, 110, 114
Literary criticism, 6–7, 99, 128–129
Mari, 28, 36
Merneptah stele, 14, 49, 69, 72–73, 103, 153, 156
Miracles, 108
Moses, 43, 45, 46, 49, 52, 54, 57, 62, 67, 76, 86, 87, 89, 100, 165, 170
Myth, 79–80, 160
Nomadism, pastoral, 35–36, 92–93, 137
Nuzi, 28, 29, 30, 31, 32, 103, 134, 135, 136
Patriarchs:
    artificial connection of generations, 41
    customs, 18, 29–33, 102
    mode of life, 34–36
    names, 18, 33–34, 136
    personifications of tribes, 67, 82, 85, 88, 153
    religion, 43, 142–143
Philistines, 41, 70, 76, 158
Prophets, 61, 62, 114–115, 151
Rameses II, 48, 49, 72, 156
Ras Shamra, see Ugarit
Seti I, 48, 72, 156, 161
Shechem, 42, 50, 85, 88, 93, 162, 163, 164
Shiloh, 69, 88
Source criticism, 9, 99
Textual criticism, 6, 13, 16
Tradition, 9, 10
Tradition criticism, 9, 27, 99
Transjordan, 66, 68–69, 83–84, 153, 161, 162–163
Tribal settlements, 65–68, 81–88
Ugarit (Ras Shamra), 28, 43, 68, 161
Zoar, 163